ESTATE PLANNING

ESTATE PLANNING

*Easy Answers to Your
Most Important
Questions*

A L E X   J.   S O L E D

C O N S U M E R   R E P O R T S   B O O K S

A Division of Consumers Union
Yonkers, New York

Copyright © 1994 by Alex J. Soled
Published by Consumers Union of United States, Inc.,
Yonkers, New York 10703.
Copyright 1984, 1988 by Scott, Foresman and Company
in association with American Association for Retired Persons
All rights reserved,
including the right of reproduction in whole or in part in any form.

Library of Congress Cataloging-in-Publication Data

Soled, Alex J.
Estate planning : easy answers to your most important questions /
by Alex J. Soled and the editors of Consumer Reports Books.
p.   cm.
Rev. ed. of: The essential guide to wills, estates, trusts, and
death taxes. c1984.
Includes index.
ISBN 0-89043-639-8 (hc)
1. Estate planning—United States—Popular works.   I. Soled, Alex
J. Essential guide to wills, estates, trusts, and death taxes.
II. Consumer Reports Books.   III. Title
KF750.Z9S6   1994
346.7305′2—dc20   93-42316
[347.30652]   CIP

Design by Ruth Kolbert
First printing, January 1994
This book is printed on recycled paper.
Manufactured in the United States of America

Estate Planning: Easy Answers to Your Most Important Questions is a Consumer Reports Book published by Consumers Union, the nonprofit organization that publishes Consumer Reports, the monthly magazine of test reports, product Ratings, and buying guidance. Established in 1936, Consumers Union is chartered under the Not-For-Profit Corporation Law of the State of New York.

The purposes of Consumers Union, as stated in its charter, are to provide consumers with information and counsel on consumer goods and services, to give information on all matters relating to the expenditure of the family income, and to initiate and to cooperate with individual and group efforts seeking to create and maintain decent living standards.

Consumers Union derives its income solely from the sale of Consumer Reports and other publications. In addition, expenses of occasional public service efforts may be met, in part, by nonrestrictive, noncommercial contributions, grants, and fees. Consumers Union accepts no advertising or product samples and is not beholden in any way to any commercial interest. Its Ratings and reports are solely for the use of the readers of its publications. Neither the Ratings, nor the reports, nor any Consumers Union publication, including this book, may be used in advertising or for any commercial purpose. Consumers Union will take all steps open to it to prevent such uses of its material, its name, or the name of Consumer Reports.

To my adored and loving wife, Ingrid,
for being astute, helpful, and supportive;
my children, Sharon L. Moser and Sheila V. Sybrant,
for being themselves, as well as for reviewing the manuscript;
and last, but not least, my late mother, Sarah Miller Pollack,
who was beloved by, and an inspiration to,
all who knew her.

Contents

APPENDIXES

Introduction

Although many of us devote a good deal of time and attention to the acquisition of property, we are often unaware that an equal or greater effort must be made to preserve and dispose of property after death.

We want to guarantee that the property we have acquired over time passes to those we intend to benefit with the least possible delay, is received with the lowest possible death taxes, and quickly becomes income producing or, if the property is not income producing, provides benefits as soon as possible.

To accomplish these objectives you must plan now. A knowledge of the basic laws dealing with property, taxes (both federal and state), and estate administration becomes essential. Knowing the ground rules will help you plan to transfer quickly and economically all of your property, whether modest or substantial, on your death.

This book will provide the information you need to participate actively in your own estate planning. Its question-and-answer format anticipates the most frequently asked questions and answers them in a way that can be understood

easily. The book is not intended to teach you to do it yourself. Rather, it is a guide to help you ask the appropriate questions of professionals. The question-and-answer format will help you understand this complex process. When dealing with wills, trusts, estates, and death taxes, many pitfalls must be avoided before one can accomplish a quick and economical transfer of property. The reader should not assume that he or she can arrange the transfer without professional help.

Estate Planning: Easy Answers to Your Most Important Questions is organized to facilitate selective use and to provide quick access to specific topics. Its detailed information will also help you determine whether the professional you consult is really trained to be of assistance. If the professional does not know the answers to most of the questions raised in this book, seek another professional.

Planning for the efficient distribution of your hard-earned dollars and property deserves your attention now if you wish to guarantee that the distribution will reflect your wishes and will occur with the least expense, complications, or delay.

Terminology

ABATEMENT The reduction of a legacy because there is not enough property in the estate to pay it.

ADEMPTION When someone is left specific property by will, and on death the property is not owned by the decedent, the gift fails (is adeemed). For example, I leave you my wristwatch. On my death, I do not own that watch. The gift is adeemed.

AFFINITY Relationship by marriage.

ANCESTORS Those in your bloodline from whom you are descended. Your mother and father, their parents and grandparents, and so on, would be your ancestors.

BENEFICIARY The one who is entitled to a benefit from an estate or trust. (Rarely is this term applied to the recipient of a gift; such beneficiary is usually referred to as the *donee*.) This term is sometimes used here interchangeably with the terms *legatee, devisee, distributee,* or *grantee.*

BEQUEST Technically, any personal property left by will. Today, this also includes all types of property left by will.

CLASS When property is left to a number of persons who are not named but who fit a general description, the property is left to a class. For example, bequests to your grandchildren or your issue would be a gift to a class.

CODICIL An instrument that revokes changes or adds to the terms of a (prior) will. A codicil must be executed with all the formalities of a will.

COLLATERALS Relatives who trace relationship to an intestate (one who dies without a will) through a common ancestor. These relatives are neither descendants of the intestate nor ancestors of the intestate. For example, your mother's brother (your uncle) is a collateral, as are your uncle's children (your cousins).

CONSANGUINITY Any relationship by blood.

CORPUS The principal or capital sum, especially of an estate or trust, as distinguishable from the interest or income derived from the principal or capital sum. (Also see pages 94–95.)

DESCENDANTS Persons who have been born through someone's bloodline.

The term includes every generation born after the individual. For example, your father is not your descendant, but your children, grandchildren, and great-grandchildren are.

DESCENT AND DISTRIBUTION STATUTES The laws of a state that set forth who inherits your intestate property and in what proportions if you do not have a will. These laws are sometimes known as intestacy statutes, or laws, of descent and distribution. When a will fails to dispose of all property owned by the decedent, such property is referred to as intestate property. When there is no will, all the property owned by the decedent is also intestate property. When an individual dies without a will, we refer to that individual as having died intestate.

DEVISE Leaving real property by will. The person who receives real property by will is called the *devisee*.

DISTRIBUTIVE SHARE The share of property that someone inherits when one dies intestate. The recipient is called the *distributee*. It is possible for someone to inherit all of the intestate's property. For example, assume someone dies intestate and has no spouse and only one child. In most states, the child inherits the entire estate. This (the entire estate) would be the child's distributive share.

EXECUTOR/EXECUTRIX The person, bank, or trust company that legally steps into the shoes of the decedent, temporarily owns all the decedent's property, and represents the estate in the eyes of the law. If the person appointed is a female, the appropriate term is *executrix*. In some states, the title given to the executor or executrix is *personal representative*. (Throughout this book the terms *executor* and *personal representative* are used interchangeably.) You may appoint more than one person to serve as executor. If the executor is a bank or trust company, it can serve as sole executor or coexecutor.

GIFTS, DISPOSITIONS, PASSES, BEQUEATHS These words are really shorthand for describing the act of having ownership of property transferred from the testator to the one the testator wishes to benefit. A lawyer would describe the property left by you to your loved ones as the *gifts* (the word *gifts* or *gift* has different meanings in different contexts; here, we are only talking about gifts by will) made by you or the property that "passes" on death from you, or the "disposition" made by you of your property, or the property that is "bequeathed" by you. You would be called the *transferor* or *testator,* and the one who receives the property would be called the *transferee* or *legatee.*

GRANTOR, OR SETTLOR The person who creates a trust during lifetime. When the trust is created by will, the creator of the trust is called the *testator,* which is the same name given to the one who makes a will. Sometimes the grantor is referred to as the *donor* or *trustor.* The one who is entitled to the benefits therefrom is called the *grantee* or the *beneficiary.*

HEIRS In most states today, the word means those who inherit property from those who die intestate (without a will). For example, if your will left all your property to your heirs, your property would be inherited by the same people, and in the same amounts, as if you died without a will. The word *heir* usually means the same as *heirs at law* or *lawful heirs*.

INTERESTED PERSON In most states, an interested person is defined by state law as a person who would inherit the property when someone dies without a will, or a person named in a will to receive a bequest.

INTER VIVOS TRUST A trust created during lifetime, sometimes called a *living trust*.

INTESTATE Someone who dies without a will. A person who dies with a will and fails to dispose of *all* his or her individually owned property is referred to as leaving property by *intestacy*. *Intestate succession* is the name sometimes given to property inherited as a result of an intestacy.

ISSUE All descendants of a particular person. The term includes, in addition to children, grandchildren, great-grandchildren, and so on, but does *not* include a spouse of any of them.

LAPSE The principle of law providing that when a person who is left property by will (a legatee) dies before the testator (the maker of the will), neither the legatee nor the legatee's estate is entitled to receive the inheritance, since it "lapsed."

However, many state laws provide that when a person is named in a will or a class is indicated, even where the named person or any person who is part of the class dies before the testator, their respective estates inherit the share left to the person or class. This type of law is commonly referred to as an *antilapse statute*.

LEGACY Any type of property that is left by will.

LEGACY, DEMONSTRATIVE A legacy of a certain amount to be paid first from a particular source. If the source is not sufficient to satisfy the legacy, then it shall be paid from the rest of the estate if there is sufficient property. For example, you leave someone the sum of $1,000 but direct that this sum shall first be paid from your savings account. If on the date of your death the account balance is only $600 but your estate has other property valued at $80,000, then the person who is left $1,000 is entitled to the balance of the savings account plus $400 from the other property.

LEGACY, GENERAL A legacy or devise by will that is paid out of the general assets of the testator's solely owned property but not from any specifically designated portion of it. For example, if by your will you leave someone the sum of $1,000 and do not limit this legacy as coming from a specific savings account, then the amount shall be paid from the general assets of the testator's estate.

LEGACY, SPECIFIC A legacy of a particular article. For example, leaving your diamond bracelet or your new automobile to someone is making a specific legacy.

LEGATEE The person who receives property by will.

NEXT OF KIN There is a disagreement as to the meaning of this phrase. The preferred view is that it means those who are the nearest blood relations. Thus, a surviving husband would not be included under this definition. Some courts interpret "next of kin" similarly to "heirs," that is, those who would inherit property if you died without a will.

PERSONAL REPRESENTATIVE See *Executor*.

PERSONALTY Personal property.

PER STIRPES AND PER CAPITA As a technical definition, *per stirpes* means "by the roots" or "by representation." It really refers to a method of distributing property. When the *per stirpes* method of distributing property is used, a group inherits the share to which their ancestor would have been entitled had such ancestor lived. This method is also referred to as a *per stirpital* method of distribution.

For example, assume you leave all your property to your "issue surviving you, *per stirpes*." Assume you have three children named Ann, Betty, and Charles. Ann and Betty are dead, but Ann has four children (your grandchildren) living at the time of your death. Betty has one child (also your grandchild) living at the time of your death. Charles has no children.

Ann's four children share equally the one-third share that Ann would have received if Ann had survived you. Betty's child inherits the one-third share that Betty would have received if Betty had survived you, and Charles inherits one-third. Note that here the word *issue* includes all your descendants, children as well as grandchildren.

Per capita means "by the head." It also refers to a method of distributing property. Thus, each member of the group inherits equal shares. For example, assume you leave all your property to your "issue surviving you, *per capita*." Assume the same facts as in the prior example. That is, you have three children, Ann, Betty, and Charles, and Ann and Betty are dead, etc. In this case, at the time of your death there are six persons living in the group. (The group consists of your issue.) These six persons are Ann's four children (your four grandchildren), Betty's one child (your grandchild), and Charles (your child). Your property would be divided into six equal shares.

The distinction between these two methods of distributing property, as applied to the prior example, is that when the property is left *per stirpes*, the property is divided into three equal shares (and Ann's four children share one of those three equal shares), but where the property is left *per capita*, the property is divided into six equal shares. Also note that under the *per stirpes* method a living parent inherits to the exclusion of any of his or her living descendants. Under the *per capita* method each living descendant would inherit an equal share of the estate.

PROPERTY Anything that may be the subject of ownership or possession. It includes real property (e.g., land), tangible personal property (e.g., furniture, art, coins, automobiles), and intangible personal property. Intangible personal property usually has no intrinsic or marketable value but is representative or evidence of value (e.g., bank passbook, certificate of shares of stock, mutual fund certificate, mortgage, promissory note).

SOUND MIND In general, this means that you, the testator, can understand the nature of the business in which you are engaged at the time you make your will, that you have a recollection of the property that you intend to dispose of, and that you understand who are or should be the natural objects of your bounty. For example, your spouse and children would be considered to be the natural objects of your bounty. Your close friends would not.

SPOUSE A husband or wife.

TENANTS OR TENANCIES As used by lawyers, the owners or possessors of property.

A joint tenancy exists where property is owned jointly by two or more joint tenants. Each "tenant" has the same interest in the property. If a joint tenant dies, his or her (ownership) interest becomes the property of the surviving joint tenant or tenants. During the tenant's lifetime, any joint tenant may sever (break up) the joint ownership either by sale or other transfer.

A tenancy by the entirety is similar to a joint tenancy, except that it can only exist between wife and husband. The most important feature of this tenancy is that, unlike a joint tenancy, the tenancy cannot be undone or changed by one of the parties acting alone; it requires the joint act of both. On the death of one, the survivor will become the owner of the whole (as in a joint tenancy). Divorce will also terminate this tenancy and convert it to a tenancy in common.

A tenant in common has a distinct and separate undivided interest in the property. A tenant in common may transfer his ownership without the approval or consent of the other owner(s). Unlike the joint tenancy or tenancy by the entireties, the deceased owner's interest does *not* pass to the surviving tenants in common. On death of a tenant in common, his or her interest passes to the owner's heirs or as provided by his or her will.

TESTAMENTARY TRUST A trust created by will. To create such a trust, there must be a direction to deal with property that is identified as the subject of the trust and to specify the beneficiary or beneficiaries who have certain rights and privileges in the trust property.

TESTATOR/TESTATRIX A male who makes a will; a female who makes a will.

TRUST A device used for disposing of property or managing property, or both. Technically, it is the name applied to the relationship created between two or more persons when one of them, the trustee, holds property for the benefit of another. As used here, the word *person(s)* includes a corporate fiduciary, such as a bank or trust company, when referring to a trustee. (See further discussion under "Trusts.")

WRITTEN INSTRUMENT While it is clear what is meant by *written,* the writing need not be in ink or by typewriter. If a pencil is used, this will satisfy the law, but pencil is not recommended. Pencil writing can be erased easily, and someone can readily insert names, change dollar amounts, and commit other frauds.

WILLS

General Information

What is a will?

A declaration that disposes of one's property after death. Such declaration is usually made in writing, and must meet certain required statutory formalities.

What is a testator?

A male who makes a will.

What is a testatrix?

A female who makes a will. For clarity, this book will usually refer to the testator (the male version); however, this reference also includes the testatrix.

What property can be disposed of by will?

All property of any kind owned solely by the one who makes the will (the testator).

Can a testator by will dispose of property that is not owned solely by him?

No. Consider this: Can I provide in my will that the car that you (the reader) own shall be left to my daughter? Certainly not! Why is this so? Simply because your car does not belong to me and is not mine to give away.

Let us reverse roles. Can you give to your son, by your will, the car that I own? Again, no! The reason is that you cannot give away property that does not belong to you.

Assume you bought six U.S. Series EE Savings Bonds some years ago. Last year, you added your daughter's name to the bonds. By registering the bonds in this manner, you provided that on your death the bonds would be paid to your daughter (the words used are "payable on death," abbreviated "P.O.D."). You now prepare a will. Because of a change in family circumstances, you provide in the will that the bonds be paid to your son. Will your son become the owner of the bonds on your death? No, because at the *moment* of your death, ownership of the bonds shifted to your daughter. Since your will could only dispose of property you owned at the *moment* of your death, at that moment you no longer owned the bonds. Of course, during your lifetime you could have made the changes by re-registering the bonds and substituting your son's name for your daughter's.

When does a will become effective?

When the testator dies and the court having jurisdiction accepts the will as the valid instrument that expresses the final wishes of the testator. The procedure leading up to and including acceptance of the will is called "probating the will."

What does *testament* mean and what is the difference between the separate words *will* and *testament* and the phrase *last will and testament?*

In earlier times, *testament* referred to leaving personal property (property other than real estate) on death, and *will* referred to leaving real property (real estate) on death. When the same instrument left personal as well as real property, the instrument was commonly referred to as the "last will and testament."

Today, the term *will* refers to personal property as well as to real property. Because of the customs and laws of some states, it is recommended that the phrase *last will and testament* be used.

What is meant when it is said that a will is ambulatory and revocable?

Ambulatory means that it does not take effect until death.

Revocable means that it is capable of being revoked. To revoke a will means to cancel, dissolve, or declare it to be of no force or effect.

A will only takes effect on the death of its maker (the testator), and every will may be revoked by its maker. Thus, if you make a will, you may change it as many times during your lifetime as you wish, or you may revoke it. However, if the maker becomes of unsound mind, he or she cannot legally change or revoke the will.

Should I have a will?

Yes, the object of a will is to dispose of one's assets as desired. The lawyer's role is to advise the client and to prepare the necessary documents so that distributing assets as one desires may be accomplished with the least delay and at the lowest possible tax rate and administrative cost.

The laws of the state in which a person resides at the time of death direct how his or her solely owned personal property shall be disposed of when that person dies without a will (*intestate*). With respect to real property (real estate), the laws of the state where such assets are located determine its disposition. In other words, the state makes a will for you. State laws that leave your property to those specified in such laws are known as "laws of descent and distribution." (Solely owned assets are commonly referred to as *probate assets*, that is, assets that are administered under the supervision of a *probate court*. For a full discussion of this subject, see the material beginning on page 52.)

Under Maryland law, for instance, if you have a wife and minor children and you die intestate, your wife inherits one-half of your property and your children inherit the other half. You must then ask yourself if this is the type of distribution that you wish. There is a summary in the Appendixes of the current laws of descent and distribution for all 50 states and the District of Columbia.

If your children inherit half your property, they are entitled to receive the property, in some states, as early as age 18. It is unwise to give large sums of money to children who are 18 years old, since at that age they may not know how to handle large sums. Appropriate language in a will can delay distribution of large sums until the children are older.

In most states, a person under age 18 is considered a *minor*. Minors usually do not have the legal capacity to enter into contracts. In the eyes of the law, the minor is considered to be under a legal disability. This legal disability disappears when the minor attains legal age (referred to as attaining *majority*). When property is left to a minor, complications arise during the time the money is held for the benefit of the minor.

Frequently, it is necessary to appoint a guardian of a minor's property. Without a will, the appointment of a guardian for a minor's property usually requires filing a petition with the court, which then may require a surety bond. With a will, you can appoint guardians of the minor's property without requiring a bond. Premiums for the surety bond are costly and are payable from the assets of the minor. Also, the minor's funds frequently may not be spent for the minor's benefit without securing a court order.

A will permits you to designate an executor of your choosing; you need not rely upon state law and eventually the courts to appoint someone to administer the estate. If you appoint someone to administer your estate, that person is called an *executor* (*executrix*), although the terminology can vary from state to state. In some states the term *personal representative* is used instead. If the court appoints someone to administer your estate, that person is called an *administrator*. In the absence of a will, any court-appointed administrator must post a bond. The premium cost varies with the size of the estate and is an estate expense. In some areas of the country where a bond is required, the bonding company will properly require that all transfers of property be countersigned by the company, regardless of the resulting delays.

If you are the sole owner of a business, at the moment of your death, this asset (the business) becomes the property of your estate. The laws of most states prohibit an estate from owning or running a business. This may then require the liquidation of the business at an inconvenient time. A will can permit the continuation of the business if you desire it. In some states, there is a requirement that a business be incorporated in order for the estate to run it. This will entail additional expense.

At the outset, you may think that all of your property is jointly owned and that there is no necessity for a will. However, you may have forgotten about property; you may have inherited additional property that is not jointly owned, or you may have the right to collect monies, such as compensation for injuries. Any of the foregoing could be a valuable asset of your estate and should be disposed of by provisions of your will.

Assuming that all your property is jointly owned with your spouse and that your spouse survives you, your spouse would certainly need a will, since she or he would become the sole owner of all of the property. If your spouse does not have a will, his/her solely owned property would be inherited in accordance with the laws of descent and distribution. You may say that your spouse can, as soon as you die, have a will made, but the possibility that you could die together or that your spouse may be incapable of making a will must be considered.

I wish to have a valid will. What is required?

The laws of most states require that you be of a certain age (usually 18), that you be of sound mind, and that the formalities required by law be followed.

Usually, the state law requires:

1. a written instrument;
2. your signature on the document, or some other person's signature for you in your presence and by your express direction; and

3. an attestation (i.e., the formal act of witnessing the written instrument at the testator's request) and signature by two or more credible witnesses in the presence of the testator.

In several states, step 2 requires that you identify the instrument as being your will and also that you specifically request the witnesses to serve as such. Another name given to step 3 in these states is *publication* of the will. Sometimes this step is referred to as *execution*. (Also see the explanation of *sound mind* on page 6.)

Shouldn't I execute several copies of the will so that if I lose the original, one of the copies can be probated?

No. As a general rule, if copies are executed, every copy must be produced in court. If all executed copies are not produced, the law assumes that the will was revoked. It is much simpler to preserve one original signed document in a safe place, such as a vault or safe-deposit box.

Assume you execute the typewritten ribbon or computer-generated copy (the original) and also two carbon copies or perhaps two photocopies of the original. At death, only the original is submitted to the court for probate. One or two signed copies cannot be found. The laws of virtually every state provide that if all of the executed documents cannot be produced, there is a presumption that the will was revoked.

This same rule applies if the copies are submitted to the court for probate.

In the absence of the original will, the presumption is that the will was revoked. (A *presumption* is a technical rule of evidence about what conclusion is to be drawn from the stated facts. As it applies to wills, if an executed document is missing, the conclusion drawn is that the will was revoked.) The presumption can be overcome. For example, if the beneficiaries can show that the original will was at all times in your attorney's hands and that the attorney never turned it over to you and cannot explain its disappearance, then if the executed copies are produced, probate will normally be approved for the copies of the will.

Where should my will be kept?

In most states, your will should be kept in your safe-deposit box at a bank (provided that the box is rented in joint names with your spouse), at your lawyer's office, or at the bank or trust company you may have named as your executor. In some states, the clerk of the probate court will hold it for safekeeping in a sealed envelope. There will be a nominal fee for this, and only you or your designated agent can have access to it during your lifetime.

However, in some states, such as New York, if your will is in a bank safe-deposit box and the box is rented in your name either as sole tenant or as joint tenant, the box will be sealed when you die. (If the surviving spouse is the joint tenant, the box is usually not sealed.) In such states, no one may have access to the box until the state tax commission authorizes its opening and its contents are inventoried. A representative of the taxing authority may be required to be present, and a substantial delay could result.

In all other states, when the box is rented in the decedent's name only, bank representatives will seal the box when they learn of the death. In such cases, a court order will be required to open the box. Usually, the order is limited to looking for and removing the will; the box is then resealed.

Your choices are as follow:

1. If you reside in a state in which the state tax representative need not be present when the box is opened, rent the box in your name and your spouse's name. On one person's death, the other may properly open the box.

2. If you reside in a state in which the state tax representative must be present, place your will in a box rented in your spouse's name and vice versa. Or, if you control a family-owned corporation, have the corporation rent the box and place the will there. In this case, be sure your spouse has corporate authority to enter the box.

3. Leave the original will with your attorney or bank or trust company (if named as executor), and keep your receipt in a place known to your family.

4. Deposit the will with the court clerk for safekeeping. During your lifetime, the contents of the will are sealed and only you, or your designated agent, may have access to the will or remove it from safekeeping. Not every state extends this service.

I can't find my original will. I think I left it with my lawyer, but I can't remember his name. How can I revoke my will?

Execute a new will and declare that the new will revokes your old will.

How else is a will revoked?

While the laws of each state determine how a will is to be revoked, a will generally is revoked as follows:

1. By your executing a subsequent valid will that says directly or indirectly that it revokes an earlier version. (Naturally, it is desirable to say so directly.)

2. By you, the testator, cutting, tearing, burning, or mutilating the original will, or by having someone else do this in your presence with your consent.

3. By your obtaining a final divorce or an annulment of your marriage. (Bear in mind the difference between a final divorce and a separation.)

4. If after the execution of the will you as testator marry, a child is born of the marriage (or one is adopted), and the child is not provided for by the will. In some states, either your marriage or the birth of a child causes the will to be revoked, or state law makes provision for the wife or after-born child.

My will was executed 10 years ago. My wife and children are all living. Do I need to bother with the will anymore?

A will should be reviewed every three to five years or even more often if your finances or family situation changes. When you first executed the will, your children may have been minors. You might have designated your mother as the guardian for the children. Ten years later, is she still physically able to care for the children?

Did you provide for trusts for your children and have they by now demonstrated financial maturity so that you would wish them to receive their shares of your estate outright? Has another child been born to you and your spouse, one for whom you failed to provide under your will? In some states, when a child is born after a will is executed (known either as an *after-born child* or as a *pretermitted child*) and you have not provided for that child in your will, all or part of the will is deemed to be revoked. Has the amount or title, i.e., the name in which your assets are held, changed so that a will that was logical and fiscally sound 10 years ago is no longer appropriate?

Give me some examples of what you mean.

1. When your mother was aged 62, she was designated guardian of your minor children. She is now living in a nursing home in frail health. Your oldest child is now 20 and your youngest child is 12.

Your oldest child should replace your mother as the guardian of your youngest child.

2. When you wrote your will, your two children were uncertain about what they wanted to do and wanted time to travel and think. Your daughter is now an attorney, happily married, and has one child. Your son is an engineer and head of a large industrial unit. Your will and your spouse's will left all the property after your spouse's death to a bank, as trustee. The wills provide that the trustee may distribute income to the children, and on the death of both, the remaining property is to be held in trust. It now appears that the children are mature and should receive the property outright.

3. When your will was written your sole assets were a home, some savings, and property in West Virginia. These assets were worth $125,000. Both you and your spouse provided that your children receive everything outright. Oil now has been discovered on your West Virginia property, and the property is worth a great deal of money. You should consider whether or not your children should inherit the property outright when you and your wife die. It may be advisable to give them their shares at periodic intervals.

4. Your simple will has language similar to the following:

I give, devise, and bequeath all the rest, residue, and remainder of my estate to my wife, Jane, if she survives me, and if she fails to survive me, to my children
surviving me, in equal shares, or all to the survivor of them surviving me.

Your wife died three years earlier. This unfortunate event does not require redoing your will, since the will says she inherits your estate only if she survives you. In view of her earlier demise, the will provides who inherits, namely, your children. You have two children. Jane, the older, is a successful practicing pediatrician. Your son, John, is a nationally known graduate civil engineer. Three years ago John began his own business. While John caused the business to be incorporated, he personally borrowed extensively and guaranteed all corporate loans. Last year, it was learned that the corporate place of business owned by it and necessary to its operations had heavy concentrations of toxic waste. The cost to the corporation to clean up the site may bankrupt the business. If the corporation becomes bankrupt, so does John.

There is a relatively little-known provision of the federal bankruptcy law that states that assets inherited by a bankrupt individual within 180 days after filing a petition for bankruptcy belong to the bankrupt estate. That is, such inherited assets will belong to the creditors of the bankrupt and not to the individual. This rule also applies to proceeds of a life insurance policy or of a death benefit plan.

In this case, and considering John's financial condition, you should consider changing your will (as well as the beneficiaries of your life insurance and death benefit plan) and leave John's share in trust for his benefit. If John does not become the outright owner of the inheritance or life insurance or death benefit plan proceeds on your death, such assets should probably be protected from any possible creditors of his bankrupt estate (if indeed he is required to declare bankruptcy, voluntarily or involuntarily).

Whether to have a trust and what terms and conditions should be included in the trust should be discussed with your lawyer.

5. When you lived in New Hampshire, you had a lovely neighbor. Her name was Violet White. She used to baby-sit for your children, provided home cooking and home remedies for illness, and looked after your house when you and your family were away for extended periods. Both you and your husband wished to remember her in your will. You therefore left her a bequest of $10,000. Mrs. White has no children and is now remarried.

What should be your concern? Under the laws of some states, even if Mrs. White predeceased you, her estate would still inherit the $10,000. In this case, the most likely recipient would be her new husband, whom you never met.

The reason for this result is that the laws of most states have an *antilapse* provision. The effect of this provision is that, *unless you provide otherwise,* any bequest to an individual who dies before you die does not lapse (fail).

What should you do? Nothing, if you are satisfied that her husband should inherit the $10,000. Alternatively, you can change that provision of your will or be sure the bequest under your will reads:

I give and bequeath the sum of $10,000 to Violet White, my former neighbor, who now resides at 10 Magnolia Walk, Concord, New Hampshire, if she survives me.

By adding the phrase "if she survives me," you have *provided otherwise.* Therefore, you have ensured that if Violet predeceases you, the bequest will be revoked.

Earlier you referred to "titling of assets." What does *titling* mean? How does one change *title?*

Title is the means by which one establishes ownership of, or an interest in, property of any kind. For example, when a deed is executed and recorded showing that Franklin Jones is the owner of a one-acre parcel of land, this act establishes his title (ownership). When a stock certificate is issued for 100 shares showing Franklin Jones as the owner, his title (ownership) is established.

Should Mr. Jones later wish to transfer ownership of the land or the shares (whether by sale or gift), he would have to change the title to such property. This is done by his executing and recording a new deed for the land. The deed would name the new owner. When this is done, the new owner would have title to (ownership of) the land. The process of naming the new owner is commonly referred to as *titling* or *retitling.*

To retitle the stock certificate, the corporation or its agent would require that the old stock certificate be returned to it together with a signed document (known as a stock power) authorizing the issuance of a new stock certificate. The new certificate would recite the name of the new owner. When this is done, the property (in this case the shares of stock of the corporation) would thereafter be owned by the named individual (or partnership or corporation).

I lived in New York when I executed my will. I now live in Maine. Must I have my will rewritten?

While not necessary, it is wise to have your lawyer review the will. If the mechanics of executing the will (the "formalities") were in accordance with New York law, then Maine law says that the document will have full force and effect in Maine. Every state has a similar rule.

However, the laws of one state for creating, defining, and regulating property rights (as distinguished from the procedural requirement—the "formalities") may be different from those of another state. It is therefore wise to have a lawyer review the will to point out any problems arising from differences in the laws of the state to which you have moved.

What laws apply to the property of someone who has died (the decedent)?

In general, the state's laws governing the decedent's principal residence determine rights to personal property as well as any tax imposition, but the laws of the state where any real property (or real estate) is located determine rights to that real property as well as any tax imposition.

The laws of a particular state may change this general rule.

Contents of Wills

Please tell me what, in your opinion, a will should contain.

1. State your full name. If you are known by any other names, list them.

Comment: Your name is Mary Smith and you own stock registered in the name of Mary A. Smith. Your estate may have difficulty reregistering the stock unless it can be shown that Mary Smith and Mary A. Smith are the same person. It is far simpler to prove the fact when it is clarified by the will.

2. State where you consider your principal residence to be.

Comment: The court that has principal jurisdiction over your will and the property disposed of by your will is the court located in the place where you have your principal residence. (Technically, your principal residence is referred to as your *domicile*.)

There are tax reasons for making this statement of your residence. The general rule of death taxation is that the state in which you reside has jurisdiction to im-

pose taxes on all of your property, other than real property. Hence, by clarifying your place of residence, you simplify for the estate representatives the determination of which state has the proper authority to tax your property. This also simplifies the decision as to which court properly has jurisdiction over the administration of the estate.

It should be noted, too, that even when you declare where your residence is, another state is free to ignore your statement and to make its own determination as to your residence. There are times, though rare, when two or more states try to tax your estate. Declaring where you reside will be helpful in preventing two states from trying to impose death taxes on your estate.

3. State that the will revokes and supersedes (takes the place of) any prior will and *codicil* (a codicil is an instrument that revokes, changes, or adds to the terms of a will).

Comment: This should be done even if you do not remember having an earlier will. Why take the chance that an earlier will was not revoked and still has legal effect?

4. Give your instructions with respect to the disposal of your body and funeral arrangements.

Comment: In many states, the representatives of your estate may not spend above a certain amount for your funeral without special authority given by your will. If this authority is not given by your will, it may become necessary to secure a court order. Giving instructions will avoid the expense and delay of requesting a court order authorizing the amount of money that has already been spent on your funeral or the amount desired to be spent. Without appropriate language in the will, the court can deny the necessary permission.

Also, if you wish to be cremated or to donate your body or any of its parts (eyes, kidneys, etc.) to medical science for research, therapy, education, or transplantation, you should clearly state that.

If you want your body to be used for scientific purposes, you should carry with you a written expression of your wishes. Otherwise, by the time your will is located, it may be too late to carry out your instructions, since you could already have been buried or cremated. Obviously, if you have a surviving spouse, he or she will know of your wishes. Eye banks, kidney foundations, medical societies, and hospitals can provide printed forms that you can sign, have witnessed, and carry with you. Some states' driver's licenses also contain optional directions for body or organ disposal.

The provisions of law relating to organ disposition are contained in the laws of every state. They are patterned after the recommendations made by a nationally recognized group. The recommendations are known as the Uniform Anatomical Gifts Act.

5. Do *not* direct the payment of all "just debts."

Comment: Too many wills are written with the direction that the estate pay all "just debts." The law is clear that debts *must* be paid, regardless of what is said in the will. So why say anything about debts?

You may then ask, What harm is done by a reference to "just debts"? Here are the answers:

a. You may owe the federal or state government money for past income taxes. The law may prohibit the collection of such taxes because the statute of limitations ran out on the debt. (A *statute of limitations* is a law that imposes limits on the time period during which someone may sue or collect debts. Such a statute also applies to federal and state governments.) But though these statutes of limitations may prevent taking action with respect to debts, they do not prevent you from voluntarily paying debts. The question raised is: When you direct by your will the payment of "just debts," have you voluntarily agreed to pay these "outlawed" debts and, therefore, is your estate then required to pay them? If you do not wish your estate to pay debts on which the statute of limitations ran out, why say so?

b. You may owe money on a mortgage.

You may have left property to a cousin, but the property may be subject to a mortgage for which you, and then your estate, are legally liable.

Do you wish to have your estate pay off the entire mortgage? If you do not, then why state in your will that all your "just debts" should be paid?

Using such language could be cause for a court suit to determine exactly what you meant—an unnecessary expense that could lead to a possible result you did not intend.

6. Direct the passing of your household furnishings, paintings, silverware, art objects, automobiles, etc., to your spouse, if living, and if not, to your then-living children.

Comment: In many states, when a residence is owned by a husband and wife as joint tenants or tenants by the entirety, the contents of the residence are considered owned in the same fashion. In such a case, the survivor will become the automatic owner on the spouse's death.

This rule (whereby the survivor becomes the automatic owner) does not apply in all states and usually does not apply when a residence is owned by you in your name only, nor does it usually apply to automobiles, a boat, or other valuable vehicles. When the survivor does not become the automatic owner, and if the testator did not specifically bequeath these objects, there could be serious and substantial adverse income tax consequences. These consequences could arise when the survivor acquires ownership of these assets. (A detailed expla-

nation of these rules can be found beginning on page 180.)

7. Dispose of the "rest, residue, and remainder" of your estate. (The words *rest* and *remainder* have been interpreted by the courts to mean the same thing as *residue.* Customarily, lawyers refer to the balance of the testator's property, after specific bequests, as the rest, residue, and remainder of that person's property.)

Comment: Residue is what is left after something is taken out. You want to be sure that the will disposes of *all* your property. If everything is not disposed of, the remaining property must be disposed of as intestate (undisposed of by will) property. State law will determine who will inherit intestate property. To avoid this and to dispose of your property as *you* wish, your will should state who will inherit the residue of your estate. (See Death Taxes for what may be desirable from the tax point of view.) To illustrate what the will should contain to be sure that your loved ones receive what you intend them to receive, here are several different situations.

When you die, your parents, wife, and three children survive you.

Assume that you wish to leave some property to your parents to supplement their incomes. You might then leave $100,000 to trustees in trust and direct them to pay the income from the $100,000 to your parents for life. On their deaths, the trust property is paid to your wife outright, and if she is not then living, to your children. When you have your will prepared, you obviously do not know who will be living on the date of your death. The language of the will should therefore cover all possibilities. In this case, your will should include language such as:

If either of my parents survives me, I give and bequeath the sum of $100,000 to Jane Doe, my wife, as Trustee. My Trustee shall pay the net income [the balance of the income remaining after all expenses are deducted] therefrom to my parents, in equal shares, or all to the survivor of them surviving me, so long as each shall live, and in addition, my Trustee may give, at any time or times, to either of my parents during such parent's lifetime, such sum or sums from the principal of the trust, including the whole thereof, as, in the absolute discretion of my Trustee, may be deemed necessary, advisable, or desirable for the health, maintenance, or support of my parents or either of them.

Upon the death of the survivor of my parents, the trust shall terminate and my Trustee shall pay over and distribute the trust, as then constituted, to my said wife if then living and if not then living to my children then living, in equal shares, or all to the survivor of them then living.

You should consider the following: If neither of your parents is living at the time of your death, there would be no reason to create the trust. Therefore, you will note that the language of the will states that you give the sum of $100,000 to your trustee only if either of your parents survives you.

When your parents die, the trust terminates (ceases) and the trust property is paid to your wife, but only if she is *then* living. "Then" refers to the date when the last person among you and your parents dies, since the trust only becomes effective on your death *and* if either of your parents survives you. There have been wills that inappropriately state that the trust property shall be paid over to the testator's wife if she survives the *testator*. She may survive you but die before the death of your parents. For example, assume you died in 1980, your wife died in 1982, and your parents died in 1984. If the will uses the (incorrect) language that the property shall be paid over to your wife if she survives you (the testator), this could cause two major problems.

First, if your wife is not living when your parents die, the property will be paid to her estate. By reason of this, the property will be needlessly subject to death taxes in *her* estate, and needlessly subject to delay and expense, since the property will be administered as part of her estate.

Second, if your wife remarries and dies without a will before your parents die, your property may be paid to her second husband. This will, of course, reduce the amount of your property that your children will receive.

There is another consideration. If both of your parents die after your death and your wife is not *then* living, you may perhaps wish to leave the property to *your* brothers and sisters or perhaps to a charity. However, if you leave the property to your children who survive *you* (rather than restrict the bequest to such children who are *then* living), the property may be left to one of your children's spouses.

This happens because even though your children are not living when the last-surviving parent dies, they were living when *you* died. The law then requires their interests under your will to be paid to their estates. If the interests are paid to the ones who are entitled to inherit such child's estate, they may then belong to such child's husband or wife. Leaving your interests to a *child's* husband or wife may be in accordance with your wishes. But if it is not, then stipulate that a child receives a share only if he or she is living at the time of the death of the survivor of your parents.

When you die, your wife and three children survive you.

In this case your will should include language such as (remember, we are not yet taking into account any tax results):

All the rest, residue, and remainder of my estate, I give, devise, and bequeath to my wife, Jane, if she survives me, and if she fails to survive me, to my children surviving me, in equal shares, or all to the survivor of them surviving me.

Please note that the language here does not take into account the fact that a child may die before you but have children (your grandchildren) surviving you. If you wish to leave property to the child or children of *your* deceased children, language similar to what appears in the next example should be used.

When you die, your wife, three children, and two grandchildren survive you.

Your will should include language such as:

All the rest, residue, and remainder of my estate, I give, devise, and bequeath to my wife, Jane, if she survives me, and if she fails to survive me, to my issue surviving me, per stirpes.

Here, you would have to know two things. First, the word *issue* means all your descendants. This includes children, grandchildren, great-grandchildren, and so on. Second, the words *per stirpes* (which is further explained on page 5) explain the portions that your descendants receive. The older generation takes a share to the exclusion of younger generations, and the younger generations take only the share that their ancestor would have taken if he/she were alive. For example, your three children are named Arthur, Benjamin, and Cathy. Arthur dies before you but leaves two children surviving you. By using the quoted language, Arthur's two children (your grandchildren) each would inherit a one-half portion of the one-third share of your estate that Arthur (the ancestor of your grandchildren) would have inherited had he been alive at the time of your death.

If you wish to leave property only to your children, then you should say:

. . . to my children surviving me, in equal shares, or all to the survivor of them surviving me.

When you die, only your wife survives you.
Your will should include language such as:

All the rest, residue, and remainder of my estate I give, devise, and bequeath to my wife, Jane, if she survives me.

It is always advisable to name your wife because you may have remarried after you signed your will. The wife you had when you first signed your will may have died before you. Therefore, if the language you used in your will only states that you leave your entire estate to your "wife," there could be questions raised about whether you intended your second wife to inherit your property. An important factor in writing a will is to eliminate questions as to what was intended. By naming your wife, there can be no questions about your intentions.

You could certainly argue that if you remarry you will redo your will. But what if you never get around to doing so or go off on a honeymoon with your new wife (before you have a new will) and die in an automobile accident? In this case, you obviously will not have clarified the matter.

When you die, only your three children survive you.

Your will should include language such as:

> *All the rest, residue, and remainder of my estate I give, devise, and bequeath to my children surviving me, in equal shares, or all to the survivor of them surviving me.*

Here, should only two children survive you, then the two children inherit your entire estate. If only one child survives you, then this one child inherits your entire estate.

When you die, only your brothers and sisters survive you.

Your will should include language such as:

> *All the rest, residue, and remainder of my estate I give, devise, and bequeath to my brothers and sisters surviving me, in equal shares, or all to the survivor of them surviving me.*

As is the case in the previous situation, only those among your brothers and sisters who are living on the date of your death will inherit from you.

The language used in each of the preceding situations is designed to be a guide only and is not intended to be complete. It is strongly recommended that a lawyer be consulted.

8. Provide for the disposal of *all* your property in the event, however unlikely, that none of your referred-to family members survives you.

Comment: Every well-written will should state what happens in the event that *none* of the persons you name, or refer to, survives you. (Professionally, this is referred to as providing for *remote contingent beneficiaries*.) For example, you, your husband, and your two children are killed in a plane crash. Who will inherit your property and your husband's property? Appropriate language should be inserted in both wills to take care of this situation.

9. Consider the source of the payment of death taxes. If no special provision is made in the will as to what assets are to be used for payment of death taxes, with certain exceptions, each asset is required to pay a proportionate part of the tax.

This may not be in accordance with your wishes. In some states, if no provision for taxes is made, they are paid from the residue.

10. If you have a minor child or children, you should appoint a guardian of the person and property of your children. The general rule throughout the United States is that the surviving parent has the power and authority to appoint a guardian for minor children in case of the survivor's death. Many people forget that the oldest child, if he or she is not a minor, may serve as a guardian of minor children.

The language of your will should be similar to the following:

> *I nominate, constitute, and appoint my then oldest legally competent child to be the guardian of the person and property of all children of mine who may be minors at the time of the death of the survivor of my spouse and me.*

11. If a trust is created under your will, you should appoint one or more trustees to administer the trust property. It is also advisable to name one or more successor trustees. The trustee may be the same individual as the personal representative.

The trustee may be your spouse, your children, or a bank or financial institution that has authority to serve as trustee. For example, savings and loan associations, stockbrokerage firms, or credit unions, with some exceptions, do *not* have such authority.

12. You should appoint one or more personal representatives to administer the estate's property. It is also advisable to name one or more successor personal representatives. (A discussion of what is a personal representative, his or her duties, and related matters is found on page 6.)

The personal representative may be your spouse, your children, or a bank or financial institution that has authority to serve as personal representative. For example, savings and loan associations, stockbrokerage firms, or credit unions, with some exceptions, do *not* have such authority.

So that I can be aware of possible problems in the will I now have or in the will I am planning to have, please describe some typical problems you have encountered or learned about in the course of your professional career.

---

1. *Gifts to charity.* In the legal profession, when the word *gift* is used in connection with leaving property on death, it really means the same as a *bequest* (leaving personal property by will) or a *devise* (leaving real property by will). When used in a will, the term gift is not limited to the kinds of transfers most people are accustomed to making during their lifetimes, either at holidays or for birthdays, weddings, or other occasions. When making a gift by will to charity, the precise name and address of the charity should be used. Too frequently, there are two charities with similar names. If there are two charities with similar names, the court will decide which you meant. Apart from the problem of which charity will eventually receive the property, the court process involved is very costly because lawyers will be hired for each charity and for your estate, and each lawyer usually receives a legal fee. Sometimes a legal fee is paid from the assets in your estate. Who pays the legal fees depends on the laws of your state as well as the discretion of the court.

In some states, when certain members of your family are living, you may not leave to a charity any property that is larger than a certain percentage of your estate. You should check this with your lawyer. Also, in some states you may not leave property to a religious organization within a certain period of time after your will is executed. The reason for this last rule is a historical one and is designed to protect the testator from undue pressures from the representatives of the religious organization.

2. *You leave your property to your children.* If you have an adopted child, is it your wish to have this adopted child included among the words *child or children?* If you have a child who, in turn, adopted one or more children, is it your wish to include these adopted children (of your child) among those included in any gifts you make to grandchildren? If, during your marriage, a child is born to your wife by artificial insemination and you are not the donor of the semen, do you intend such child to be included among your children?

In most states, by statute, the word *child* is defined to include adopted children (as well as under certain circumstances children born before the parents have married each other). Yet, if one of your children is adopted, be certain that he or she will inherit the property you intend such child to inherit based on the laws of the state. It is therefore wise to consult your lawyer about these matters.

3. *You make a gift to your issue.* When you refer to your *issue,* the word includes all your descendants. But the real question here is whether you wish to leave your property to descendants living at any time during your lifetime or only to those living when you die.

For example, you have three children who are named Al, Bob, and Cathy. Al had one child; Bob and Cathy each have three children. Al and his child both die before you. Is it your intention to leave property to the estate of Al or perhaps to the estate of his child (both your issue), even though they are not living at the time of your death? Undoubtedly not.

There are certain rules that lawyers and the courts follow that state what happens when you leave *class gifts* (class gifts are gifts to a number of persons who are not named but who fit a general description). The usual rule of construction in the United States is that when you make a gift to a class, in this case to issue, the persons who inherit are those who are living at the time of your death. However, why leave these interpretations open to question or to possible changes in the law or court rulings? Always be specific!

If you wish only Bob and Cathy to inherit your property, you can arrange this by saying in your will that you leave your property "to my issue surviving me, per stirpes." By adding the words *per stir-*

pes, you have indicated in a shorthand way that if Bob or Cathy is living, then the children of Bob and Cathy do not inherit the parent's share.

By stating "to my issue surviving me," you have indicated that those who inherit property from you must be living at the time of your death. Thus, since Bob and Cathy are both living, they would inherit your property, but neither Al's estate nor his child's estate would inherit your property. Unless you clarify your wishes, it is possible for Al's estate to inherit a share. His share may then be inherited by his wife, since his wife may be entitled to inherit all or part of his estate.

These are only a few examples of similar problems that can arise.

4. *You leave your property to "A and his children."* This language is not specific enough. You probably intend to leave your property to A if he is living at the time of your death, but if he is not then living, to his children if living at the time of your death. However, too often wills are written with imprecise language, and the courts then have the problem of trying to understand what you intended.

Did you really mean that if A has three children living when you die and A is also living, your property would be divided into four shares? Or did you mean that A receives all of it if he is living when you die and that if he is not living, his children inherit his share? Or did you mean that A inherits one-half and his three children inherit the other half?

To complicate this matter further, assume that A at one time had four children, one of whom is now dead. Was it

your intention to leave one part to this dead child's estate?

Because of imprecise language, the answers to these questions are not clear. Obviously the will should be more specific. You should state that you "give, devise, and bequeath all of my property to A if he survives me and if he fails to survive me, to his children surviving me, in equal shares, or all to the survivor of such children surviving me."

5. *You leave your property to your brother, John, and his wife, Mary, if both survive you.* The problem here is that you do not specify the shares that each owns nor do you specify the form of ownership. If both of them are living at the time of your death, do they inherit your property in equal shares or as joint tenants with the right of survivorship? If they own the property equally, then on the death of one of them, the other does not inherit all the property remaining; however, if they own it as joint tenants, the survivor of John and Mary will own it all.

Do not leave the determination of what you intended to a court; clarify this in your will.

6. *You leave all your tangible personal property to your brother, Frank, if he survives you.* By definition, *tangible* refers to something that you can touch and feel. Usually when tangible property is left to someone by will, what is meant is household goods—flatware, clothes, furnishings, etc. All too frequently, people forget that they own other "tangible" property. For example, do you intend to leave your brother, Frank, your automobile or perhaps your speedboat? What about your bicycle or perhaps your expensive golf cart? They, too, are tangible personal property.

More important, you may be the owner of a stamp collection or a valuable painting. Is it your intention to leave this to your brother? It is not necessary to list each item, and this is usually *not* done, but you should consider the preceding comments before you and your lawyer write your will.

Some wills written by a lawyer state that the testator leaves all his or her *personal property* to an individual. In these cases, the lawyer forgot (or never knew) the distinction between *tangible personal property* and personal property. The term personal property is much broader than tangible personal property. For example, if you own stocks in a company, savings bonds, passbooks, or certificates of deposit, these items would be personal property. When the clause of the will is read, the context of the gift indicates that the intention was to leave the personal household furnishings (tangible personal property) and not *all* personal property. Yet, wills are invariably strictly construed. This means that when the term personal property is used, most courts state that they are bound by the language the testator used and are not free to speculate as to what was meant. Therefore, if you use the phrase personal property, this language could be binding on the disposition of your property.

7. *You leave a house to your cousin Fred.* The house has a mortgage, which could have been placed on the house after you wrote your will or perhaps even before you wrote your will. In many states, the law provides that when property is specifically left to someone by will and the property has a mortgage on it, the person receiving the property is entitled to have the mortgage paid off from the balance of your estate. This is known as *exoneration.*

But aside from this rule, you should consider whether this result is what you wish. Is it your intention to have your estate pay off the balance of the mortgage at the time of your death so that Fred receives the house free from the mortgage? Or is it your intention that Fred receive the property *subject* to the mortgage (in other words, Fred will have to pay it off)?

Since it is your property that you are leaving, your wishes should prevail, and this matter should be considered by you and included in your will.

8. *You are angry with your sister Joan because you felt that when your father died and she took the grandfather clock, she cheated you. Your will states that Joan shall receive nothing from your estate because she cheated you years ago.* This statement is defamatory, and Joan can sue your estate for libel and collect damages if she proves the statement to be false. The damages she can recover may be the entire amount of your estate. A will is an inappropriate place to express such sentiments.

9. *You leave your entire estate to your first cousin William. Your will requests that William use the funds for the benefit of all your cousins.* The question that arises here is whether William *must* use the property for the benefit of the cousins. In other words, have you imposed a trust upon the property so that the property is not really owned by William but is held by him for the benefit of your cousins? Or are you really expressing the hope that he *may* do so, but that the decision is strictly at his discretion?

For example, you leave your property to your husband. You then state that it is your "wish and will" that your husband give your daughter, Kathy, $10,000 when she marries to help set up her household.

When Kathy marries, is your husband *obligated* to pay her $10,000? Does the language "wish and will" mean that your request is mandatory, or is it merely the expression of a hope that is not legally binding on your husband?

The courts always wish to determine and enforce the intention of the testator; therefore, it is important for you always to be specific in your will. Whether your wishes are mandatory and legally binding or merely expressions of a wish that is not binding should be made clear by appropriate language. (The technical term used by the courts when the language is not binding is *precatory*.)

10. *Every will should take into account the effect of death taxes. This is done by either directing the source from which death taxes shall be paid or deciding to do nothing about such direction.* The general rule is that if nothing is said about death taxes, the property inherited is reduced by its proportionate share of death taxes. A simple example of this rule is where A inherits $75,000 from your estate and B inherits $25,000. If the total tax is $12,000, then A's share of the tax will be $9,000. This is because A inherited three-quarters of the total of $100,000, and his share must therefore bear the burden of three-quarters of the taxes. Since three-quarters of the total tax of $12,000 is $9,000, this amount will be allocated to A's share.

In one actual case, an individual died with considerable wealth, and the only property owned by the testatrix in her individual name, that is, the only probate asset, was a farmhouse with the surrounding land, worth approximately $75,000. Everything else the testatrix owned was in joint names. The death taxes of this particular estate amounted to $60,000.

The will of this testatrix directed that all death taxes be paid from the rest, residue, and remainder of her estate. She also provided that the farmhouse was to be held for the benefit of her longtime employee and friend, Mary, who was the housekeeper. Mary was to be able to live in the house rent-free for her lifetime and without the payment of any repair or insurance expenses. The only expenses Mary would have would be utilities and property taxes. The testatrix felt that with the small savings that Mary had, plus Social Security and lifetime cash gifts that she made to Mary, Mary was well provided for. However, all her plans were spoiled, since the will directed that taxes be paid from the rest, residue, and remainder of her estate. Because the only property in the rest, residue, and remainder of her estate was the farmhouse, this farmhouse had to be sold to pay death taxes. This was an unfortunate outcome and resulted because the testatrix did not consider or understand the consequences of the particular tax clause.

What the testatrix should have done was to set aside money to pay the death taxes or to have said nothing about them at all. If nothing were said about taxes, everyone who received property on the death of the testatrix would have had to pay a portion of the taxes imposed on the estate. That is, even those who inherited jointly owned property would have had to pay a proportionate part of the taxes. Then, perhaps, one acre of the land inherited by the housekeeper could have been sold to raise the cash to pay her proportionate part of death taxes, leaving the farmhouse and most of the land intact for Mary's benefit.

11. *You leave 1,000 shares of stock to your son. At the time you made your will, you owned 1,000 shares. Since then, there have been two stock splits. In addition, you reinvested the dividends by purchasing additional shares of the same stock. At the time of your death, you own a total of 8,000 shares.* Is it your intention that your son receive only 1,000 shares, as you stated in your will? Or is it your intention that he receive all shares owned on the date of your death or all the shares that originated with the first 1,000 shares that you owned?

The laws of most states originated in England. Throughout history, the courts of England as well as those of the United States have had to decide literally thousands of cases involving meanings of wills. During this time, rules, called *rules of construction,* have evolved. These rules of construction were designed to help the courts decide what the testator meant in each case. Yet it is obvious that there is no rule of construction that is as precise as clear instructions from you, the testator. If what you meant by the direction in your will was that your son shall inherit all the shares of this stock owned by you on the date of your death, then say so.

There is a further problem if, on the date of your death, you do not own any shares. This problem arises because of a rule of law known as *ademption.* In general, this rule states that where specific property no longer owned by the testator on the date of death is left to someone, the beneficiary receives nothing because the gift is considered to be *adeemed,* or "wiped out." In this case, clarification is needed as to whether you as testator left your son the 1,000 shares of stock owned when you executed the will. In other words, was there a specific bequest? If so, since the 1,000 shares were not owned on the date of death, the gift would be adeemed. On the other hand, did you as testator intend that your son receive 1,000 shares of this stock on your death, whether or not you owned the shares on the date of your death? That is, is the executor required to go out and purchase 1,000 shares of the stock for your son?

If it is your desire as testator that your son receive the equivalent of the value of the 1,000 shares as of the date of your death, whether or not you own these shares on the date of your death, you should be specific and say so in your will.

12. *You make a gift to your daughter, Suzanne, if she is an adherent of the Jewish faith at the time of your death.* Theological authorities, just as lawyers, judges, etc., have varying opinions as to what constitutes being an "adherent of the Jewish faith." Do you intend to leave property to your daughter only if she is practicing the dietary laws at the time of your death? Is it your intention that your daughter be required to observe the Sabbath as set forth in the Bible? Your daughter may have married someone outside the Jewish faith. If she did marry outside the Jewish faith but was nonetheless an adherent of the Jewish faith in important respects, was it your intention that she should or should not inherit any part of your property?

Suppose you provided in your will that your estate was to be divided among your nieces and nephews who survive you *and* were Catholics who abided by the laws of the Roman Catholic church. Would a niece who practiced artificial birth control be entitled to inherit a share of your property? Was it your intention that instead of abiding by all the laws of the Catholic church, she would inherit a share if she were a practicing Catholic?

If you are not clear as to what you mean, it may be necessary to have a court decide what you intended. A court proceeding is costly and time-consuming. In addition, the court may reach a conclusion that may not be in accordance with your wishes.

13. *In your will you leave property in trust for the benefit of your children.* Many problems can arise in this type of situation. For example, you provide that the trust shall give income to your son, John, but the will fails to mention when the trust terminates (ends). In such a case, John may never receive principal, and he would receive income only during his lifetime. Then, on John's death, the problem arises as to who is then entitled to the trust principal when the trust terminates.

If you provide that the trust terminates on John's death and the trust principal is to be distributed to John's children, Christine and Richard, in equal shares, the will should clarify whether they must be living at the time of John's death. If this is not specified, the laws of most states provide that if a descendant is dead at a time when he or she is entitled to possession of any property, his or her estate would inherit the designated share. This occurs because of a law known as the antilapse statute: the share of the dead person does not "lapse," or fail, but is nonetheless inherited by that person's estate. Therefore, if Christine dies before John but has a husband who is living, it is possible for Christine's husband to inherit all of her share or perhaps one-half of her share. This result may follow (1) if Christine's will left all her property to her husband or (2) if she left no will, because the laws of intestacy specify who will inherit all of Christine's property interests. (Most states provide that when an individual dies without a will, survived by a spouse and children, the surviving spouse inherits one-half the property left by the decedent.)

In most cases it is natural for people to leave their property to their spouses and then to their descendants, but not to spouses of their descendants. If Christine has children, you would most likely wish them (your grandchildren) to inherit *your* property before Christine's husband does so. If Christine has no children, it is possible that you would wish Richard to inherit Christine's share before Christine's husband does so.

The appropriate language to use to benefit your descendants would be language similar to the following:

The trust shall terminate upon the death of my son, John. Upon termination, my Trustee shall pay over and distribute the trust principal, as then constituted, to my then-surviving issue, per stirpes.

The suggested language does several things.

1. It specifies what property shall be distributed (namely, the principal then held).
2. It specifies that the ones who shall inherit are those living at the time of John's death (to "my then-surviving issue"; the word *then* refers to the date of John's death).
3. It specifies how the division shall be made by the use of the phrase per stirpes (Christine's living children inherit the one-half share that Christine would have inherited had she been living at the time of John's death).

Another example: You provide for disposition of the trust principal to your son, John. You provide that he shall receive one-third of the trust principal at age 21, one-third at age 25, and one-third at age 30. This is clearly incorrect because the language used does not dispose of all the property. An illustration will readily show why this is so.

Assume the property is at all times worth $10,000. Then at age 21, John will receive $3,333 (one-third of $10,000), leaving a balance of $6,667. At age 25, he will receive another one-third of the

principal, $6,667, or $2,222, which leaves a balance of $4,445. Finally at age 30, he will receive one-third of $4,445, or $1,482, which leaves a balance of $2,963. This balance of $2,963, you will note, is left in the trust, and you have not made provision for its distribution. Appropriate language should take care of this situation.

Another example: You provide that all the trust property is held until John dies or attains age 35, whichever occurs earlier, but if John dies before age 35, the property shall be distributed to his wife Mary.

At the time you created the trust under your will, John was married to Mary. However, when John dies, say at age 34 (before he is entitled to all of the principal), he is no longer married to Mary, having been divorced from her for the last six months. No consideration was given to whether or not Mary would be John's wife at the time John died. Appropriate language should therefore be inserted to take care of this situation.

In addition, language should be inserted that requires Mary to be living at that time. If this is not done and you live in a state where there is an antilapse statute, then Mary's estate would inherit the property. In this case *her* closest relatives would inherit the property. This means that if there are no children of John and Mary then living (your grandchildren), *her* parents and *her* brothers and sisters would inherit your property.

Perhaps you provide that all the income shall be distributed to your son John. No provision is made for distribution of principal.

Were you alive and were your son in

need of large sums for his health, support, or education, you would pay whatever was needed. Why then limit distributions from the trust to income only? If no provision is made for distributing any sums from the principal, the trustee would be unable to distribute principal. When preparing the will, you should consider giving the trustee discretion to distribute principal. If it is your desire to be restrictive in this regard, you can do this by limiting the trustee's exercise of such discretion to "emergency needs" for your son's health, housing, etc.

14. *In your will you leave property in trust for the benefit of your wife Joan and on her death the property is to be paid over to her children.* As obvious as it may seem, you will note that this provision does not take into account the fact that your wife may remarry and have additional children by a second husband. The will here leaves the property to her children and is not limited to your descendants. If it is your desire to leave your property to *your* descendants, then say so directly or by using language similar to the following:

> *If my wife Joan survives me, the trust shall terminate on the death of my wife Joan. On termination, the trust principal, as then constituted, shall be paid over and distributed to the children then surviving of the marriage of my wife Joan and me, in equal shares, or all to the survivor of such children then living.*

15. *It should be clear that a will disposes of property owned by you at the moment of your death.* Assume that the principal asset you own is a stock certificate representing the ownership of one-third of the stock of a family-owned corporation. Your two brothers own the other two-thirds of the stock.

The stock was inherited from your parents, and for the last 20 years you and your brothers ran the business in harmony. Each of you took an equal salary. If the business were sold to an outsider, each of you would receive approximately $250,000.

On your death you leave your entire estate to your wife of 25 years. The most important asset you leave to her is the stock certificate. What can she do with the stock certificate? Will she receive income from it? Since the stock certificate only represents a one-third interest in the corporation, the other stockholders really control the business. The economic benefits from the corporation are controlled by your two brothers. They can withdraw all or most of the profits in the form of salaries and other employee benefits. They may declare no dividends on the stock, preferring instead to use the money in the business. Can your wife sell the stock to an outsider? Legally yes, but who would buy it when the stock really has no current value?

Can your wife compel your brothers to sell the business to an outsider so she will have at least the benefit of the use of the $250,000? The answer is no.

This seemingly valuable asset is really almost valueless because it may give your wife no present income or capital. The stock is then only a piece of paper that seemingly represents something worth $250,000, but in reality does not.

What should have been done?

a. A stockholder's agreement should have been entered into that *requires* the corporation or the other stockholders to purchase the stock of any deceased stockholder. In this way, the stock would be sold to or redeemed by the corporation or the other stockholders. The estate would then receive $250,000, and, in turn, your wife would really receive what you thought she should receive, namely $250,000.

This agreement is commonly referred to as a *buy-sell agreement* or a *stockholder's redemption agreement*. The purpose of this agreement is to turn a piece of paper, the stock certificate, into an asset worth its proportionate share of the business. Without the agreement, the stock has little economic value. Your brothers would then end up owning 100 percent of the business without any interference or claims by your wife.

b. An agreement could have been entered into whereby your wife would be entitled to be employed by the corporation at the same salary as your brothers, or perhaps she would be entitled to a continuation of your salary as a form of deferred compensation based on your past employment.

It must be recognized that a stock certificate represents only a percentage ownership of a corporation. Unless this stock represents a majority interest in the corporation, or contractual rights requiring the purchase of the stock or liquidation of the corporation, the actual dollar value of the stock is severely limited.

The point to be noted here is that while a will may be well written and have provisions that appear to be 100 percent suitable, unless care is taken to see how the document (or instrument) will work with the assets you own, all your plans may not work out.

16. *The maker of the will must remember how its provisions will be implemented.* For example, in one instance, the principal asset owned was stock in a successful restaurant. The decedent was the owner of 40 percent of the stock. He was the manager and received a yearly salary of $45,000 plus the use of a car. When he died, the other stockholder hired another manager, his nephew, for $60,000 per year, and the stockholder took a salary of $30,000 for himself as a part-time employee.

After paying these salaries the corporation had no profits to pay as dividends. The wife of the 40 percent stockholder inherited his stock but could not turn it into cash. All she had was a piece of paper (the stock certificate) that said she owned 40 percent of the stock of the corporation that owned the restaurant.

If the restaurant were sold, her share would have come to $250,000, but she had no way of forcing the 60 percent stockholder to make the sale. Had there been a stockholder's agreement or employment agreement, she would have been protected.

The lesson to be learned is that you should look at your assets and see if they have economic value apart from the will. If not, try to make them productive after your death. These principles also apply to other potentially valuable interests such as partnerships, as the following example illustrates.

Suppose that during his lifetime Hal was a one-third partner with his two cousins in a large resort hotel operation. Hal was in charge of the food operation, one cousin was in charge of the front desk and grounds, and the other cousin was in charge of the office and finances. The three cousins each lived on the premises with their families, rent and tax free, and each drew a salary of $80,000 yearly.

There was a short partnership agreement. After all, nothing elaborate was needed among cousins. To keep the business in the family, the agreement provided that as long as any of the cousins lived, the partnership would continue. Nothing else of importance was in the agreement.

When Hal died, the two remaining cousins voted to hire their two sons to replace Hal at an annual salary of $40,000 each. Hal's wife was not an employee and was asked to leave.

As in the past, after salaries, cars, etc., the partnership had no profits to distribute to Hal's widow and family. On a financial statement the one-third partnership interest had great value because of the value of the land and buildings, but it had little value to Hal's family. Hal's family could not force the partnership to dissolve or to sell its land and buildings. In addition, his family could not derive any income from the partnership, as there was none.

Had Hal, or his advisors, given any thought to this situation, he would have realized that a will is like a funnel. The funnel is only as good as the assets one can "pour" into it. In this case, the partnership interest was not well protected.

17. *From time to time people change their minds about the amount of property they wish to leave someone.* Assume you leave $10,000 to your good friend and neighbor, Sybil. After a bitter argument you decide to eliminate this bequest to her. You take out the original of your executed will, and in ink you cross out the statement about the bequest to her. You also decide to change two other gifts at the same time. The gift to your godchild, Eunice, is increased from $10,000 to $20,000, and the one to your cousin, Franklin, is reduced from $7,500 to $5,000.

The gifts to Eunice and Franklin were changed by your crossing out in ink the figures in your existing will and inserting the new amounts.

Your acts create problems. Most states require strict compliance with the formalities of execution for a will to be valid. Also, different state laws set forth how a will is to be revoked. When you strike out a gift or change its amount, what has really happened? The act may be a revocation of part of the will.

Some states permit a revocation of part of a will. Thus, in these states the gift to Sybil can be revoked. In those states that do not permit a partial revocation, striking out Sybil's name and the dollar amount or the entire sentence will really have no legal effect.

When you changed the amount, you did not insert the new amount with the formalities required for execution of wills. In those states that permit a partial revocation of a will, a further complication arises. Since the new amount has no legally binding effect, the question is whether you intended that the prior gift (the gift of $10,000 to Eunice) be revoked, but only if the $20,000 gift becomes legally binding. Or did you intend to revoke the old gift completely whether or not the new gift was valid?

It may be easier to answer the last two questions when an amount is increased than when it is decreased. In the case of the gift to Eunice, in which the amount is increased but the increase is not effective, you would have wished Eunice to have at least the lower amount. However, in the case of the gift to Franklin, you reduced the gift from $7,500 to $5,000. Would you rather that Franklin receive nothing instead of $7,500? Even if the court does decide the question in the way you would have wished, a court proceeding is an expensive matter, far more expensive than it would cost to redo your will or prepare a codicil. (See page 2 for a definition of *codicil*.)

Once a will is executed, no changes should be made in it without consulting with your attorney. Usually the easiest way to make changes is to do so by codicil.

I have a bank account, and I have named my sister Jane as joint owner of it. At the present time, I really want to leave the money in this account to my sister Mary. Can I do so by will?

No. A will only disposes of property individually owned by you at the moment of your death. When you have a joint bank account, at the moment of your death the joint owner becomes the sole owner. (See page 66.) Therefore, your will does not operate to affect ownership of this account. (There is an exception to this rule with respect to *Totten Trusts*, which are discussed in the section headed Trusts. Also, there may be exceptions for certain kinds of bank accounts in certain states. Your lawyer should be consulted.)

I have named my sister Jane as the beneficiary of my life insurance. I now wish to name my sister Mary as the beneficiary in place of Jane. Can I do so by will?

No. The insurance company that issued the policy is bound by the contract that you made with it to pay the beneficiary you named on the form provided to you. At the moment of your death, you do not own this policy or its proceeds; at the moment of your death, the named beneficiary becomes the owner.

If you do not name a beneficiary at all, the contract with the insurance company, with rare exceptions, provides that it will pay over the insurance proceeds to your estate. If the proceeds are paid over to your estate, then of course you will have the right to dispose of the proceeds by your will.

When I bought my U.S. Series E Bonds, I named my sister Jane as the person to whom all the bonds will be paid on my death. I now wish to name my sister Mary as the beneficiary. Can I do so by my will?

No. The payment of the proceeds of U.S. savings bonds is governed by United States Treasury regulations. These Treasury regulations provide that the proceeds will be paid to the beneficiary you designated during your lifetime. Whatever you write in your will with respect to leaving these bonds to someone is not legally controlling and would not accomplish what you want.

What do I do to make the changes that I desire?

In the case of the bank account, you should go to the bank and fill out a new signature card, instructing the bank what you wish done with your money on your death. If you are named as the only owner of the account, then on your death the proceeds will be paid over to the executor of your estate and, in this case, the language of the will would tell the executor how to distribute this money.

For the insurance policy, contact your insurance agent or the home office of the insurance company and ask for a change-of-beneficiary form. Then insert the name of the beneficiary you desire, sign the form, and mail it to the agent or the insurance company. The change will be recorded by the company, which will then send you an acknowledgment that this has been done. This is the simplest way to handle the matter. The insurance proceeds can of course be paid to your estate, and in such a case, the language of the will shall take care of who gets the proceeds.

In the case of the savings bonds, a change-of-beneficiary form is available at the bank or at the regional office of the Federal Reserve Bank. If you follow the instructions on this form, you can make whatever changes you desire.

Lately I have not been getting along too well with my second wife. I would rather leave all my property to my children. Can I do so?

Usually not. For the purpose of this discussion, we must first assume there is no written agreement between you and your current spouse that provides for what happens to your property upon the death of either of you. If there is such an agreement, it is really a contract that is binding on you. If you break the agreement, the court will enforce it even after your death and may require the executor of your estate to satisfy its provisions. This type of agreement is called a *prenuptial agreement* (when it is entered into before marriage).

In general, each state has its own laws as to what amount of your property must be left to your spouse. Except for such laws, every person is generally free to leave his or her property to whomever he or she wishes.

At one time, many state laws protected the wife by giving her *dower* rights in the property of her deceased husband. These dower rights took many forms. As a rule, a dower right took the form of giving the wife an interest for life (called a life estate) in the real property owned by her husband at any time during the marriage. The protection of the laws was extended in such a way as to give such dower rights even if the husband disposed of the property during his lifetime. This is why a wife may have been asked to sign a deed in the past when property was sold. The effect of signing was to give up any dower rights in the property. Protection for the husband, similar to dower rights, was extended in the form of giving him *curtesy* rights in the property of the deceased wife.

The majority of states now have abolished or greatly modified dower and curtesy and have instead given certain rights to the surviving spouse. (Remember, *spouse* refers to one's husband in the case of a wife and to one's wife in the case of a husband. *Surviving* refers to the one who outlives the other.) These rights take different forms in each state. Usually they provide that the surviving spouse is entitled to a certain percentage of the estate of the dead spouse. If this is not given by will, then the surviving spouse can elect to take the minimum share provided for by that state's law.

An example of this situation would be when the husband dies first and leaves the following assets:

A house that is jointly owned with right of survivorship to his wife and is worth	$150,000
An insurance policy insuring his life, with his wife named as beneficiary. She receives from the insurance company the face amount of	200,000
Stock of a corporation that is worth	300,000
	$650,000

The husband's will leaves his wife $75,000 and the balance to his children by a first marriage. As pointed out earlier, the will can only dispose of property owned by the husband individually at the moment of death. It is clear that the wife will become the sole owner of the house, since it was titled in her name and her husband's name as joint tenants with right of survivorship. She survived him and at the moment of his death she became sole owner. The proceeds of the insurance policy, or $200,000, will be paid to his wife by the insurance company, since she was named as the beneficiary of the policy.

Let us assume that Maryland law applies here. Maryland law states that a surviving spouse (whether male or female) may elect to take, instead of property left by will, one-third of the probate estate if there are surviving issue and one-half if there are no surviving issue. Here the wife was left $75,000 under the will but actually received a total of $425,000 by reason of the husband's death (the house plus the insurance proceeds plus the $75,000 bequest). Yet the law now permits the wife to "elect against" the will. She will therefore be entitled to receive $100,000 (instead of the $75,000 bequest), which is one-third of the $300,000 he left in his probate estate, in addition to the house and the insurance proceeds. (The effect of death taxes has not been taken into account in order to simplify this illustration.)

I have left my spouse $150,000 by naming her the beneficiary of my

pension plan. Since I own $100,000 in stocks and bonds in my own name, may I leave all $100,000 to my children?

Probably not. The laws of several states usually provide that the property you own individually is subject to the laws dealing with the minimum share your spouse is entitled to. Regardless of the amount of property (other than individually owned property) that you leave your spouse, your spouse is still entitled to the "minimum share" provided for by state law from your individually owned property (the property controlled by the terms of your will).

The stocks and bonds are individually owned by you, and the laws of most states provide that your spouse would be entitled to her statutory or minimum share from these assets.

I live in California. Do these rules as to how much I must leave my spouse apply to me, too?

No, but the rules as to what you own are different, too. Arizona, California, Idaho, Louisiana, Nevada, New Mexico, Texas, Washington, and Wisconsin have community property laws. In general, these laws provide that all property acquired by either the husband or wife during the marriage is community property. (The marriage is considered something like a partnership or "community"; this community property is, in general, limited to property acquired during the

marriage.) The following are usually not considered community property:

1. all property owned before marriage
2. all increases, profits, and income derived from property owned before marriage
3. property acquired by either the husband or wife by gifts, devise (that is, inherited under the terms of a will), or descent (that is, inherited from someone who dies without a will)

The important legal effects of property being considered community property are as follows:

1. Each party to the marriage is considered to own one-half of such property.
2. One party to the marriage cannot dispose of any part of the community property to third parties during his or her lifetime without the consent of the other party.
3. On the death of one party to the marriage, the dead party (the decedent) is not restricted from leaving his or her share of the community property to whomever he or she wishes.

These rules are subject to modifications that are not uniform for each of the states mentioned. In general, the principal rules are

1. You and your spouse may, by written agreement, vary the rules; however, Louisiana prohibits this.
2. In Washington, the surviving spouse is entitled to 100 percent of the com-

munity property and 50 percent of the *quasi-community property*. In the other community property states that recognize the concept of quasi-community property, the survivor is entitled to one-half of such property.

Quasi-community property is property that was acquired by the decedent (deceased) in another state, which would have been treated as community property in Washington had it been acquired by either one of you had you then lived in Washington (instead of the other state). For example, you saved $30,000 from your salary while working in Nebraska, and you inherited $40,000 from your sister while living in Nebraska. Had you acquired the $30,000 while living in Washington, the money would have been considered community property. Therefore, the $30,000 is considered to be quasi-community property. The $40,000 would not be considered community property because it was inherited. Therefore, it is not considered to be quasi-community property. It is considered to be separate property.

3. Wisconsin's system of law constitutes a slight variation of the community property system but substantially with the same consequences. Instead of the quasi-community property concept, Wisconsin refers to such property as *deferred marital property,* and the surviving spouse is entitled to one-half of such property.

4. Louisiana's rules are based on the civil law, which, in part, provides that children are entitled to inherit a certain portion of your property. This is known as *forced heirship.*

With respect to disposing of property that is not community property, the law varies from community property state to community property state. It is therefore wise to consult an attorney in your state for the answers to your questions.

I remarried 15 years ago. Since then, my children will not talk to me. I wish to leave them nothing under my will. May I do so?

Yes. In every state except Louisiana, you may disinherit children and leave them nothing. Louisiana requires that you leave some property to your children.

If I wish to leave my children nothing in my will, must I name them and leave each one dollar?

In most states, no. However, in a number of states, if you die leaving children who are not named or provided for in the will or otherwise, the children not named are entitled to take some share of your estate as though you died without a will (intestate).

Even in those states where you need not name a child whom you disinherit, you should do so when a child is born after you make your will. If you do not do so, the child will take that part of your estate as though you died intestate.

In general, if a child is left nothing by will, it is wise to name the child. This advice is based on the general rule that in order to make a will, you have to be legally competent and of sound mind. The courts have adopted a simple test to see if someone is competent. The test determines whether the person has a general knowledge of his or her affairs and knows the natural objects of his or her bounty. A child is usually the natural object of one's bounty. Therefore, if your children are not named as the ones eventually to inherit your estate, an argument can be raised by them that you were not competent to make a will.

To be more specific, let us discuss the following example. You are a widower who has lived with a woman for two years and wishes to leave her all your property. Your children will receive nothing. If you do not mention your children in your will, they may contest the will. They can state that since you did not provide for the natural objects of your bounty, your children, you were not competent to make your will. If the court decides that you were not competent, you will have died intestate (without a valid will), and all your property will go to your children.

In general, the question of your competence is one for the trier of fact, which would be a jury or a judge. If the jury or judge can be convinced of your incompetence, the one you wished to benefit, your female companion, may not be benefited.

To prevent this, simply name your children and leave them each one dollar. They can still claim you were incompetent but cannot do so on the basis that

you were not aware of the natural objects of your bounty. (Also see the discussion of *undue influence* on page 112.)

I was married years ago. The marriage ended in divorce. I want to treat my children by my first marriage equally with my children by my second marriage, but I want to be certain my first wife receives none of my property directly or indirectly. What can be done?

Let us assume that there is no agreement between you and your first wife to leave her some of your property by will. If there is such an agreement and you do not fulfill your agreement, your first wife will then be a creditor of your estate. If there is a separation agreement, you should show it to your lawyer to review in preparing your will.

The principal problem arises if you leave, say, 20 percent of your estate to your two children by your first marriage. If you leave this percentage to them as outright owners, they may do with the property as they see fit. They can then give the property to their mother (your first wife). Also, we must assume that a child of yours could die without leaving a spouse or children surviving him or her. If the child dies without a will (remember, the child may be legally incapable of making a will because of age), in most states the surviving parents inherit all of such child's property. In each case, then, the child's mother (your first wife) would essentially be inheriting your property.

Consider leaving such children's shares in a trust and either not giving them any income during the life of their mother (which is designed to prevent their mother from benefiting from such income) or giving them income but not giving them principal until the death of their mother.

Please explain how one can ensure that one's wishes are carried out by the use of an *in terrorem* clause.

An *in terrorem* clause provides that if any beneficiary should contest the terms of the will, any legacy to such person shall be void. Such a clause conditions a bequest on compliance with the requirements imposed by the decedent. Unless the conditions are illegal or against public policy, the courts will enforce such conditions. Still, the courts do not favor such clauses and will enforce them only with apparent reluctance.

Therefore, such a clause will usually not be enforced unless the condition imposed precisely fits the facts of the case. For example, assume you were to bequeath real property to your niece but state that you will only do so if she does not contest your will. If she were to file suit seeking clarification of the terms of your will, the courts would undoubtedly state that seeking clarification is not the same as contesting the will, and therefore the bequest is valid.

As another example, you bequeath $100,000 to your nephew on condition that he not marry within 10 years of his college graduation. Many courts would consider such a condition as a hindrance to marriage and in violation of public policy and would refuse to enforce it.

In general, then, *in terrorem* clauses are valid but are strictly construed to avoid making the bequest invalid. Note that the laws of many states now provide that if a person has good reason to contest a will, a clause intending to penalize someone for contesting the will is void.

My husband died without a will. We have two children. Under the laws of my state, I inherit half the property and my children inherit the other half. I am the estate's personal representative. One of the items owned by my husband when he died was a 26-foot power boat worth $50,000. I will be retitling the boat next week so that I will be the sole owner of it, giving my children an equivalent amount of cash. Later on, after all taxes are paid, the estate will be distributed. Should I transfer ownership of the boat to myself now?

The answer to this question depends on what income the estate has and the timing of the distribution. It is therefore important that you first have your accountant or your lawyer analyze what the taxable income of the estate will be. To the extent that there is income from the estate during the period in which you distribute the boat to yourself, you may be legally required to report the income for income tax purposes. The explanation that follows will clarify this statement.

Though an estate, if large enough, is

required to pay death taxes, it may also be required to pay income taxes. For example, an estate sells the business it owns and collects $100,000 by reason of the sale. The estate's representative invests the $100,000 in a certificate of deposit at a bank. The interest from the $100,000 is $10,000 per year. This $10,000 is income that is subject to federal income tax.

Now let us assume that the estate distributes the $10,000 to the beneficiary who is entitled to this income. The estate will now receive a deduction for the $10,000 and will have no taxable income. However, the beneficiary will be required to report the $10,000 as income and pay the appropriate income tax on this amount.

The technical tax name given to what income the estate or the beneficiary must report for income tax purposes is *distributable net income,* or *DNI.* (DNI does not quite mean the same thing as taxable income. But for purposes of this book we will be treating DNI as though it meant taxable income.)

Not everything that an estate receives is part of its taxable income. An example of this is the prior situation in which the business was sold. The $100,000 received would not be taxable income if the business was valued at $100,000 for estate tax purposes. (Why not? Because the amount received was equal to its basis, that is, its value for estate tax purposes. There is no income when something is sold for the same amount as its basis; all that occurs is the recovery of principal.)

One further rule: An estate's taxable income is figured on its income for its taxable year. Most of us report our income on a calendar-year basis. This means that whatever money or property we receive as income between January 1 and December 31 of any year is our taxable income for that year. An estate is considered to be a new taxpayer that comes into being on the date of the decedent's death. At this time, the estate has the right to pick its taxable year. The estate representative has the choice whether to have the estate's taxable year end on December 31 or at the end of any other month. Once the choice is made, a change cannot easily be made.

Now let's apply these rules to your question about transferring ownership of the boat. Let us assume your husband died on February 15. Assume, too, that the income of the estate will be $48,000 per year on the average, or $4,000 per month.

If the estate chooses December 31 to close its taxable year, then it will have income of $42,000 (the income for February being only $2,000, since it is for one-half month). If you distribute the boat, worth $50,000, to yourself on February 28 of the year your husband died, the law will require you to report all of the income of the estate generated during this period as your income. Since the income of the estate for the period ending December 31 is $42,000, you (the beneficiary) will be required to report this $42,000 as your income. In general, any distribution by an estate constitutes taxable income to the extent there is any taxable income in the year when the estate makes such distribution.

To pursue this matter further, assume that you distribute to your children $50,000 ($25,000 to each) in cash and that it is also distributed on February 28. Since the income of the estate is $42,000 (the distributable net income, or DNI), the law now requires that this income be apportioned among you and the children. Since you received 50 percent of the total amount distributed, you would report 50 percent of the $42,000 of DNI, or $21,000, as income in your taxable year ending December 31. Each of your children would also report $10,500.

If no distribution is made by the estate, then the $42,000 of income is taxable to the estate at its applicable rate. When the $42,000 is taxed to you (or to you and the children), the estate gets a deduction for this amount and the estate will have no income tax to pay.

To answer the question, you must consider your other income and the other income of your children. Then your accountant or your lawyer would prepare tentative income tax returns for the estate, you, and your children, showing what the total taxes would be both ways, that is, if a distribution is made and if a distribution is not made.

The reader should be aware of two possible variations to the above. The first one, based on the facts just given, is to have the estate pick a taxable year that ends February 28. If the estate income (DNI) for this short period is only $2,000, and the boat worth $50,000 is distributed on February 28, you would be considered to have income of only $2,000. The balance of the value of the boat, or $48,000, would not be considered income. The reason is that you are only taxable on income to the extent of the estate's taxable income (DNI) for its taxable year. Since the estate's DNI here was $2,000, this is the limit of the income that you will be taxed on.

The second possible variation is for the estate to select as its taxable year the period ending January 31 of the following year. In this case, the income for the eleven and a half months (from the preceding February 15) would presumably be $46,000. If the boat is distributed to you on February 28, though you would be required to report $46,000 as your income, the income would have to be reported by you only in the following year. This is possible because of another rule that says that income received from an estate is income to the beneficiary only in the year of the estate ending within the beneficiary's tax year. This enables you to defer paying taxes for a substantial period of time.

The reader should note that most of the rules just mentioned also apply to the taxation of income from trusts. These rules are complex, and their application to your situation requires the assistance of an experienced accountant and a lawyer.

Do be aware, however, of an important exception to the taxability of distributions from an estate. The exception provides that when a will bequeaths a specific item or cash, referred to as a *specific legacy*, the recipient is not considered to have received any taxable income from the estate. This is another reason to have a will and to be certain that the will specifically bequeaths tangible personal property to the extent desired.

Types of Wills

I have heard about a joint will. What is it?

One document that is usually signed by husband and wife and that represents the will of each party. This document is sometimes referred to as a "joint and mutual" will. In a joint will the terms usually provide that the one who dies first leaves everything to the other. Then, on the death of the second party, everything is left to specified persons, usually children.

A joint will sounds like a good idea because it could save me legal fees. Also, it saves the bother of having two pieces of paper. Do you approve of joint wills?

No. First, it takes more time for the lawyer to draft (write) a joint will than to draft two separate wills. The more time it takes, the higher the legal fee. Second, many state courts have found that a joint will is really a contract for the survivor to leave his or her property the way the will read on the death of the first of you to die. In such cases, there could be substantial adverse tax consequences as a result of the Internal Revenue Service disallowing the estate a marital deduction. If you really want to contract to leave your property a certain way, then say so, and ask your lawyer to prepare an appropriate agreement.

May I have an *irrevocable* will?

Yes, but even though it is called irrevocable, it is generally considered to be revocable as a will. An understanding of the previous sentence requires the recollection of an earlier statement. That is, that a will is a revocable instrument. On the other hand, an irrevocable will (if legally enforceable) is inconsistent with the idea that a will is always revocable.

The vast majority of the courts in all jurisdictions now state that a will that is called irrevocable can indeed be revoked. However, the irrevocable will may be

SAMPLE AFFIDAVIT

STATE OF _____

COUNTY OF _____

Each of the undersigned, individually and severally, being duly sworn, deposes and says:

The within will was subscribed in our presence and sight at the end thereof by _____, the within named testator, on the _____ day of _____, 19_____, at _____.

Said testator at the time of making such subscription declared the instrument so subscribed to be his last will.

Each of the undersigned thereupon signed his name as a witness at the end of said will, at the request of said testator and in his presence and sight and in the presence and sight of each other.

Said testator was, at the time of so executing said will, over the age of 18 years, and, in the respective opinions of the undersigned, of sound mind, memory, and understanding and not under any restraint or in any respect incompetent to make a will.

Said testator, in the respective opinions of the undersigned, could read, write, and converse in the English language and was suffering from no defect of sight, hearing, or speech, or from any other physical or mental impairment that would affect his capacity to make a valid will. The will was executed as a single, original instrument and was not executed in counterparts.

Each of the undersigned was acquainted with said testator at such time, and makes this affidavit at his request. The within will was shown to the undersigned at the time this affidavit was made, and was examined by each of them as to the signatures of said testator and of the undersigned.

The foregoing instrument was executed by said testator and witnessed by each of the undersigned affiants.

Under the supervision of _____, attorney-at-law.

_____

_____

Severally sworn to before
me this _____
day of _____
19_____

_____

Notary Public

considered a contract, and if valid as a contract, can be enforced as such.

What is a self-proved will?

In many states, when a will is probated the witnesses must appear personally before the court or before a representative of the execution of the will. In an attempt to simplify this procedure, the laws of many states now provide that when an affidavit is signed by the witnesses setting forth the facts about the will's execution, their personal appearance in court is not necessary. A will that is submitted to a court for probate and has this affidavit attached or presented separately is called a self-proved will.

What is a living will?

A living will is a separate document in which a person, while competent to do so, expresses a wish that his or her life not be prolonged by artificial, extraordinary, or heroic measures. This type of will does not involve disposing of one's property.

Is a living will legally binding?

Yes. While every state now has a law authorizing a living will, in some states the legislation does not permit the withdrawal or withholding of nutrition and hydration (that is, food and water, usually). At this time the law is not clear whether legislative permission is necessary for a person to require that nutrition and hydration be withdrawn or withheld.

What does such a will look like?

Each state that has adopted, or approved, the living will has its own suggested form. Use of the form is optional and its language may be modified. Maryland's suggested form is shown on p. 49.

May I designate another who can make decisions regarding my health care?

Yes.

How is this done?

Bear in mind that the laws of each state vary somewhat. In general, you do so by executing a document appointing a health care agent (sometimes called a "surrogate"), whose decisions are required to be followed by the health care provider.

Maryland law, for example, has a suggested and optional form to accomplish this. The document may contain special limiting or mandatory instructions to your health care agent, all as desired by you.

What is a durable power of attorney relating to health care?

It is a written document that gives another person (known as the surrogate), as a substitute for the patient, the power

LIVING WILL

If I am not able to make an informed decision regarding my health care, I direct my health care providers to follow my instructions as set forth below. [Initial those statements you wish to be included in the document and cross through those statements that do not apply.]

A. If my death from a terminal condition is imminent, and even if life-sustaining procedures are used, there is no reasonable expectation of my recovery—

_____ I direct that my life not be extended by life-sustaining procedures, including the administration of nutrition and hydration artificially.

_____ I direct that my life not be extended by life-sustaining procedures, except that, if I am unable to take food by mouth, I wish to receive nutrition and hydration artificially.

_____ I direct that, even in a terminal condition, I be given all available medical treatment in accordance with accepted health care standards.

B. If I am in a persistent vegetative state, that is, if I am not conscious and am not aware of my environment nor able to interact with others, and there is no reasonable expectation of my recovery within a medically appropriate period—

_____ I direct that my life not be extended by life-sustaining procedures, including the administration of nutrition and hydration artificially.

_____ I direct that my life not be extended by life-sustaining procedures, except that if I am unable to take in food by mouth, I wish to receive nutrition and hydration artificially.

_____ I direct that I be given all available medical treatment in accordance with accepted health care standards.

C. If I am pregnant my agent shall follow these specific instructions:

By signing below, I indicate that I am emotionally and mentally competent to make this Living Will and that I understand its purpose and effect.

_____   _____
          (Date)   (Signature of Declarant)

The Declarant signed or acknowledged signing this Living Will in my presence, and based upon my personal observation, the Declarant appears to be a competent individual.

_____   _____
        (Witness)   (Witness)

            (Signature of two witnesses)

and authority to make medical decisions relating to the rendering of medical treatment and health care.

Though there are not many court decisions dealing with such powers, the principle is that the holder of the power can make medical decisions in place of the patient when the patient is disabled and cannot make such decisions. The holder appears to have the power not only to authorize medical care and treatment, but also to direct withdrawal of such care and treatment.

A durable power of attorney relating to health care is considered a broader and more desirable grant of authority than a living will. This is so because the living will authorization is limited to those situations where the patient has a terminal condition and death is imminent. Also, with a durable power of attorney, the holder of the power is available to make specific health care decisions based on the then-known facts and some knowledge of what the patient wants.

The President's Commission for the Study of Ethical Problems in Medicare and Biomedical and Behavioral Research stated that such durable powers of attorney are preferable to living wills, since they have broader application and provide a better vehicle for patients to exercise self-determination.

Without appointing an agent, may I also leave specific instructions to the health care provider that are required to be followed?

Yes. You may do so in writing and may even issue oral instructions. Maryland's law provides a suggested and optional form for the written instructions.

What happens if, as a result of an auto accident or other cause, I am not terminal (that is, my death is not imminent) but a "vegetable." Can I issue similar directions?

Yes. The United States Supreme Court recently decided a case involving an individual who was in such a state. Medically, this condition is called being in "a persistent vegetative state." It is defined as a condition in which a person exhibits motor reflexes but evinces no indications of significant cognitive function. That is, there is no behavioral evidence of either self-awareness or awareness of the surroundings in a learned manner. The court concluded that an individual has the constitutionally protected right to direct what medical care shall be given, withheld, or withdrawn.

Following this decision, in states where the laws do not specifically so provide, many attorneys now suggest to their clients that the following language be inserted in their living wills:

It is further my wish and direction that if I am in a persistent vegetative state, no nutrition or hydration shall be administered. The determination of whether I am in a persistent vegetative state shall be made by two physicians who have personally examined me, one of whom shall be my attending physician.

I have heard about *holographic* wills. What does that term mean?

Generally, a holographic will is a will that is *entirely* in the handwriting of a testator and is signed and dated. The laws of each state specify when and under what conditions such wills may be made. The main difference between wills that are holographic and other wills is that, when permitted, holographic wills need not have attesting witnesses. Many states permit such wills only when a testator is in the U.S. armed services and makes the will while outside the United States.

What is a *nuncupative* will?

Oral wills are also called nuncupative wills. While all states require that the will be in writing, there are cases in which this requirement is waived. The usual exception is when a will is made on one's deathbed, in which case an oral will is permitted. An oral will is one in which the testator states his or her final wishes in front of appropriate witnesses. (The laws permitting oral wills also usually require three witnesses, death within a certain period of time after making such a will, and certain other conditions.) Few states authorize nuncupative wills.

Courts

What is meant by probate?

Probate is the procedure required by law whereby the court having jurisdiction accepts (or rejects) an instrument as being the will of the decedent.

What does one's probate estate consist of?

Property owned by the testator in his or her own name as sole owner at the moment of death. The will disposes of this property, and this property is therefore the probate estate.

While the testator may own one or more life insurance policies insuring the testator's life, if a beneficiary was named, that beneficiary becomes the sole owner of the insurance proceeds at the moment of death. Therefore, the will of the testator has no control over ownership of the proceeds. If the beneficiary is the estate of the testator, then the provisions of the will would control the ownership of the proceeds. During his or her life-

time, the owner of the policy has control over who is named as beneficiary. Lawyers, the courts, and others will sometimes refer to the probate estate as the "estate."

Note: The term *estate* is also used to refer to assets of a judicially declared incompetent individual, of a minor, or of a bankrupt or insolvent individual. Here, we are only concerned with a decedent's estate.

What do you mean by the court having jurisdiction?

Jurisdiction is the legal authority granted by state law to an appropriate court to exercise its power over the particular subject matter.

Why is it necessary to give any court jurisdiction over my property?

The right to leave property by will to the person or persons of one's choice is not a constitutional right. This right is given by state law. State law requires that before ownership of property is turned over to the person or persons you name in your will, all debts you may have and also all federal and state death taxes must first be paid. The courts are given jurisdiction to see that these objectives are fulfilled.

When the court assumes jurisdiction over wills, the important end results are

1. to establish who is entitled to property or the benefits from it and to transfer ownership of property to the person or persons entitled to it;
2. to see that the ones entitled to it do indeed receive the property or, as directed, the benefits from the property;
3. to pay all debts due from the deceased person whose estate is being administered and to give creditors time to notify the estate's representative of the existence of such claims; and
4. to pay all federal and state death taxes that are due.

What is the name of the court that has jurisdiction?

Each state gives the court a different name. In some states it is called the *orphan's court,* in some the *probate court, surrogate's court,* the *prerogative court,* or the *court of ordinary.*

Sometimes, the language used in a will has to be clarified by the courts to determine what the testator meant. In such cases, jurisdiction may be given to different courts (other than those named above) to answer the questions raised. The courts that have such jurisdiction are called by various names. Some of the names used are *superior court, circuit court,* or *supreme court.*

What happens to a will that is not accepted by the appropriate court?

The will is not legally binding on anyone. However, members of the family may consider themselves morally bound by the wishes expressed in the will.

If the will is not accepted by the court, it is as though the maker of the will died without a will (intestate). In this case, state law determines who is entitled to the property owned by the decedent.

What do I do to be certain that my will is accepted for probate?

Be sure that you follow the law of the state in which you live or in which you sign your will. Each state has its own requirements for a valid will. An example would be the requirement that the testator be of a certain minimum age. Among the requirements are those related to the procedure that must take place when the will is signed. Required procedures are sometimes called *formalities.* They must be followed strictly.

In addition, if your principal residence is in Arkansas, Ohio, or North Dakota, your will may be validated during your lifetime. The procedure to accomplish this validation is known as *antemortem probate.*

Please tell me a little more about antemortem probate.

The process is similar to a court trial. The testator asks for a court determination that his will is a valid and binding one. The obvious principal advantage of the procedure is that thereafter no one can contest that will on the grounds that the testator did not have the required legal capacity or that it was executed under undue influence of anyone. The disadvantage is that since the will then becomes known to the family, it can cause anguish and disharmony.

What is the procedure to be followed on someone's death so that ownership of the decedent's property shall pass to those named in the will or, if there is no will, as provided by state law?

When there is a will, the procedure to accomplish this is known as the probate process, and the process varies from state to state. In general, courts have a printed form usually called petition for probate. Probate means "to prove," and probate is the means whereby an instrument is proven to the satisfaction of the court as being the decedent's will.

When a petition is filed with the court, the court, through its employees, sends notices of the petition to all the interested persons named in the petition, or the petitioner does so. Interested persons are those named in the will, those who would inherit property if there were no will, and in some states, those who are named in a prior will or codicil. This gives those persons an opportunity to challenge the probate of the instrument that the court is asked to accept as the will of the decedent. This procedure is designed to determine if the instrument that is offered for probate really represents the will of the decedent. If the instrument is not accepted as the will of the decedent, then it is as if the decedent died without a will. The person who files the petition is usually the person or persons named in the will as the executor(s) or personal representative(s).

After the will is probated, the property owned by the decedent is administered under the general supervision of the court that approves the probate of the will.

If the decedent dies intestate (without a will), a petition is submitted to the court requesting that the court issue an order giving the petitioner legal authority to represent the estate of the decedent and act on its behalf. This petition is usually called a petition for letters of administration. As is the case when there is a will, after the petitioner is appointed, the court will supervise the administration of the estate's property.

Once the court approves the petition (either to accept the will or appoint the petitioner as the estate representative when there is no will), it will issue an order. The order will accomplish the following: (1) When there is a will, it will accept the document as being the decedent's will; and it will appoint the legal representative of the estate, called the personal representative. (2) When there is no will, it will appoint the legal representative of the estate, also called the personal representative.

When there is a will, the personal representative is required to administer and dispose of the estate property in accordance with the terms of the will. When there is no will, the personal representative is also required to administer and dispose of the estate property in accordance with state law.

The court procedure involved when one dies with a will is similar to the procedure if one dies without a will. To simplify the explanation, the following discussion will generally refer to both procedures as though the decedent died testate (with a will).

Is anyone else required to receive notice of the petition for probate?

Yes. Creditors must be notified. If they are known, or can be identified after reasonable diligent effort, actual notice must be given to them. For this purpose, a creditor should be considered as one to whom a debt is now due or will become due, is absolute or contingent, or is liquidated or unliquidated. A *contingent* debt is one that is dependent on some future event. A *liquidated* debt is one where it is certain how much is due. An *unliquidated* debt is one where the amount due is not determined, such as damages in a personal injury lawsuit.

In addition, in some states, persons who are adversely affected by a will or any codicil are required to be notified. For example, assume that in your will you leave a gift of $5,000 to your friend. You later execute a codicil whereby you reduce the amount of the gift to your friend to $2,000 or you eliminate this gift

entirely. Your friend is adversely affected by the codicil. In many states, he would be considered a person who must be notified of the petition to probate the will and codicil.

Who submits the petition for probate?

In general, it is submitted by the executor or personal representative named in the will. The petition could also be submitted by a surviving spouse or a child. Basically, any interested person or creditor can submit the petition.

When the decedent dies without a will, state law specifies which person or persons are entitled to petition the court to be appointed as the personal representative. In general, those persons most closely related to the decedent are the first ones entitled to be appointed. When more than one person is equally entitled to be appointed (such as children), the court may appoint all or may choose among them.

I have received a notice from the court that my mother's will is about to be probated. My mother left her entire estate to my sister. At the time my mother executed her will, she was living in my sister's house. I feel that the will should not be probated because the will represents my sister's wishes rather than my mother's. What can I do about this?

It should be noted that not everybody may come into court to object to the probate of a will. Those entitled to do so are usually interested persons or those adversely affected by a codicil. When one does object to the probate of a will, documents are filed with the court stating that the offered document is not the will of the decedent. In some states, this procedure is known as *caveating* a will. (*Caveat* is Latin for "let him beware"; therefore, a caveat is a notice to the court to beware and not to accept the instrument as the will of the decedent.) The procedure is similar to any court trial, and the one who objects to the will has the burden of proving his or her contentions. In such cases, consult a lawyer.

What are the grounds for contesting a will?

The grounds for contesting a will can generally be divided into two parts: mechanical defects and substantive defects.

A document becomes a will only when it is admitted to probate. In order to be probated, it is essential that the document be executed in compliance with the formalities of state law. A failure to follow any of the formalities would be considered a mechanical defect.

Most states require that the will be signed in the presence of witnesses, that the witnesses be considered attesting witnesses (in most states this requires that they, at the request of the testator, certify that the testator executed the will), and that the witnesses sign the will in the presence of the testator and in the presence of each other. If any of these formalities is not present, the instrument may fail because it does not represent the will (intent) of the decedent.

For example, you are home ill and you sign your will in the presence of your brother, who serves as a witness. Your brother then takes the will and alone goes next door to your neighbor and asks your neighbor to serve as a witness. You are not present when your neighbor signs as a witness. Your will would be defective because you did not sign the will in front of both witnesses, who, in turn, did not sign in your presence and in the presence of each other.

Another example: when you signed the will, six pages had been typed and were ready for your signature. You and the witnesses signed as each should have. The next day, upon rereading your will, you noticed that on page three of the signed will you made a gift to your friend of $3,000 and you really meant to leave your friend only $1,500. Rather than go back to your attorney, you retyped page three with the exact language of the first will but substituting $1,500 for $3,000. This will is defective because the formalities of execution were not satisfied. Some courts would admit to probate everything except page three, or they might admit to probate everything except the change.

How would anyone know about these mechanical defects?

If called upon in court, the witnesses would have to testify about the facts. Also, copies of the will may be in existence, and the copies may be different from what is offered as the original. These are only two of the ways that mechanical failures can be disclosed.

What do you mean by substantive defects?

In order for a document to be accepted by the courts as a will, the person signing the will must be of "sound and disposing mind" and capable of executing a valid deed or contract. If any of these elements is missing, there would be a substantive defect.

Give some examples of substantive defects in a will.

You may show that your mother signed her will by reason of fraud or by undue influence exercised upon her by your sister. Your mother may have been without the mental capacity to execute a will. Your mother may have thought that she was executing an agreement of some sort rather than her will.

With respect to undue influence, you would perhaps want to show that in a prior will you were treated equally with your sister, that the attorney who drafted your mother's first will was her attorney of many years' standing, and that the attorney who drafted the last version of the will was your sister's personal attorney, or that your sister placed unfair pressure on your mother to sign a will leaving everything to her.

The preceding is not intended to be a complete statement of the law on this subject. It is important that you consult your lawyer if you wish to contest a will.

The important thing to remember is that each state has a time limit during which you *must* file the appropriate pa-

pers to contest or caveat (serve notice to the court) the probate of a will. If the time limit is not strictly observed, you would not be able to contest the probate of the will even if you had a good case.

The court has now accepted the will for probate, or if there is no will, has approved the petition for appointment of the estate's personal representative. What happens now?

If you are appointed the personal representative, you will need to establish your legal authority to "step into the shoes" of the estate; therefore, the court will issue a document under its seal called *letters of administration, letters testamentary,* or some other similar name.

Some courts issue *certificates of letters* (as they are called) proving your authority. In some states, you must order (and pay for, at estate expense) certified copies of the letters you will need to submit to various banks, stock transfer agents, and others who ask for them. These certificates, or certified copies, of letters are evidence that you are the legal representative of the estate and, as such, are legally entitled to act on its behalf, to take possession of the estate assets, and to have temporary ownership of the property while the estate is being administered.

Before the letters are actually issued, you may have to file a bond. The purpose of a bond is to insure the estate beneficiaries and the taxing authorities against losses resulting from improper administration. The laws of most states require the filing of a bond for every estate unless waived. By choice, most wills that appoint a personal representative waive this requirement. Even when the bond requirement is waived by the testator, many states still require a bond to ensure payment of their state's death taxes. This bond is commonly referred to as a nominal bond. However, when a person dies intestate, there is no will that permits the bond to be waived. Therefore, in the majority of states, when a person dies intestate, a bond will be required.

When a bond is required because a person died intestate, or the will does not waive the requirement of a bond, the amount may be equal to the estimated value of the estate or twice the amount of the estate. The premium cost of a bond of $100,000 is approximately $460 per year until the estate is closed. The premium cost of a nominal bond is $75 to $100 per year. The cost of a bond is one reason why it is important to have a will that can waive the bond.

Witnesses

Tell me more about witnesses. Would it be advisable to have three witnesses?

The states of South Carolina and Vermont require three witnesses. However, even these states provide that a will is valid with only two witnesses if the will was executed in a state that allows only two witnesses. For example, New York law provides that a will executed there needs only two witnesses. Thus, a Vermont resident may execute a will in New York with only two witnesses, and the courts of Vermont will accept the will. If you own real estate in South Carolina or Vermont (where three witnesses are required) and are a resident elsewhere, it is advisable to have three witnesses.

Can my husband be a witness to my will?

In most states, there is no legal objection to this. In some states, such as New York, however, a witness is legally prevented (disqualified) from inheriting any property under the will when that witness is necessary to prove the will. For example, if there are only two witnesses to the will and one of them is your husband, the will is valid but your husband may not inherit anything under the terms of your will.

On the other hand, many states do not permit an interested person to become a competent (also called a credible) witness. An interested person becomes a disqualified or incompetent witness. In states that apply this rule, the will would not be valid; the witness may not even waive the right to receive property under the terms of the will so that he or she can become a qualified witness.

In general, it is preferable to have two disinterested witnesses. These witnesses should be persons who can testify in court if it is necessary to prove that all legal formalities in connection with the execution of the will were satisfied.

What do you mean by *interested persons*?

An interested person is an individual who has a direct and immediate financial interest in establishing the validity of your will. For example, if you were to leave $10,000 to your sister in your will, she would be an interested person because she would have a financial interest in assuring that the will is probated.

What happens to my will if the laws of the state in which I live and make my will provide that an interested person is an incompetent witness, but an interested person becomes one of the two required witnesses?

Since your state required two competent witnesses and the interested person becomes an incompetent witness, your will does not have the required number of witnesses. Therefore, the will cannot be admitted to probate and will have no binding legal effect.

Please explain these phrases:

YOU SIGN THE INSTRUMENT, OR BY SOME OTHER PERSON . . .

The usual procedure is for you, the testator, to sign the instrument, using your full name, in ink. If you are unable to write your name, you may place an *X* mark or your initials on the instrument as long as it is later shown that you in-tended the document (instrument) to be your will. If you cannot do that—for example, if you had a stroke and your hands are paralyzed—you can have another person sign your name. The other person must sign at your request and in your presence. In a few states, having another person sign at your request and in your presence may not be acceptable, so a lawyer should be consulted.

IT BE ATTESTED AND SIGNED BY . . . WITNESSES

Generally this means that the witnesses must intend to act as witnesses and in doing so must fulfill all the statutory requirements necessary to the legal execution of a will.

THE WITNESSES BE CREDIBLE

The word *credible* is the equivalent of *competent* and means a person who could legally testify in a court to the facts to which he or she attests.

Please give me an example of what you consider to be the correct language to use when the witnesses sign their names to my will. I understand this language is called an attestation clause.

The foregoing instrument, contained on this and the ( ) preceding typewritten pages, was on the date last above written, signed, sealed, published, and declared by the above-named Testator, (insert name), as and for his Last Will and Testament, in the presence of us, who at his request, in his presence and in the

presence of each other, have hereunto
subscribed our names as witnesses.

_____ *Address* _____

_____

_____ *Address* _____

_____

(If the person making the will is a female, substitute the word *Testatrix* for *Testator* and, of course, *her* for *his*. Also, if the will is executed in a state that requires three witnesses, add another line on which the third witness is to sign.)

Do the witnesses have to know how I disposed of my property?

No. All that is required is that they see you sign the document. In some states, they do not even have to see you sign, as long as you acknowledge to them that the signature is yours.

ESTATES

General Information

What does my estate consist of?

An estate generally consists of two parts:

1. property you own outright in your own name as sole owner
2. property you do not own outright in your name as sole owner, but in which you have some financial interest

What is the practical difference between the two types of property ownership?

Property owned by you outright in your own name as sole owner has these characteristics:

1. Ownership of the property passes to whomever you designate in your will.
2. The property is usually subject to supervisory control by the courts.
3. The property is always subject to federal and state inheritance, estate, or similar taxes.

Property not owned by you outright in your own name as sole owner, but in which you have some financial interest, has these characteristics:

1. Ownership of the property does not usually pass to another under your will.
2. The property is usually not subject to supervisory control by the courts.
3. The property may or may not be subject to federal and state inheritance, estate, or similar taxes.

For example, if the title to a property is registered in your name as sole owner, the property is an item that can be disposed of by will. (By "disposing of" property, we mean stating who becomes the owner after your death.) But if you, the testator, have the property registered in your name as joint owner with another, then on your death the *survivor* becomes the sole or individual owner of the item. Since the survivor becomes the owner at the moment of your death, your will cannot dispose of the property because you do not then own it.

Give me some examples of the two categories of property in an estate.

One category includes bank accounts (checking and savings), certificates of deposit, savings certificates, etc., for which you are shown as sole owner of this property. If stock is owned by you individually (in your sole name), whether the stock is in a publicly held company or in a privately held company, you may effectively dispose of it by will.

If you are listed as a joint owner of stock or bank accounts (the second category of ownership), the surviving owner becomes sole owner on your death. In such a case, you do not own the stock or the bank account at the moment of your death and thus cannot dispose of it by your will. Proceeds of life insurance, when you have designated a beneficiary other than your estate, would also be treated as property that you cannot dispose of by your will. This is so because at the moment of your death, the person named as beneficiary becomes the sole owner of the proceeds.

Note: In many states a joint bank account or certificate of deposit does not always become the sole property of the survivor. The creator of the account may have intended for the survivor to become the sole surviving owner. Yet, when similar cases have been litigated, many courts have concluded that the creator of the account only added the other person to assure convenience and assistance in making withdrawals and carrying on other bank business.

In this latter case, there would not have been a gift during lifetime nor, according to some courts, was it intended that ownership of the account or certificate be shifted to the surviving joint owner. Therefore, since neither the account nor the certificate constituted a will, many courts have decided that the account or certificate belongs to the estate of the decedent (and therefore must be disposed of by the decedent's will). (See also the discussion of Totten Trusts, pages 124–25.) You should discuss this situation with your lawyer.

Administration of an Estate

What is meant by administration of an estate?

An estate consists of property owned by a deceased individual at the moment of death and owned only in the decedent's name. The process involved in collecting the assets belonging to the estate; safekeeping and investing these assets; paying the estate's debts, taxes, and expenses; and distributing the balance of the estate to those entitled to it is called *administering* an estate. This entire process is sometimes referred to as *settling* an estate or probating an estate.

Where is an estate administered?

In the county of the state where the decedent was "domiciled" at the time of his or her death. The term *domicile* refers to that place where a person has resided with the intent to make that residence his or her fixed and permanent home. A person may have several residences (for example, one or more vacation homes) but only one domicile. For simplicity, we will usually refer to a person's residence, but we will mean domicile.

The place of principal residence (domicile) is the place where the principal administration (sometimes referred to as *domiciliary administration*) takes place. When a decedent also owns property located in another state, administration of this other property frequently will be required in the other state. When this occurs, the administration is called *auxiliary* or *ancillary* administration, which means administration that is secondary to the principal place of administration.

What is a public administrator?

When someone dies *intestate* (without a will), the laws of every state provide who is first entitled to the privilege of being the administrator of the estate. Usually this means that the spouse is first entitled to this privilege, then children, then grandchildren, then parents, and so on.

If none of these persons is alive or able to serve, some states have a publicly appointed official who then serves as administrator of the estate. This official is called the *public administrator*. Each of the counties of New York City has a public administrator.

The public administrator's duties are similar to those of a personal representative or executor: to collect the estate property, to pay all outstanding debts and taxes, and to distribute what remains to those who are legally entitled to it.

What is a *fiduciary*?

The word describes someone who has a relationship with another that involves a duty to act for the benefit of the other party. The one who has this duty is called the fiduciary. Thus, a guardian of your children, the trustee of a trust created under your will, or the executor of your estate, among others, is considered to be a fiduciary.

Instead of the court appointing an executor, I have read somewhere of courts that appoint fiduciaries with names such as *administrator cum testamento annexo, administrator de bonis non,* and *administrator cum testamento annexo, de bonis non.* What are they?

If a will does not name an executor or if the executor does not serve and there is no successor executor appointed or capable of serving, the court appoints an individual or trust company to serve in this capacity. This fiduciary is called *administrator cum testamento annexo,* which means "administrator with will annexed."

In some states when someone dies intestate, the fiduciary appointed to administer the estate is called an *administrator*. (In other states, the title of the person who is appointed to administer the estate, whether or not there is a will, is *personal representative*.) If the administrator fails to complete the administration for some reason (death, resignation, incapacity, or removal), the court appoints an individual or trust company to serve in this capacity. This fiduciary is called *administrator de bonis non,* which means "administrator of goods not administered" (that is, not administered by the previous administrator).

If an executor fails to complete the administration of an estate being administered pursuant to the terms of a probated will and there is no successor executor appointed or capable of serving, the court appoints an individual, bank, or trust company to serve in this capacity. This fiduciary is called *administrator cum testamento annexo, de bonis non,* which means "administrator with will annexed, of goods not administered" (that is, not administered by the previous administrator).

Who do you recommend to be my named fiduciary?

As guardian of a minor child: a relative or friend, even your oldest child, who has the interest, warmth, love, and intelligence to take care of your children and has the ability (physical and financial) to do so. This guardian determines where the minor child lives, goes to school, what medical care is administered, etc. The guardian of the property fulfills functions similar to a trustee. Though each of these functions can be performed by different people, if you trust someone with custody of your child, you should trust him or her with custody of that child's funds. Therefore, the guardian of the person should be the same person as the guardian of the property.

As trustee: one or more persons, a bank, or a trust company with the skill, experience, and intelligence to manage funds and possibly business enterprises over what may be an extended period of time.

State laws limit those who may serve as trustees, some states being more restrictive than others. Not every bank has the legal authority to act as a trustee.

Your spouse or one of your children would be suitable, provided that this person either has the ability to manage the trust property or the experience or skill to select a suitable attorney, bank, broker, or accountant to assist with the several tasks. An attorney or accountant would be a good choice, depending, of course, on experience and ability. A bank or trust company—serving alone or with a member of your family, the attorney, or the accountant—would also be suitable.

As executor, or personal representative: the duties of this individual are usually of a relatively short duration, as contrasted with those of a trustee, who may serve for an extended period. Nevertheless, the comments about the trustee are applicable here. The only possible exception is that there is less need to have more than one person serve as executor.

A fiduciary is entitled to commissions or fees for serving in that capacity. Such commissions or fees are paid from the assets that the fiduciary administers. When appointing someone, this should be taken into account.

I wish to appoint my sister as guardian of the person and property of my minor children. You said that the guardian should have financial ability to serve. My sister's heart is big but her purse is small. Are you suggesting she not be appointed?

No, but funds may be needed for your children's care. If you left enough property, the income from the property would be adequate to take care of the children's needs. On the other hand, if you died without accumulated earnings or property, the guardian would need the means to feed, clothe, and educate your children. You should be realistic and face this problem while you are alive and should plan accordingly. Consideration should be given to purchasing life insurance for this purpose.

What does a guardian do?

There is a difference between a *guardian of the property* (in some states referred to as a conservator) and a *guardian of the person*.

The guardian of the property of a minor is the one who manages funds or property. The guardian of the person determines where the children live, what schools they attend, what clothing and medical care they receive, etc. In other words, the guardian of the person stands in the shoes of the deceased parents. When preparing wills, we, of course, do not know whether the husband or wife will be the survivor. It is therefore desirable for each parent to state his or her wishes on who shall be the minor children's guardian. Any such designation will take place after the death of both parents. Ideally, both parents can agree upon a suitable person. Also, if possible, it is advisable to name one or more successors to the named guardians.

What is a personal representative?

A personal representative is the individual or individuals, a bank or trust company, or a combination of these, who legally steps into the shoes of the decedent, temporarily owns all of the decedent's property, and represents the estate in the eyes of the law. In some states, the name given to the personal representative is *executor* (if a male) and *executrix* (if a female).

Who appoints the personal representative or the executor?

The testator has the privilege to name the personal representative. (The testator is the one who makes the will.) The court will then issue an order confirming the appointment. If the testator does not name a personal representative or names a person who cannot serve, state law provides whom the court may appoint. (Technically, the testator nominates the personal representative, and the actual appointment is made by the court.) If the decedent dies without a will or if the document is not accepted as the decedent's will, state law dictates whom the court may appoint.

I have appointed my friend John to serve as my personal representative. Under what circumstances would he be unable to serve?

Clearly, John has to be alive and willing to serve. The usual situations prohibiting him from serving are the following: he has not reached the age of majority; he has been convicted of a serious crime; he is not a United States citizen; or he is a judge of a court. In some states, such as Florida, a nonresident is prohibited from serving as a personal representative unless the person named is closely related to the decedent.

My sister designated me as executor under her will. I am not in good health and do not wish to serve as such. Am I required to serve?

No. If you do not wish to serve, for whatever reason, you are not required to do so. In such event, you should file with the court an executed renunciation. A renunciation constitutes a relinquishment (giving up) of your right to serve as executor. This renunciation only affects your right to serve as executor; it has no bearing on your right to inherit under your sister's will. When signing the renunciation document, read it carefully to be sure that the language is limited to your right to serve as executor (and *not* your right to inherit under your sister's will).

Do you have any recommendations as to whom I should appoint as my personal representative?

Do not appoint anyone who may have a substantial conflict of interest. For example, there could be a conflict of interest if you appoint as your personal representative your partner in a business or the sole surviving stockholder of a corporation. The conflict could arise if there is an agreement that your partner, the corporation, or the surviving stockholder would have to compensate your estate for your interest in the partnership or corporation based on certain flexible and indefinite formulas provided in the agreement.

In this case, there would likely be a conflict of interest because it would be in the financial interest of your partner or the surviving stockholder to interpret the agreement so that the smallest possible amount is paid to your estate for your interest. Since it is the job of your personal representative to fulfill your intentions and to negotiate for the best possible price, placing your partner in this position creates the potential for a conflict between a personal financial interest and a personal representative's duty.

I wish to appoint my attorney instead of my spouse as executor (or personal representative) of my estate. Since either party would be entitled to commissions for serving as executor, what difference can it make to my family?

There would obviously be more money left for your family if your spouse served as executor. On the other hand, an executor who is an attorney can relieve the family of many burdensome administrative details and, by appropriate after-death tax planning, can save the estate money. Only you, the testator, can determine whether the expense of having a non–family member serve is worthwhile.

Assume you died in 1993, a resident of Maryland, and left a (probate) estate of $200,000. In Maryland the maximum executor commissions (and those usually allowed) are 9 percent of the first $20,000 of the estate and 3.6 percent of the balance. The commissions would be:

9 percent of $20,000	$1,800
3.6 percent of $180,000	+ 6,480
	$8,280

If your spouse inherits the entire estate and your attorney serves as executor, your spouse would receive:

Estate	$200,000
Less the commissions paid the attorney	(8,280)
	$191,720

If your spouse serves as executor, your spouse would receive:

Estate	$200,000
Less the commissions (which should be waived; see below)	(0)
	$200,000

If your spouse serves as executor and accepts the commissions, your spouse would receive:

Estate after deducting commissions	$191,720
Plus the commissions	+ 8,280
	$200,000

Two things should be noted about the previous examples:

1. An attorney who serves as executor will, in most cases, also perform all legal services as part of the services as executor. Thus, if your spouse serves as executor and the services of an attorney are used (which is usually required as a practical matter), the amount your spouse eventually receives will be reduced by the attorney's fees. Such fees are usually a minimum of one-half the commissions allowed by law. If the attorney serves as the executor, then, depending on the state, the fee may be taken into account in calculating the commissions.

2. It is usually inadvisable for a spouse who serves as executor to claim and receive commissions. If commissions are paid, they become taxable income to the recipient. If the executor will inherit the entire estate, why pay income taxes on property that will be received anyway? (Unless a federal estate tax will be due, in which case the deduction on the federal estate tax return can be larger than the income tax on the commission.)

Am I restricted in my choice of executor or trustee?

In general, no. However, in some states a nonresident of that state may not serve as executor unless he or she is closely related to the decedent. For example, in Florida a nonresident of Florida at the time of the decedent's death is disqualified from serving unless the person is a close relative; however, this prohibition against nonresidents has been questioned by at least one Florida court as a violation of U.S. constitutional provisions. However, the Supreme Court of Florida has upheld the constitutionality of its laws. Nonresidents of Florida are now barred from serving as executors of a nonrelative's estate, but there is no such restriction for trustees. You should consult with your attorney about necessary qualifications in your state.

How are the duties of a personal representative, or executor, carried out?

When the will is probated, the court will issue to the executor *letters of administration,* or as they are called in some states, *letters testamentary.* These letters are evidence of the executor's legal authority to represent the estate.

What are my duties as personal representative or executor?

Your duties are to have the will probated, collect the assets, give notice to the public of your appointment so that unknown creditors may notify you of their claims, give direct notice, by mail or by personal service, to known creditors, pay whatever taxes are due, and as soon as possible, distribute the remaining assets to the persons who are legally entitled to them. Assets that are held for any length of time should be invested to ensure their safety and to secure adequate income from them.

A good broad statement of the duties of a personal representative follows:

A personal representative is a fiduciary who is under a general duty to settle and distribute the estate of the decedent in *accordance with the terms of the will and with as little sacrifice of value as is reasonable under all the circumstances. The representative shall use this authority while fairly considering the interests of all interested persons and creditors.*

How do I go about my duties?

The answer given here is based on the assumption that you are going to do the work yourself. Usually, you hire a lawyer to take care of the administration of the estate. In some states, a bank or trust company will perform the ministerial function for you even though it is not named as personal representative.

Whether a lawyer does the work or you do the work, the following are the steps that are necessary to accomplish the collection of assets. (This assumes that the closest member of the family will have arranged for the funeral and the burial of the body. If there is no member of the family, then the personal representative usually undertakes this responsibility.)

1. Some states require that an estate receive a tax waiver issued by the state taking authority before assets are turned over to the personal representative. New York is one such state. (By requiring a waiver, a state is notified of the possibility of a tax liability. This enables the state to be sure that its taxes are paid.) In New York, the personal representative fills out forms supplied by the state tax commission. The waivers are usually issued promptly. A separate waiver is required for each asset of the estate.

One of the first steps is to request tax waivers in the case of any decedent who resides in a state that requires them. The waiver permits the stockbroker, bank, insurance company, or whoever has property belonging to the decedent to release such property to the estate's personal representative.

2. With respect to checking and savings accounts owned in the decedent's own name at the time of death, the personal representative of the estate now becomes their owner. As the estate representative, you should collect the balance remaining in these accounts. To do this, the certificate or certified copy of the letters issued by the court must be submitted to the bank (hereafter we will refer to this certificate as *letters*), together with the tax waiver(s) if the state requires this. Some banks may require a death certificate in addition, but this is not the usual case.

As personal representative, you are the short-term manager of the estate and therefore have a choice whether to leave the money on deposit with the institution or institutions, or to withdraw it and place it in another bank or banks. If you decide to remain with the original bank, you should have the bank account titled in your name as personal representative. The account, as well as all the estate assets, should be registered substantially as follows:

(Your name), Personal Representative of the Estate of John Doe, deceased, or

Estate of John Doe, (your name), Personal Representative.

(Variations of the foregoing are acceptable.)

If you decide to move a savings account to another bank, be careful that the estate does not lose interest by reason of premature withdrawal.

A death certificate is a certificate issued by a state or local health department that certifies the death of the decedent. The certificate will usually be required by insurance companies, the Social Security Administration, and others. The funeral director customarily orders copies as an accommodation to the family. They usually cost from one to two dollars each.

3. If there are certificates of deposit, you should deal with them as you would with the checking and savings accounts.

4. It is important to note that the estate should have its own checking account. This enables you to keep a record of whatever is received and paid out. Therefore, all receipts should be deposited in this account, and all payments should be made by check from this account.

5. With respect to stocks, bonds, and mutual fund shares, each institution has its own requirements to enable the assets to be titled in the name of the estate. The illustration that follows, dealing with stocks, generally applies to bonds and mutual fund shares as well.

On the right-hand side of every stock certificate is the name of a transfer agent (usually a bank). The transfer agent's job is to have certificates properly issued to parties entitled to them. When a person dies, ownership of his or her stock shifts to the personal representative as the representative of the estate (the representative is, of course, holding the stock in a form of trust fund for the benefit of those entitled to receive it).

The transfer agent (or bank) will require *letters* dated within 60 days of the date you are requesting that they make the transfer. (As noted earlier, the transfer agent may also require that you obtain a tax waiver.) The transfer agent will ask for an affidavit of domicile, which is an affidavit that establishes the state in which the decedent resided at the time of death. Not every transfer agent requires this affidavit. Upon receipt of this document, the transfer agent will issue a new certificate showing you, the personal representative, as the owner. (The precise form of registration is similar to that set forth above in 2.) The transfer agent will also ask you to provide the federal identification number issued to the estate.

If a stock certificate is lost, the transfer agent will replace the certificate if you first submit a bond insuring the agent against claims by third parties for the value of the certificate. The premium cost of such a bond is usually 3 percent of the value of the certificate that is lost. It is therefore important when mailing certificates to send them by registered mail and to insure them for at least 3 percent of their value. If the certificates are hand delivered to a local office of a brokerage house, and if the house is taking care of retitling the certificates, always get a receipt for the stock. The same procedure applies to bonds and mutual fund shares.

6. A federal identification number should be requested. This number is called a federal employer's identification number (even though the estate may not actually employ anyone) and is issued by the Internal Revenue Service (IRS). A request for this number is made on Form SS-4, which will be supplied to you by the local office of the IRS. The number is required on tax returns. Banks, transfer agents, and others will request this number, and it is wise to obtain the number as soon as possible.

7. Federal law requires each personal representative acting for an estate to send a notice thereof to the IRS. This is done on Form 56, which can be secured from the local IRS office.

If the IRS is not notified, the personal representative may not receive timely notice of any change the IRS makes in the decedent's income tax returns. The IRS is authorized by law to mail the notice to the last known address of the decedent. The last known address would be the one shown on the decedent's last return. If the decedent left a spouse and the spouse remained in the old residence, notice would eventually be received by the spouse. However, the spouse may have moved, or there may be no spouse.

Federal law also provides that any taxpayer who receives a notice of a proposed assessment may contest the claimed tax before payment by going to the United States Tax Court. However, in order to go to the United States Tax Court, the taxpayer (or personal representative) must file a petition with that court within 90 days of the mailing of any proposed assessment. If Form 56 is not filed, then you, as personal representative, may never receive the notice of the proposed assessment, or the notice may arrive too late for you to do anything about it in the Tax Court.

If the estate is damaged because you failed to send this notice, you personally may become liable to reimburse the estate for any damages.

8. If the decedent lived in a rented house or apartment, you would have to consult local law and the lease, if any, to determine what is necessary to terminate the lease. Check the terms of the lease to see if there is a security deposit and if you are entitled to receive this as an asset of the estate. You must take possession and dispose of any household goods in the residence. Before disposing of these contents, they should be appraised.

An appraisal establishes the value of the household goods for tax purposes. Sometimes, too, if the will does not bequeath the household goods to specified individuals, it would be advisable for you to get an appraisal before selling them at a private sale. If a beneficiary contests the selling price as being too low, you can establish that you sold the goods for their appraised value. In this connection, bear in mind that in some states household goods are considered to belong to a surviving spouse, where there is one, and if none, to any surviving children.

The laws dealing with the selection of appraisers vary from state to state. In Maryland, official court appraisers are available, but it is not necessary to use them. You may select your own appraiser. In other jurisdictions, you would

seek outside help to choose an appraiser. The appraiser should be one who is qualified and is so recognized by the taxing and court officials.

If the will disposes of the household goods, you should arrange with the beneficiaries to have the merchandise picked up or delivered to them. It may be necessary for you to store the household goods until you can dispose of them at an appropriate time.

During the time when household goods are owned by the estate, you should be sure that there is adequate insurance against fire, theft, etc.

If there are valuable paintings, jewelry, a coin or stamp collection, or valuable books, it is your job to take possession of these assets and dispose of them in accordance with the will. If the will has not provided for this, sell them at the highest possible price. In some states, the law encourages you to distribute the actual assets rather than to sell property. It is also your job as personal representative to distribute these assets as fairly as possible to those who are entitled to them.

As a practical matter, the personal representative should consult with the members of the family or others entitled to the property to see if an agreement can be reached as to who receives what. Unfortunately, in many families, agreement cannot be reached, and there have been bitter contests as to who is entitled to the favorite grandfather clock, tea service, china service, painting, etc. When this happens, your state laws should be consulted. In some states, you must make the decision about who receives what assets. Usually, this can be done with the court's approval.

9. If the decedent owned a car, you should either transfer ownership in accordance with the terms of the will, reregister it in your name as personal representative (in some states it is not necessary to reregister it until the next license renewal date), or perhaps sell the car at the best obtainable price. If the decedent rented a car, it is your job to minimize the financial drain of the lease.

10. At the present time, most people are covered by Social Security. If the decedent was covered, the decedent's spouse would be entitled to a lump-sum death benefit. If there is no spouse, any children may be entitled to the benefit, and appropriate application should be made.

If the decedent was a veteran or a railroad employee, there may be veterans or Railroad Retirement benefits. The personal representative should apply for any benefits due the estate.

11. The decedent may have had a safe-deposit box. As the estate representative, you should enter the safe-deposit box to take possession of its contents. In some states, such as New York, the bank representatives will not allow you to enter the box until you receive a tax waiver from the appropriate tax agency. Also, an official representative of the taxing agency may be required to be present. The official will inventory the box's contents. In some states, an officer of the bank must be present to inventory the contents of the box.

Customs and laws vary throughout the United States as to the procedure necessary to gain entry and secure possession. Ease of entry may depend upon the name in which the box is rented. Rental may have been in the name of the decedent only, the decedent may have rented it jointly with a spouse, or the decedent may not have even been the one who leased the box but merely had power of attorney granted by someone else. If I were the sole personal representative, I would want the surviving spouse, if any, or one or more of the children to accompany me when I open the box. If there were no surviving spouse or children, I would ask the principal legatee to do so. I would then inventory the contents of the box. I would not wish my integrity to be questioned concerning a missing piece of jewelry or cash that was supposedly in the box.

12. The decedent may have owned brokerage accounts, and the stockbroker may have held stock for the decedent as agent on behalf of the decedent.

Stock could be held in the name of the decedent only, and the certificates representing the stock could be lying in the vaults of the stockbrokerage company. On the other hand, if the decedent actively traded in securities, the stockbrokerage firm may just have registered whatever stock was purchased in the name of a "nominee." Registering the stock in the name of a nominee is merely a way to let the brokerage firm sell the stock quickly when called upon to do so.

In any event, where there is such an account, there would be monthly or perhaps quarterly statements showing the status of the account, what monies are owed to the brokerage company or to the decedent, and what stocks are being held for the account of the decedent.

Possession of these assets should be secured. Before turning over these assets to you, the stockbroker must be assured that you are legally entitled to them. The broker may therefore ask for *letters* and a death certificate.

13. The decedent may have owned life insurance on his or her life. If the life insurance is to be paid to a named beneficiary, the named beneficiary should apply for the benefits by direct application to the insurance company. Each company has its own forms for this purpose.

If no beneficiary is named, then you, as personal representative, should submit the application to the insurance company and receive the proceeds. If you receive the proceeds, they must be invested so that you receive the maximum return on the money consistent with safety and the terms of the will. Do not deposit the proceeds in a checking account and promptly forget about your duty to the beneficiaries. Your duty is to safeguard the assets and make them productive until the time of distribution.

If the estate is required to file a federal estate tax return, bear in mind that you must attach to the return Form 712, which is issued by the insurance company. Request Form 712 when you apply for the insurance proceeds.

Even if insurance proceeds are not payable to the estate, there may be estate taxes due because of such insurance. You may be required to collect a proportionate part of the taxes from the beneficiary. Consult with your lawyer about this rule.

14. If the decedent owned real estate, you should retitle the property in your name as personal representative, pay the taxes, and manage the property or hire somebody to manage it. Be sure to collect any rents that are due.

It is your job to secure appropriate and proper insurance for any property. Therefore, even if the decedent had insurance on the property as of the date of death, you should review the insurance to see if it is adequate. Also, notify the insurance company to change the policy to show that you, as personal representative, are the owner.

The personal representative also has to decide whether to hold the property for eventual distribution to the beneficiaries of the estate or to sell the property. If a sale is made, the personal representative decides the terms of the sale. The terms of the will or state law may restrict or prohibit such a sale except for cash.

In some states, ownership of real estate passes directly to the beneficiaries on the death of the decedent. In these states, the personal representative need do nothing about securing possession of the real estate. However, the representative may be required to have it appraised for tax or other purposes.

15. If the decedent owned promissory notes, mortgages, royalties on oil or gas interests, or perhaps royalties for artistic endeavors such as books, movies, or paintings, it is the job of the personal representative to collect these assets. Sometimes it may become necessary for the personal representative to go to court to enforce these ownership rights, as any litigant might.

16. If the decedent was employed at the time of death, the personal representative should collect salaries or whatever other benefits are due. If the decedent was a stockholder in a corporation and the stock is sold, the personal representative should try to get the highest price for the stock. It may be that the stock was held subject to the terms of a stockholder's agreement (sometimes referred to as a buy-sell agreement or stockholder's redemption agreement). If so, the terms of the agreement must be followed.

The decedent may have been the principal stockholder of a corporation, in which event the personal representative would have to determine whether the business should be continued or sold. The decision must be based solely on what is in the best interests of the beneficiaries of the estate. In the absence of any statement in the will, state law must be reviewed to see whether the business may be continued. The laws of most states prohibit the continuation of a business beyond a short period of time after the death of the owner, the idea being that it would be too risky to continue a business without the owner.

17. If the decedent was self-employed, the personal representative should collect whatever accounts receivable are

due, perhaps try to sell the business, and sell assets owned by the business.

In most states, unless there are specific instructions or authority in the will, any unincorporated business may not be continued for any lengthy period of time. Some state laws provide that if it is advisable to continue to operate a business, the business must be incorporated.

18. The decedent may have been in the process of litigation at the time of death. In such a case, it is the duty of the personal representative to pursue such litigation. Usually, a personal representative has authority to settle such litigation or any claims.

19. If the decedent owned U.S. Savings Bonds, the bonds should either be cashed in or distributed, depending on the terms of the will. Check on available tax options and consequences of various ways of handling the bonds.

20. The decedent may be entitled to union benefits or disability insurance claims. The facts should be reviewed to determine whether or not the estate is entitled to such benefits.

21. The estate may be entitled to proceeds from a qualified pension plan. In such an event, application must be made with the trustees of the plan. In this connection, investigate the several tax options available.

22. If the decedent was a general partner in a partnership, the partnership interest must be disposed of as set forth in the partnership agreement. If there was no partnership agreement, the laws of most states provide that a partnership ends on the death of a general partner. When the partnership ends, the remaining partner or partners must liquidate the partnership assets. After liquidation they must account to the deceased partner's estate for the decedent's interest in the partnership. The accounts submitted by the surviving partners should be carefully reviewed.

23. Determining other assets, aside from asking family members, is usually best made by looking at the checkbooks and income tax returns of the decedent for the past several years. Checkbooks would disclose what checks were issued in payment of assets, and tax returns would show sources of income that would enable the personal representative to trace these assets.

After all the assets are collected, what should be done with them?

It is essential that every asset be safeguarded, invested (on a short-term basis) to secure the maximum return possible but with absolute safety of principal, and, at the proper time, distributed to those entitled to them. Remember that the personal representative is a fiduciary, that is, one who is in a position of trust acting on behalf of persons entitled to benefits. Accordingly, the law provides that the highest responsibilities are imposed upon a fiduciary.

In discharging these duties, it is es-

sential that a careful inventory be maintained of all assets belonging to the estate. Most courts will require that the personal representative make and, in most instances, file a document called an inventory (in addition to a later accounting), which sets forth all of the assets owned by the decedent at the time of death. Most courts have forms that can be used for this purpose.

Unless this inventory is filed at the right time, the court can remove the personal representative or impose a fine or other sanctions. Embarrassment will be avoided if the personal representative consults the appropriate laws and rules shortly after appointment to determine the duties of the position.

May I sell estate assets?

Yes, unless the will prohibits this. As personal representative, you may determine that estate assets should be sold as a means of protecting or enhancing their value. While most states encourage the distribution of assets in kind to the legatees entitled thereto, the most important consideration must be the preservation and safekeeping of assets.

There may come a time during administration of the estate when you will find it prudent or desirable to sell an asset. This may be because there should be greater diversification, or there may be danger of loss or opportunity. The impact of income taxes should be considered in your decision making. This is so, since an estate is required to pay income taxes.

When assets are sold, there may be a gain or loss, which is measured by the difference between the *basis* of these assets and the net selling price. Usually, basis is equal to cost (minus depreciation where applicable).

When a person dies, the law states that the property owned by the decedent as of date of death acquires a new basis equal to the value of the property as valued for estate tax purposes. When an estate tax return is required to be filed, the value of the property is its fair market value. When an estate is not required to file a federal estate tax return, the new basis of estate assets is also the fair market value of such property as of date of death. (For a discussion of *fair market value,* see page 170.)

Thus, when an estate owns stock that is valued on the decedent's date of death at $1,000, the estate's basis for the stock is also $1,000. It is immaterial that the decedent may have paid substantially less or more for the stock. The new, or stepped-up, basis for the stock is $1,000. (If the decedent paid more for the stock than its value at date of valuation, usually date of death, the basis for the stock may be "stepped-down.") Therefore, if the estate sells the stock for $1,000, there will be no gain (or profit) because the basis of the stock, that is, its artificial cost, is equal to the selling price of $1,000. If the stock is sold for $900, the estate will have a loss of $100.

This basis rule, known as *uniform basis,* also applies to everyone who inherits such property in kind. This is so whether the property is inherited under the provisions of the will or under the

Tax-Saving Suggestion

Consider selling assets during your lifetime that would give you a tax loss deduction. Consider selling securities or other assets before your death, if doing so will give you a capital loss. Such a capital loss will therefore enable you to reduce your income taxes in the year of the sale, subject, of course, to the income tax rules pertaining to limitations. For example, your capital loss will be used as an offset against capital gains, and any remaining capital loss will be used as an offset against $3,000 of ordinary income.

An example of using this technique is as follows. Your mother is the owner of a substantial number of securities. She is terminally ill. If you, her daughter, hold a power of attorney from her, you can lawfully sell securities owned by your mother. By selling those securities whose value is less than their cost, you may be able to save income taxes in your mother's final income tax return.

Why do such assets "usually" acquire a new basis? Because the carryover basis is not available for assets that are considered to be "income in respect of a decedent." (Also see page 179.)

intestacy laws. For example, if the basis of stock to the estate is $1,000, and the estate does not sell it but distributes the stock to a legatee, the basis of the stock to the legatee is $1,000.

To simplify the explanation, we referred to basis as applied to securities (stocks). The rules about basis also apply to any other assets that are part of a decedent's gross estate for tax purposes. This could be cars, jewelry, a business, art, real estate, collections, etc.

Is there anything else I should know about uniform basis?

Yes. In general, and without trying to discuss every facet of this complicated subject, you should know:

1. When the *estate* purchases an asset during its administration, the basis of the asset is its cost to the estate. The fair market value of the asset as of date of death is immaterial to determining its basis.

2. If the asset acquired from the decedent is a depreciable asset, then the depreciation that is allowable must be taken into account. For example, at the moment of death, the decedent owned a small commercial building, which was rented to a business. The building had a fair market value of $100,000 and the land on which it stood had a fair market value of $30,000. The decedent died July 1. For income tax purposes, the estate elected a taxable year ending December 31. Assume that the allowable depreciation for the building for the July 1 to De-

cember 31 period is $2,500, the basis of this property as of December 31 would be $127,500. This is arrived at by subtracting $2,500 from the $100,000 and adding the land value of $30,000.

3. Assets that are included in the decedent's estate for estate tax purposes, even though not owned by the decedent, also acquire the new (uniform) basis. For example, the decedent created an inter vivos (or living) trust and retained the right to the income therefrom for his lifetime. The trust was revocable during the decedent's lifetime. On the decedent's death, his two children became absolute owners.

The basis of all trust assets became its fair market value as of the decedent's date of death (or alternate value date, if elected). (Also see page 176).

When may I distribute estate assets?

The laws of most states provide that creditors have a specific time period during which they may file claims for any debts owed them. If you make distribution before the time has elapsed for creditors to file claims with the estate, you may be personally liable to these creditors for any estate assets prematurely distributed to beneficiaries. This is so because the laws of all states provide that creditors are entitled to be paid before any estate assets are distributed to beneficiaries.

Both federal and state laws are also very strict about death taxes being paid in full before any estate assets are distributed. The personal representative should be certain that sufficient estate assets are retained to pay all tax claims. If this is not done, the personal representative will be personally liable for payment. You may distribute estate assets while the estate is being administered and before the estate is finally closed. However, *final* distribution of estate assets should only be made when the time period for the filing of claims by creditors has expired, and all taxes have been paid.

When is an estate closed?

An estate is closed when a final accounting is rendered to the court (in a state where this is required), the accounting is approved, all payments or distributions as set forth in the accounting are made (to all creditors and legatees), all taxes have been paid (federal and state death and income taxes), and all court fees have been paid.

In a state where no accountings are required, an estate is closed after all estate assets have been collected and accounted for, all payments or distributions have been made to all creditors and legatees, and all taxes and court fees have been paid. Distribution of all estate assets should be made to the legatees at the earliest possible time thereafter.

When would it be advisable to distribute assets before an estate is closed?

Subject to retaining enough assets to pay all creditors and all taxes:

1. When the estate owns a business that requires skilled family management; where the estate could not successfully run the business; where any sale of the business would not realize the maximum potential value, or any combination of the above.

2. To effect an overall income tax savings. For example, a child may be in the lowest income tax bracket (a student who has no other income), whereas the estate would be in a higher bracket. (The subject of income taxation of estates and trusts constitutes a separate and complex body of law and should be discussed with a lawyer or accountant.)

3. Present need of a spouse or other legatee.

Must I, as personal representative, pay every claim that is presented to me?

Certainly not. You need pay only valid and proper claims. Your duty is to examine the claim to see that it is presented on time, whether it should be paid in whole or in part, or rejected. Every state has a time limit (usually six months) during which time claims must be presented. If a claim is presented late, this would be a proper basis for denying the claim. Taxing authorities are not required to file claims and usually do not.

If a claim is rejected in whole or in part, or if you take no action on it, creditors will have rights to contest this action before the court that appointed you.

May a claim be paid even if no formal claim is filed?

In general, yes, but in a few states the filing of a formal claim, in the proper form and within the specified time period, is required.

Where the personal representative has a claim against the estate (which the personal representative is administering), prudence suggests that a formal claim against the estate be filed with the court. If this is not done, upon the request of the legatees or other unpaid creditors, the court could refuse to approve the payment of the personal representative's personal claim. The laws of your state should be consulted.

Give me some examples of problems that could arise if I distribute the assets of the estate too soon.

1. Assume a wife survives her husband and is entitled to his entire estate. I am the personal representative of the estate, and you, the wife, ask me to turn over the entire estate to you 60 days after my appointment as personal representative. If I do what you ask and if creditors do file claims on time, I am personally responsible to them because I made premature distribution of the estate assets.

I can seek reimbursement of these amounts from you, of course, but you may have moved, or you may have made some imprudent investments and lost all the money. At best, I would spend a lot of money to recover the distribution from you, and at worst, I would never be able to recover anything. In any event, I could be personally liable for the premature distribution.

2. Assume similar facts, but this time I turn over the estate to you 10 months after date of death and after I have filed the federal and state estate tax returns.

The taxing authorities come in one year after I filed these returns and establish that there was an omission of assets from the return that neither you nor I knew about, or perhaps they say that the land we valued at $1,000 per acre was in reality worth $10,000 per acre. On this basis, the tax would be substantially higher than the tax we had paid when the returns were filed.

The assets from the estate have already been distributed to you, and both the federal and state governments can properly sue me personally for these distributions that I made prematurely. The actual distribution should never have been made until the returns were accepted as filed. If there is any contest over the amount of tax claimed, this controversy should be resolved first. Accordingly, I may be personally liable for the tax.

Are there any other problems that I may be confronted with?

Yes. Despite all your efforts, the language of the will may not be clear enough to enable you as personal representative to distribute the property. You may require the assistance of the courts to interpret or to construe the will. This help is obtained by beginning a proceeding in court called a *construction proceeding*. These illustrations point out when construction problems may arise:

1. A $2,000 bequest is made under the will to cousin John. A problem may arise if the testator has two cousins who are named John. The question is which John was intended to be the beneficiary of the $2,000.

2. The testator leaves the remainder of his property, after the death of his wife, to his children in equal shares. At the time the testator made the will, and when he died, he had three children; by the time his wife died, one of the children was already dead. The question is whether the dead child's estate will inherit one-third of the estate, since the will was not clear as to whether that child had to survive the wife in order to inherit the one-third share. This situation requires that the courts construe the will to determine the testator's intent.

3. The testator left a bequest of $5,000 to the First Memorial Methodist Church. When the will was executed, there was a First Memorial Methodist Church in the community where the testator resided, and in the adjoining town there was a church with a similar name of which the testator was a member. The will was not clear as to which church was meant and you, the personal representative, may not distribute the bequest to one of the churches without seeking a construction of the will so that the court may determine the testator's intent.

A construction proceeding usually requires that a complaint be filed setting forth the facts about what is contained in the will and asking the court to construe the meaning of the language. This proceeding obviously requires the preparation of additional documents by an attorney, at extra cost to the estate, and will further delay any distribution to be made by the personal representative.

When a proceeding of this nature is begun, every possible person who is interested in the outcome of the proceeding must be notified. The problem becomes further complicated when persons who may be interested in the settlement of the estate are not yet born or perhaps are minors. In this event, the court, upon the request of the party seeking construction, would be duty-bound to appoint a guardian for the unborn persons or the minor or minors. This is so because of a basic rule of law that persons who have not appeared before the court, personally or represented by counsel, are not bound by the proceeding. Therefore, it is important that the personal representative bind everybody who could possibly have an interest in the outcome of the court proceeding.

The testator gave no instructions in his will concerning his burial wishes. The funeral home has now submitted a bill for $5,600. Am I, as personal representative, required to pay it?

Laws vary from state to state on this matter. In general, funeral bills are to be paid before any other amounts are distributed. However, in many states, when a funeral bill exceeds a certain amount, the court must approve it before it may be paid. Therefore, you should check your state's laws before paying any funeral bill.

The decedent signed a contract during his lifetime to purchase some property from another person. As personal representative, am I bound by this agreement?

Yes, to the same extent as the decedent was. However, since you are acting on behalf of the estate, only the assets of the estate, and not your personal assets, are subject to any financial responsibility.

I am the personal representative of my late brother's estate. He died in 1986. He left one-third of his property to his children, Mary and Harry, and two-thirds to his wife. In 1984, two years after my brother executed his will, his wife gave birth to another child, Charles. Is Charles entitled to any share of the children's one-third?

In most states, Charles would be entitled to take the same share that he would have received had your brother died without a will (intestate). In this case, Charles may even receive a greater share than the other children. For example, assume your brother lived in a state that provides that when a person dies intestate, the wife is entitled to one-third of the estate and the children receive the other two-thirds. Assume also that your brother's estate is valued at $150,000. Charles, as one of three children, is entitled to

one-third of two-thirds (two-thirds of $150,000 is $100,000), or $33,333.

Since the balance left for distribution is $116,667, your brother's wife will be entitled to the amount left to her under his will, or two-thirds of $116,667. This amounts to $77,778. The balance left for Mary and Harry is $38,889, and each will receive $19,444.50 (one-half of $38,889), even though Charles receives $33,333.

Many states now provide that an after-born child takes the same share that the other children do. In this case, each child would inherit $16,667 (one-third of $50,000). A child born after a will is executed, and not named, referred to, and there is no indication of an intentional omission, is known as a *pretermitted child*.

The testator died on July 1. On June 15 he signed his will and left 90 percent of his property to a charity. He left a wife and one child. Am I, as personal representative, required to distribute the property as the will provides?

In many states, when a spouse or children survive, no more than a certain percentage of a decedent's estate may be left to charity. In other states, if a will is executed within a certain number of days before death, the amount that may be left to charity is also limited.

My late husband's will left to his sister some jewelry that he inherited from his mother. I am the estate's personal

representative. **What do I do with this jewelry?**

This jewelry is specifically left (*bequeathed*) to his sister, and therefore it is your job to hand it over to the sister. You should get a receipt to document the transaction.

The balance available for distribution from my husband's estate to our two sons is $50,000. I am the personal representative. After the appropriate waiting period, may I distribute $25,000 to each son?

In general, yes. It is possible, however, that during your husband's lifetime, he gave one of your sons $10,000 or so and treated this amount as what the law calls an *advancement*. This is essentially an advance against the inheritance that the beneficiary is entitled to if the decedent died without a will. It reduces the amount to be distributed upon death. Therefore, if there were indeed an advancement, this advancement must be taken into account before making distribution. The laws of most states require that if there is an advancement, written confirmation of this must exist on the date of death. Note that the advancement rule usually applies only if the decedent died without a will.

I am the personal representative of my husband's estate. My husband's will was probated. We have two daughters, Sharon and Sheila. In his will, my husband left a bequest to our daughter Sharon in the amount of $25,000 but stated in his will that if there is in existence at the time of his death a promissory note from her, the face amount of the note shall be deducted from the bequest. He also left a bequest to our daughter Sheila in the amount of $25,000. He also stated in his will that if there is in existence at the time of his death a promissory note from Sheila, the note shall be discharged and considered satisfied. I have possession of the two notes mentioned. Each note is dated one year ago and is for $10,000 and specifies that no interest is due. The estate's administration is completed and I am ready to make distribution. Who receives what?

Sharon is entitled to receive $15,000 and Sheila is entitled to receive $25,000. If your husband's will did not refer to the promissory notes at all, you, as estate personal representative, would be required to collect $10,000 from each child or you could offset the outstanding debt against each $25,000 bequest.

One of my sons is a minor. As personal representative, may I distribute his share to him?

A minor is incapable of giving the personal representative a release for any distribution made to him. The personal representative should never distribute estate property directly to a minor.

Until relatively recently, the laws of most states provided that when property was to be distributed to a minor, it was necessary to have a court-appointed guardian for such a minor. This was a time-consuming, costly procedure. Many states now provide that when a minor is entitled to a distribution, the personal representative may make the distribution by giving the property to a custodian under the Uniform Transfers to Minors Act (formerly named the Uniform Gifts to Minors Act).

In most states, even those that have not simplified the procedure, provisions protect the personal representative from a later lawsuit for acting improperly in turning over to a minor, or perhaps to his or her parents, property that is valued either below a certain dollar amount or that consists of household furniture and goods.

My husband left his tractor to my son, Frank. About two months before my husband died, he sold the tractor to pay some of his hospital bills. Is it necessary for me to buy an equivalent tractor and turn it over to my son?

No. The bequest here was *adeemed*. Property is adeemed when the property is no longer in existence as of the date of death. Therefore, the bequest to Frank fails, and you need do nothing about this matter.

As another example, let us assume that your husband left 100 shares of stock to his mother if she survived him. Your husband's mother survived your husband, but when your husband died, he no longer owned this stock. This language is a classic illustration of a gift to

someone that is intended to take effect only if the property is in existence as of the decedent's date of death. Therefore, the *bequest,* or the gift as it is sometimes called, is considered to be adeemed. This principle of law is also sometimes known as the *doctrine of ademption.*

When my husband died, our residence was titled as tenants by the entirety. I believe that at the moment of death, I became sole owner of the residence, since I survived my husband. My question concerns a $40,000 mortgage that was left on the residence when my husband died. Am I now responsible for paying this mortgage?

Assuming that you signed the mortgage obligation, you are personally liable to the lending institution for this $40,000. If you did not sign the mortgage, you are not personally liable to pay it. However, the property is subject to the mortgage, and, unless you pay it, the property can be sold to pay the mortgage debt.

In some jurisdictions, there is a rule of law known as the *doctrine of exoneration.* This means that you are entitled to be exonerated from your husband's estate for one-half of this debt of $40,000. In other words, your husband left you with a debt of $40,000, and the entire burden of this $40,000 falls upon your shoulders. However, if this rule applies in your state, you are entitled to be reimbursed for one-half of the $40,000 by the other assets contained in your husband's estate. This right to exoneration, or to being relieved of part of the financial burden, is treated as a debt owed to you by your husband's estate. Accordingly, as personal representative, you are entitled to pay yourself $20,000, which payment is treated like any other debt. This payment is due before you make distribution of any assets in the estate to any beneficiaries. If you intend to exercise your right to exoneration, a formal claim should be filed.

What is meant when a gift, or bequest, is considered to be *abated*?

When there are insufficient assets to satisfy a bequest, the bequest, or gift, is reduced proportionately. The laws of most states set forth the priorities concerning who takes what first. An illustration will clarify this statement. Assume that the testator provided that from the monies on deposit with a specific bank, he leaves $25,000 to your son Frank and $25,000 to your son John. At the date of your husband's death, there is only $40,000 in the bank account referred to. It is obvious that there is not enough money to satisfy this bequest from the source named, and therefore, the law provides that each bequest of $25,000 must be abated, or reduced, by the sum of $5,000.

I have heard the expression *family allowance*. What does it mean?

Virtually every state requires that some amount of money or property be set aside for the benefit of a surviving spouse and minor children. The intent is to provide for the family during the period when the estate is being administered.

The family allowance takes many forms, and therefore it is important that the personal representative learn what the allowance is in the state where the estate is being administered.

In some states, the *homestead* (the principal residence) is set aside as the family allowance. In some states, it is a specific sum of money, household furnishings, tools, animals, etc. In yet other states, the allowance is a regular cash stipend for a fixed period of time.

I am the personal representative of my brother's estate. He left a bequest of $5,000 to a cousin if she survived my brother. She survived my brother by 10 days. Am I now required to pay the $5,000 to her estate?

In many states there are laws dealing with this subject. The answer to your question depends on the state in which your brother resided at the time of his death.

For example, in Maryland there is a law that says a legatee (a person who under the terms of a will would receive property) who fails to survive the testator by 30 full days shall be considered to have died before the testator. When someone dies before a testator, that person is not entitled to inherit under the will. These rules can be changed by the terms of the will. In this case, your cousin will be considered to have died before your brother and is therefore not entitled to her legacy.

This rule (requiring someone to survive by a specified period) has an exception. This exception is known as the *lapse rule.* It says that when a bequest, or gift, is given to someone who is named or referred to, if that person dies after the will is executed but before the testator dies, the bequest, or gift, is still valid. That is, the bequest, or gift, does *not* lapse. Therefore, had your brother given $5,000 to his cousin by will, but not required that she survive him, the lapse rule would have been effective. This would have meant that her estate would be entitled to the $5,000.

As interpreted under Maryland law, your brother's will requires that his cousin actually survive by 30 full days. Since she died within ten days, the lapse rule does not apply in this case.

My brother died a resident of Maryland but had real estate in another state. How do I, as personal representative, get possession of this asset?

You were appointed the personal representative by a Maryland court. The estate is being administered under the laws of Maryland, and therefore Maryland is considered to be the principal place of administration. Your authority as personal representative does not extend to real property in another state.

It will be necessary for you, or someone who is qualified by the laws of the other state, to apply to the state in which the real property is located for an appointment as the ancillary personal representative in that state. Maryland is the state in which you are the principal, or domiciliary, personal representative.

Whoever is appointed would then proceed with the ancillary administration of the estate in the state where the property was located at the time of death. This involves all the same procedures that are involved in the administration of an estate in the state where the decedent was domiciled at the time of death; that is, advertising notice of appointment (for the benefit of creditors), collecting the assets, paying debts, and paying taxes.

In the last few years many states have liberalized their laws in this area. They have permitted personal representatives appointed by another state (called *foreign personal representatives*) to come into their state to administer assets located there, without requiring the foreign personal representative to secure appointment as the ancillary personal representative.

For example, assume the domicile of a decedent is in New York. Her estate is being administered there. The personal representative there (called an executor in New York) learns of property located in Maryland. The *letters* issued by the New York court are sufficient authority for the New York executor to collect any Maryland assets belonging to the estate. Maryland requires only that the New York executor (the foreign personal representative) advertise a notice of his appointment and pay any applicable Maryland death taxes. The New York executor is not required to go through the probate process again, nor is he required to secure *letters* issued by a Maryland court; his authority is already established by reason of having the New York *letters.*

Please review the rules with respect to distribution of estate assets.

All of the estate assets, including income from such assets, shall first be used to pay administration and funeral expenses, debts of the decedent, and any taxes for which the estate is liable.

What is left is then distributed in the following order:

1. Specific and demonstrative legacies. A *specific legacy* is a gift of some specific item that can be identified. For example, a gift of the decedent's rocking chair to his daughter is a specific legacy.

A *demonstrative legacy* is a gift of a dollar amount or a quantity of material, payable from a certain source. For example, a gift of $1,000 to be paid from decedent's account at the credit union is a demonstrative legacy.

2. A general legacy payable to a surviving spouse. A *general legacy* is one that does not specify the source from which it is to be paid. For example, a gift of one-half of the decedent's gross estate to his (or her) surviving spouse is a general legacy.

3. A general legacy payable to others.

4. Residuary legacies. A *residuary legacy* is what is left after all of the above, including expenses, debts, and taxes, are paid.

If there are insufficient assets in an estate to pay all the legacies, the residuary legatees are the first affected, and then the others shown here are affected in the reverse order of this listing. In other words, some of the legacies may be abated.

What happens if there are insufficient assets to pay all of a decedent's debts?

Each state sets forth, in its laws, which debts must be paid first. As a guide, the laws of most states provide for payment of debts and expenses in the following order:

1. court fees
2. funeral expenses
3. costs and expenses of administering the estate, including compensation of the personal representative, legal fees, and real estate brokerage commissions
4. family allowance
5. taxes due by decedent
6. reasonable medical, hospital, and nursing expenses for the last illness
7. rent for the last three months in arrears
8. wages, salaries, or commissions due for the prior three months in arrears
9. all other claims

In general, the law prohibits preferring one claim in any of the above categories over another claim. For example, assume the assets were sufficient to pay in full all of the first eight items. There is a balance of $3,000 and the claims due, belonging in category 9, total $15,000. In this case, each of the creditors shall be entitled to only a portion of each claim. You may not pay 100 percent of the claim of one claimant, leaving less for distribution to the other claimants in category 9.

What tax returns must be filed, when are they due, and where are they to be filed?

For citizens or residents of the United States, the following applies:

1. The final federal income tax return of the decedent and payment of the tax are both due as though the decedent lived for the entire year. Thus, the return is due by the fifteenth day of the fourth month following the close of the taxable year in which the person died (April 15 for calendar year taxpayers).

An automatic extension of time can be secured by filing Form 4868 and paying the tax that is estimated to be due. The place of filing is the appropriate office of the Internal Revenue Service based on the legal residence or place of business of the person making the return. For the final state income tax return, consult your state tax authority.

2. A notice of qualification as personal representative should be filed with the IRS as soon as possible. Federal Form 56 is available for this purpose. The form is filed in the office of the Internal Revenue Service where the decedent's return is filed.

3. A federal estate tax return is required when the gross estate (not taxable estate) plus adjusted taxable gifts exceed $600,000. (If death occurred prior to 1987, the amount is less.) The return is filed on Form 706, which will be supplied, on request, by any Internal Revenue Service office. The return is due within nine months after the date of the decedent's death. The place of filing is set forth in the instructions for the return. Payment of the tax is due when the return is filed. (See Death Taxes.) Form 706 is also required, even if the gross estate is less than $600,000, when there is due a generation-skipping transfer tax or if the estate has any excess accumulation in qualified plans (to figure the "increased" estate tax).

The due date of the return and payment of the tax may be extended. Federal law and the regulations of the Treasury Department should be consulted to determine when an extension is available.

4. If the decedent made a gift in any year prior to his death and failed to file a gift tax return, you may be required to do so on behalf of the decedent. (A transfer to a political organization or to an educational organization or medical care provider is not considered a gift.) Form 709 is also required where there is a generation-skipping transfer subject to this tax.

Here are the rules concerning gifts:

1. Any gift of any amount to a spouse who is a U.S. citizen does not require a return, except as noted in d, below.
2. If the gift is less than $10,000 per year to anyone, no return is due, except as noted in d, below.
3. If the gift is more than $10,000 per year to anyone, a return is due.
4. If the gift is of a *future interest* in any amount to anyone, a return is due.

A *future interest* is a property interest whose use, possession, or enjoyment will begin in the future.

5. If the gift is to a spouse who is not a U.S. citizen and the gift exceeds $100,000, a return is due. If less than $100,000, no return is due.

The return is on Form 709, supplied, on request, by any Internal Revenue Service office. The return is due on or before the fifteenth day of April following the close of the calendar year. However, when death occurs in the year in which a gift is made, the return is due when the estate tax return is due (usually nine months after date of death) or on April 15, whichever is earlier. The place of filing is set forth in the instructions to the return. Payment of the tax is due when the return is filed.

The due date of the return and payment of the tax may be extended. Consult federal law and Treasury Department regulations to determine when an extension is available.

Note: Forms 706 and 709 have separate instruction forms. Ask for them. Also, request from the Internal Revenue Service a free copy of Publication 448. It is titled "Federal Estate and Gift Taxes." All forms and publications can be secured by calling the IRS at 1-800-829-3676.

In addition to these tax returns, must any other returns be filed with taxing authorities?

Yes. The estate is a separate taxpayer. Accordingly, the personal representative must keep records of income and expenses of the estate to permit the preparation and filing of federal and, in many states, state income tax returns for the estate.

The estate federal income tax return is filed on Form 1041 and is known as a Fiduciary Income Tax Return. This return must be filed when the gross income of the estate for the taxable year is $600 or more, or when any beneficiary of the estate is a nonresident alien.

The form and instructions are available from any office of the Internal Revenue Service. Also helpful is the free pamphlet "Tax Information for Survivors, Executors, and Administrators" (Publication 559).

The return and the tax are due by the fifteenth day of the fourth month following the close of the taxable year. The place of filing is set forth in the instructions. The taxable year begins on the date of death. For example, if the decedent died on March 15, the taxable year of the estate begins on March 15. A time extension may be granted upon application.

Is it necessary to keep any other types of records?

Yes. The value of the property owned by the estate as of the date of death must be determined in order to determine what death taxes must be paid. Estates also have the option of having the property owned by it valued as of another date. This other date is called the *alternate valuation date*, which for federal purposes is usually six months after date of death.

The states that impose an estate tax usually follow the federal rule in this regard.

The personal representative should determine the value of all the assets of the estate as of date of death and as of the alternate valuation date. This is done to arrive at the values that would be most favorable to the estate and to the beneficiaries.

In terms of estate taxes, the lowest values should be used; however, higher income taxes might be levied at some time by reason of using the lowest values. (See the discussion concerning taxes on page 176.)

Keep records accounting for every transaction affecting the estate. These would include, in addition to income received, amounts paid for expenses, taxes, repairs, payments made on sale of any property, and every other conceivable receipt or payment made by or to the estate.

A personal representative should account for all estate transactions to the beneficiaries of the estate. In many states, accounting to the beneficiaries or the court, or both, may be required.

Where would I find a definition of income?

For federal income tax purposes, the rules are set forth in that part of the Internal Revenue Code known as Chapter 1, Subchapter J. While the deductions and exemptions of an estate are different from those available to an individual, gross income is determined in the same manner as for an individual. For state in-

come tax purposes, the laws of most states follow the federal rules concerning the definition of income.

Where can I find rules explaining the differences between income and principal from the nontax point of view?

Most states have now adopted as part of their laws the revised Uniform Principal and Income Act. The text of the act can be found among the laws of each state that enacted it into law. A copy of the act can be secured from the National Conference of Commissioners on Uniform State Laws, 676 North Saint Clair Street, Chicago, IL 60611.

In summary, the act provides that income is the return, in money or property, derived from the use of *principal*. Principal is the property that has been set aside by the owner or by the person legally empowered to do so.

The property that is set aside shall be held in trust and eventually delivered to the *remainderman* (the person entitled to principal, including income that has been accumulated and added to principal). While the principal is held in trust, the income from the principal shall be paid over to the *income beneficiary* (the person to whom income is presently payable or for whom it is accumulated for distribution as income) or accumulated, depending on the terms of the trust.

When a corporation distributes its own shares of stock, whether by a stock split or a stock dividend, this is considered principal unless the corporation declares that the distribution is being made instead of giving an ordinary cash dividend.

You must remember, however, that each state has its own laws on this entire subject. Therefore, it is important to consult the laws of your state to be sure of what is income and what is principal.

When does the right to income arise?

The following is reprinted from the revised (1962) Uniform Principal and Income Act:

1. An income beneficiary is entitled to income from the date specified in the trust instrument or, if none is specified, from the date an asset becomes subject to the trust. In the case of an asset becoming subject to a trust by reason of a will, it becomes subject to the trust as of the testator's date of death even though there is an intervening period of administration of the testator's estate.

2. In the administration of a decedent's estate or if an asset becomes subject to a trust by reason of a will

  a. receipts due but not paid at the date of death of the testator are principal;

  b. receipts in the form of periodic payments (other than corporate distributions to stockholders), including rent, interest, or annuities, not due at the date of the death of the testator, shall be treated as accruing from day to day. That portion of the receipt accruing before the date of death is principal and the balance is income.

3. In all other cases, any receipt from an income-producing asset is income even though the receipt was earned or accrued in whole or in part before the date when the asset became subject to the trust.

4. On termination of an income interest, either the income beneficiary whose interest is terminated or his estate is entitled to

  a. income undistributed on the date of termination;

  b. income due but not paid to the trustee on the date of termination;

  c. income in the form of periodic payments (other than corporate distributions to stockholders), including rent, interest, or annuities, not due on the date of termination, accrued from day to day.

5. Corporate distributions to stockholders shall be treated as due on the day *fixed by the corporation for determination of stockholders of record entitled to distribution or, if no date is fixed, on the date of declaration of the distribution by the corporation.*

Please set forth, in general, the rules as to who is entitled to income earned by an estate.

The following is reprinted from the revised Uniform Principal and Income Act:

1. Unless the will otherwise provides, and subject to subsection 2, below, all expenses incurred in connection with the settlement of a decedent's estate, including debts, funeral expenses, estate taxes, interest, and penalties concerning taxes, family allowances, fees of attorneys and personal representatives, and court costs shall be charged against the principal of the estate.

2. *Unless the will otherwise provides, income from the assets of a decedent's estate after the death of the testator and before distribution, including income from property used to discharge liabilities, shall be determined in accordance with the rules applicable to a trustee under this Act and distributed as follows:*

a. *To specific legatees and devisees, the income from the property bequeathed or devised to them respectively, less taxes, ordinary repairs, and other expenses of management and operation of the property, and an appropriate portion of interest accrued since the death of the testator and of taxes imposed on income (excluding taxes on capital gains) which accrue during the period of administration;*

b. *To all other legatees and devisees, except legatees of pecuniary bequests not in trust, the balance of income, less the balance of taxes, ordinary repairs, and other expenses of management and operation of all property from which the estate is entitled to income, interest accrued since the death of the testator, and taxes imposed on income (excluding taxes on capital gains) which accrue during the period of administration, in proportion to their respective interests in the undistributed assets of the estate computed at times of*

distribution on the basis of inventory value.

3. *Income received by a trustee under subsection 2 shall be treated as income of the trust.*

Is the personal representative entitled to compensation, and if so, in what amount?

Every state allows compensation, sometimes called a commission or fee. The amount of compensation varies from state to state and is based on the value of the probate estate. Commissions vary from 2½ percent of receipts plus 2½ percent of payments (Georgia) to 3 percent (and less, on a declining scale) of the value of the probate estate exceeding $300,000 and higher percentages for values below $300,000 (New York).

It is important to remember that compensation can be—and frequently should be—waived. Why? Compensation, when received, constitutes income and is subject to income tax. Many times the personal representative is the surviving spouse of the decedent. As surviving spouse, he or she will inherit all or most of the estate. Perhaps the children will inherit part of the estate. If the surviving spouse takes compensation, it will be subject to income tax. When no amount is taken as compensation, the surviving spouse will receive the same, or practically the same, inheritance, but it will not be subject to income tax.

For example, the decedent dies a resident of Maryland and leaves a probate estate of $100,000. This estate consists of stocks, bonds, and cash. The wife is appointed personal representative under her husband's will. The will leaves everything to her outright.

Under Maryland law, she would be entitled to commissions of $4,680, subject to the approval of the court. (For purposes of this illustration, assume there are no debts, taxes, or expenses of any kind.) If she takes the commissions, she would receive the following from the estate:

Commissions	$4,680
Balance of estate	+95,320
	$100,000

The commissions are subject to federal and Maryland income taxes, at the applicable rate.

If she waived her commissions, the spouse would receive the entire estate of $100,000, but if she applied to the court for commissions and accepted them, $4,680 will be needlessly subject to income tax.

What legal fees can I, as personal representative, expect to pay?

The fees are based on several factors and may be subject to the approval of the court. The most important factor is the time devoted to the matter, and this depends upon the attorney's work. Variable factors are: Is there a caveat to the will? Is there litigation? Is the estate involved in running a business? Is a federal estate tax return required? Are there complex legal problems requiring extensive legal research? Are there disagreements with the taxing authorities? Are there problems determining the price to be realized by the estate when closely held stock must be redeemed? Will contracts be required in connection with selling estate assets? Will extensive work be involved in disposing of a professional practice?

Fees vary from attorney to attorney and from region to region. As a general rule, an estate can expect to pay a fee of at least one-half the statutory commission rate payable to a personal representative plus something extra to handle assets that are not part of the probate estate. For example, a probate estate may consist of $50,000 in assets, but property subject to taxation may involve hundreds of thousands of dollars. Dealing with these nonprobate assets may require many hours of work for which legal fees are necessarily incurred.

Any legal fees paid for work on probate assets are an expense of the estate. In addition, legal fees for work on other assets that are part of the gross taxable estate may be an expense of the estate if the will so directs.

My father died and his bank was appointed personal representative. Last month I received $38,000 from the bank as a final distribution from Father's estate. What may I do with this money?

Anything you wish. This sum now belongs to you. If you deposit the money in a bank account and are entitled to interest income, the income will be subject to income taxes.

You should be aware that some distributions from estates are considered to be income rather than principal. If they are income, you may have to pay an income tax on the distribution. (This matter is discussed at greater length beginning on page 179.)

What does a spouse's right of election mean?

Under the laws of most states, a surviving spouse is entitled to a certain minimum portion of a decedent's estate. In some states, no matter what amount of property is left to a surviving spouse, the spouse has a right to take a share equal to the share the spouse would have received had the decedent died without a will.

Thus, a surviving spouse can file a document with the court that is supervising the estate and elect to take the following:

1. In those states giving that person a minimum amount, the spouse can take any additional sum necessary to make up the minimum amount.

For example, assume that the husband leaves to the wife $20,000 under his will and that under that state's laws, the wife is entitled to one-third of the estate, or $50,000. The surviving spouse could then demand and be entitled to receive the difference between $20,000 and $50,000, or $30,000. If, in this example, the husband left the wife nothing under the husband left the wife nothing under his will, then by exercising the right of election, the wife, who is the surviving spouse, would be entitled to $50,000.

2. In those states in which the surviving spouse has a right of election regardless of what is left under the will, the spouse can take the amount that the laws of such states allow to surviving spouses.

For example, if the minimum amount to which the surviving spouse is entitled is one-half the estate and the estate amounts to $150,000, then by filing the right of election, the surviving spouse would be entitled to $75,000.

States that give a surviving spouse this right of election require that the election be made within a certain stated period of time. This varies from state to state. It is essential that the election be filed within the mandatory period set forth by the laws of the state administering the estate.

I have heard of small estates. What are they?

They are estates that consist of property of no more than a certain sum. This sum varies from state to state and may be $5,000 to $20,000, or it may be smaller or greater than either of these figures. When the valuation at date of death is below the stated amount, the estate may be administered under the statutes for the administration of small estates.

When an estate is administered under such an act, administration is simplified. The forms are less complicated, court fees are considerably reduced, there may be no death taxes to pay, and the waiting period necessary before assets can be distributed is waived or substantially reduced.

What is independent administration?

In some states, such as Maryland, when a will is probated and the property is being administered, periodic reports in the form of accountings must be filed with the court. In other words, there is active court supervision of the administration of the estate. In some states (New York is an example of the other extreme), after a will is admitted to probate, except for the procedure for fixing the tax, there is virtually no court supervision of the administration of the estate unless an interested party requests such intervention. In some states, such as Illinois, a great degree of administration independent of the court is allowed, usually when the estate is below a certain dollar amount, so that virtually no documents need be filed with the court unless, of course, an interested person requests court intervention. When such intervention is requested, full court supervision of the estate is required. The idea behind independent administration is to help reduce the costs of administering estate property.

TRUSTS

General Information

What is a trust?

A *trust* is a device used for disposing of and/or managing property.

It requires:

1. trust property that is held by the trustee for the beneficiary
2. a trustee, that is, the person or corporation who holds trust property and has legally enforceable duties and responsibilities to deal with it for the benefit of another
3. a beneficiary, that is, the person for whose benefit property is held in trust

In general, the trustee is the owner of the legal title of the trust property. Even though the trustee has legal title, the benefits of such ownership belong to the beneficiary.

The relationship between a trustee and the beneficiary is usually referred to as a *fiduciary* relationship. The fiduciary relationship requires the trustee to act with strict honesty and solely in the interest of the beneficiary. The classic statement of what is required of a trustee was expressed by Justice Benjamin Cardozo in the leading case of *Meinhard v. Salmon,* decided in 1928 in New York, as follows:

> *A trustee is held to something stricter than the morals of the marketplace. Not honesty alone, but the punctilio of an honor the most sensitive, is then the standard of behavior.*

The beneficiary's interest is a property interest in the trust property even though the "legal interest" is owned by the trustee. Although we think of a beneficiary (sometimes referred to by lawyers as the *cestui que trust*) as a live named person, this is not always the case. A beneficiary can be one or more persons not yet born or someone who is part of a class of persons. For example, I create a trust during my lifetime. I provide that the income shall be paid to my wife for her lifetime and upon her death the income shall then be paid to my son for his lifetime. Upon the death of the survivor of my wife and son, the trust property shall then be paid over to my son's children then living, in equal shares, as outright owners.

When I created the trust, my son had one daughter. He may have more children. Because I provided that the trust property shall be paid over to his children living at the time of the death of the survivor of my wife and son, that is the time when it is determined who will be the eventual beneficiaries. Therefore, my son's children who are later born are possible beneficiaries too, even though they were not named in the trust instrument. We do not *now* know how many children there will be, nor do we *now* know what shares each will take.

The provisions of the trust are sometimes referred to as the *terms of the trust*. They are set forth in the *trust agreement* or *trust instrument*.

The *trust property* is referred to by different names. Sometimes it is called *trust estate*, *trust principal*, *trust corpus*, or *trust res*.

How is a trust created?

In general, a trust is created by:

1. An oral declaration by the owner of personal property that he holds it, as trustee, in trust for another person. For example, I own a bond and declare that henceforth I am the trustee thereof for the benefit of my cousin, Jane

Should I create a trust in this manner?

No.

Why not?

To do so would create a legal nightmare in proving the trust, the terms of the trust, transferring legal title to the bond, proving who is taxed on the income from the bond, etc.

If the owner of personal property wishes to hold the personal property in trust for another, the transfer of ownership (from the owner to himself, acting in the capacity of trustee) should be done in writing.

In any event, an oral declaration of trust for real property is ineffective. The law (known as the *Statute of Frauds*) requires any such trust to be in writing.

2. A transfer during lifetime by the owner of property to a trustee. The trustee may be a third person (individual or corporation) or the transferor. This type of trust is called a *living trust* or *inter vivos* trust. (*Inter vivos* is a Latin phrase meaning "among the living.")

3. A transfer of property pursuant to the terms of a will. A trust created by will is known as a *testamentary trust*.

4. Where a person has a power of appointment and exercises same. Even though the holder of the power of appointment (also known as the *donee*) does not own the property, he may exercise his power over the property to transfer it to a trustee for the benefit of another. The trustee may also be the beneficiary.

The power of appointment may be one that may be exercised during lifetime or by will.

Each of the acts requires that the person creating the trust have the legal capacity to do so. Also, any act of transferring property to another as trustee should be accompanied by a written instrument setting forth the trust terms.

A person has *legal capacity* to create a trust if he is competent to make a will or enter into a contract and is not otherwise legally incompetent, for example, does not have mental capacity, is an infant (except where state law permits an infant to do so). (Also see the discussion of *sound mind* on page 6 and *undue influence* on page 112.)

What is a *power of appointment* and when should it be used?

A power of appointment is giving someone the legal authority to determine who shall own property. Tax reasons for giving or withholding a power of appointment are explained under Death Taxes. There are also nontax reasons for giving someone a power of appointment.

For example, let us say that by will you leave all your property in trust for the benefit of your wife during her lifetime, and thereafter for your children. Your wife is 10 years younger than you are, and you have three children. Although you wish your wife to benefit from your property during her lifetime, you do not wish to direct that the trust property shall be left on your wife's death to your children in equal shares. You realize that your wife may survive you by 10, 20, or 30 years. During that time, the financial situation of your children may change. One child may become wealthy and have no need for your funds, another child may be physically disabled

and require the extra assistance that your funds can provide, and another child may be incapable of handling money.

Who, then, is in the best position to make the determination 20 years after your death? Obviously, your wife is. In such a case, you can give your wife a power of appointment, which grants her the authority (gives her the power) to "appoint" the property, that is, to designate who shall be the owner of the trust property after her death.

There are several types of power of appointment. You may give this power so that it may be used (exercised) only on the death of the one who has the power. (This is known as a *testamentary power of appointment*.) In this case, the one who has the power can only exercise it by will. You may give this power so that it can be used during the lifetime of the person who is given the power. (This is known as an *inter vivos power of appointment*.)

You may grant the power so that the one to whom it is given may appoint the property only among a limited group of persons, such as your children. This type of power is known as a *special* or *limited power of appointment*. If the power is such that the one who has the power can appoint the property to anyone in the world, including the one who has the appointing power (the donee), then this type of power is known as a *general power of appointment*.

The one who gives the power to another is called the *donor*. The one who receives the power is called the donee. The person who is favored by an appointment of the property by the donee is called the *appointee*. If the donee does not choose to exercise the power, the person who takes the property is called the *taker in default.*

Note: Strictly speaking, the donee of a power of appointment is not the owner of the property subject to the power. The donee is simply the agent of the donor of the power. Therefore, when the power is exercised, the ownership or use of the property that is transferred is considered to have passed from the one who granted the power (the donor) and not from the donee of the power.

As a practical matter the effect of this rule is that the property that is subject to the power of appointment is not considered part of the estate of the donee. Accordingly, such property is not administered as part of the donee's probate estate, nor is such property subject to claims of the donee's creditors.

A principal exception to this result is where the power of appointment is a general power. By definition, a general power of appointment enables the donee of the power to appoint the property to anyone, including the donee. In such a case, if the donee's will exercises the power, the usual rule is that the property would be subject to the donee's creditors, if his other assets are inadequate to pay the creditors.

For tax purposes, the property that is subject to a general power of appointment is always considered as owned by the donee and taxed accordingly.

What you have just explained with respect to how to create trusts does not seem to apply to what I have read about constructive and resulting trusts.

Please explain why there is this discrepancy.

Except for the brief comments that follow, an explanation of constructive and resulting trusts is beyond the scope of this book. The previous discussion of how to create a trust was therefore limited to an overview of how to create *express* trusts.

A so-called *constructive trust* is a device created by the courts to redress a wrong or to prevent unjust enrichment. It is not created by the express intent of the creator of the trust. A constructive trust is a means used by the courts to correct a fraud. It does so by imposing a constructive trust on the fruits of the wrongdoing. When the wrongdoer may not in good conscience continue to hold title to the property wrongfully acquired, the court declares the property to be held in (constructive) trust for the benefit of the party who is wronged.

A *resulting trust* is one where there is an inferred or presumed intent from the facts of a transfer of property. It arises when it is clear from the property transfer that the transferee was not intended to become the beneficial owner of the property. For example, I transfer stock to A to sell it 90 days later and to divide the proceeds between B and C, in equal shares. In the meantime B dies. I never intended A to become the beneficial owner of one-half of the proceeds. Since B is deceased when A sells the stock, A holds one-half of the proceeds in a resulting trust for my benefit. If I am also then deceased, one-half of the proceeds would then belong to my estate.

I will now create a living trust. I can always revoke it if I so desire. Is this correct?

Yes and no. It all depends on the state that has jurisdiction over the trust. In general, the power to revoke a trust is not implied. Thus, unless the applicable state's laws permit its revocation, if the trust instrument specifically does not provide for revocation, the trust is irrevocable.

There are exceptions to this rule. The principal ones are as follows:

1. if the settlor is the sole beneficiary;
2. there was a mistake in failing to include in the trust terms the power to revoke; and
3. when the trust was created as a result of fraud, undue influence, or duress.

A related question is whether the power to revoke includes the power to modify, remove trustees, add trustees, or remove property from the trust.

The simplest and suggested way to create certainty is for the trust instrument to specify what is desired. Language similar to the following should appear to resolve any questions:

The Settlor expressly reserves the right from time to time during Settlor's lifetime, by notice in writing, addressed to the Trustee, to alter, amend, terminate, rescind, or revoke this Trust Agreement, in whole or in part, or to remove any Trustee.

or

This Trust Agreement is irrevocable, and the Settlor relinquishes all right to alter, amend, revoke, or terminate the same.

If I do reserve the power to revoke the trust agreement, will this be binding on all?

Yes. However, please bear in mind that if you become disabled or incompetent, you may be unable to exercise the power of revocation.

Our son, John, is the typical movie version of the absentminded professor. He is intellectually interesting, generous, kind, and well adjusted. He is totally unconcerned with material things. He has no experience, interest, or concern with financial matters. His wife, who is as dear to us as a daughter, has the same personality and interests. We are concerned that upon the deaths of my wife, Mary, and me, whatever he inherits from us will be rapidly depleted by imprudent investments, gifts, and perhaps overreaching by financial "consultants." Do you have any suggestions?

Under your respective wills, you should provide that on the death of the survivor of you and Mary, whatever is left should be held in trust, with a *spendthrift clause* provision. This type of trust is sometimes referred to as a *spendthrift trust*.

The trust provides that income shall be payable to your son and daughter-in-law so long as either shall live. The trust also provides that the trustee, in the trustee's sole discretion, may invade principal for the benefit of your son, his wife, or any of their children to meet their health, education, or support needs. At the death of the survivor of your son and his wife, the trust shall terminate. Upon termination, the remaining trust principal shall be paid over outright to their surviving children.

The spendthrift clause prohibits your son (and his wife) from mortgaging or assigning their anticipated future income or principal. In addition, their creditors may not seize the income or principal before they actually receive the income or principal.

Though the spendthrift clause may not protect the sums actually paid over and received by your son (or his wife), the restraint so placed on the trust income and principal will have the desired effect of protecting them to a substantial degree from their own imprudence.

In a few states, and they are in the minority, such clauses have limited protective ability. This matter should be discussed with your attorney. Depending on the amount of your assets, your attorney may recommend creating such a trust during your lifetime (a living or inter vivos trust) and declare the trust to be governed by the laws of a state that recognizes the validity of a spendthrift clause. In most cases, this latter suggestion is not feasible because of greater complexity, and higher costs and fees.

The idea of a spendthrift clause appeals to me for another reason. I am an obstetrician, which, as you know, is a profession that is high risk in the sense of being subject to malpractice lawsuits. Even though I now have malpractice insurance, I am concerned that the coverage may be inadequate. Also for economic reasons, I may have to cancel the coverage. I will therefore create an irrevocable living trust with a spendthrift clause for my benefit and fund it with all my assets. Have I accomplished something?

Since your motive in creating the trust was to insulate your assets from possible future creditors, the answer is no. Any spendthrift clause in a trust created for one's own benefit is not valid to insulate the trust assets from either existing or future creditors.

If such a trust were created for your benefit by your parents, either during lifetime or by will, the assets would, in most states, be protected from creditors' claims until the assets were paid over to you.

At my age, my requiring nursing home care is a real possibility. I would like to have my children and grandchildren inherit my assets, which are now approximately $200,000. If I created a trust for the benefit of my family, but gave the trustee sole discretion to pay income or principal to me, would it be correct to say that my nursing home expenses would be paid by the

federally funded program known as Medicaid? Please explain what the program is and give me your comments.

The trust you propose to create is known as a Medicaid Qualifying Trust (or MQT). The name given to this type of trust is actually misleading, since such a trust would disqualify you from receiving benefits.

Medicaid is a federal statute, primarily administered by the states, which provides financial help for health care costs to the aged and disabled, among others, who are financially needy. In order for an individual to be considered "needy," his or her income and capital must fall below a certain minimum amount. Without considering certain excluded items, for example, a house, the minimum amount of capital is between $12,000 and $60,000. These amounts have been indexed for inflation. Thus, in 1992 the maximum amount was $68,700, and in 1993, $70,761. For this purpose, one-half of your spouse's individually owned assets is considered as owned by you.

Your concern then is that nursing home costs will quickly consume most of the $200,000 you have saved all your lifetime. You want to be sure that your spouse is financially comfortable and that as much as possible will be left for your children and grandchildren.

To anticipate this possibility, you propose creating a trust with all your assets. If the trust is created more than 30 months before your application for Medicaid benefits, any complete disposition of your assets is permissible. The key here is "complete disposition." However, what you propose is not a complete disposition. You want to give the trustee, who could be one of your children, the discretion to pay over to you whatever principal the trustee deems appropriate.

Several years ago, Congress closed the availability of this device. They did so by declaring that when a trustee has discretion to pay you principal, this principal is considered as being owned by you outright. Therefore, since it is "owned" by you, it is available as a capital resource and is to be taken into account to consider whether or not you are needy.

What is a testamentary trust?

A trust that is created by the terms of a will. This type of trust is distinguished from a trust created during lifetime. A trust created during lifetime is called an inter vivos, or living, trust.

Do the rules as to revocability also apply to testamentary trusts?

Since the testamentary trust is created under the terms of your will and is first created after your death, during your lifetime you can revoke the will. By doing so the trust never becomes effective.

In addition, you may insert conditions in your will that could revoke the trust upon certain conditions or the happening of an event or the failure of an event to occur. The term *revoke*, as used here, has the same result as though the trust were terminated. For example, by will you leave $150,000 in trust for your surviving spouse. Your spouse is entitled to all the income for life plus such discretionary payments from principal as the trustee deems appropriate for your spouse's health, maintenance, or support. You provide in your will that the trust shall terminate (end) upon the remarriage of your spouse. Your spouse remarries. The trust will then terminate and be paid over or dealt with as provided by your will.

Or, for example, under the terms of your will you leave $100,000 in trust for the benefit of your daughter, Jane. Until termination, she is to receive all the income. You provide that the trust shall terminate on the earlier to occur of (1) Jane's death, (2) Jane's graduation from college, (3) Jane's failure to be in regular attendance at college for a consecutive period of one year, and (4) five years after your death. Jane graduates four years after your death. The trust will then terminate and be paid over or dealt with as provided by your will.

Or, you could give a third person the power to terminate the trust. This power is essentially the power of appointment. (See pages 105–106.)

Why create a testamentary trust?

Some of the nontax reasons to have a testamentary trust are as follows:

To have professional management of property for the benefit of your loved ones. For example, assume you die, your husband is already dead, and you leave two children, aged 10 and 12. If you live in a state where the children attain their majority (legally become adults) at age 18, you have to ask yourself if you wish them to have control of their inherited property at age 18. If the answer is no, you may consider creating a trust under your will to let them inherit your property in various stages, such as one-third at age 21, another one-third at age 25 (actually one-half of the balance), and the balance at age 30.

To protect your loved ones from their own unwise acts. For example, you die and leave all your money outright to your wife. She remarries. Her new husband convinces her to invest most of the money in a very speculative business, and all is lost. If the money had been left in a trust, your wife would have had to request the money from the trustee. Depending on the language you used in your will when you created the trust, the trustee could say yes or no to a request for additional funds from your wife. But even if she had the right to demand all the funds (that is, the trustee would have no choice but to pay the money over to her when she requested it), at the very least this would give the trustee an opportunity to talk with your wife and give her the benefit of the trustee's advice.

To give someone the benefit of the use of the income from the trust but have it pass eventually to another party. An example of this is a provision for your parents, leaving $100,000 in trust for their benefit during their lifetimes. On their deaths, the trust property is then paid over to your wife, if living, and if not living, to your children.

Please discuss some aspects of creating a living trust.

There are tax and nontax reasons for creating a living trust. The tax reasons are discussed in the section on taxes. The principal nontax reasons are as follows:

1. To avoid probate.

a. The probate process can cause delay in transferring assets from a decedent to the trustee, especially when minors have an interest in the property. In New York, for example, if a minor has an interest in the estate property, the surrogate's court will appoint an attorney to represent the minor's interests before it will probate the will. The New York lawmakers perceived that the parent of a minor may have an interest in the will that might not be in the best interests of the minor. The job of an attorney appointed to represent a minor is therefore to investigate the facts and best represent the minor's interests. Essentially, the attorney is to consider whether or not there is any legal basis for opposing probate of the will. Naturally, this takes time and adds extra fees and costs to the probate process.

If a trust is created during lifetime, the delay and costs noted above are avoided because there is already a trustee or a successor trustee appointed by the creator of the trust. (The creator of the trust may be called the *grantor, settlor,* donor, or *trustor.*) Shortly after a trust is created, all the property is titled in the name of the trustee. Thus, when the creator of the trust dies, there is no reason to go through the probate process for the trust property.

b. If you own real estate in another state, it will be necessary on your death to have your will probated in that other state. Why is this necessary? Because only the state where the real estate is located has jurisdiction to convey its title. Assume you own real estate in Florida, are unmarried, and have a daughter to whom you wish to leave your possessions. On your death, this real estate is titled in your name. In order to transfer ownership to your daughter, it will be necessary to probate the will in Florida. When the will is probated in Florida, ownership or title to the property will pass to the administrator. This process is called *ancillary administration.*

The Florida administrator could be your daughter or someone else, such as a bank or an attorney. The administrator would eventually be required to distribute the property to your daughter. This process of ancillary administration will be responsible for additional costs and will delay your daughter's receipt of the property.

A living (inter vivos) trust would save the costs and delay since, at the moment of your death, the trustee would already own the property and could distribute it to your daughter without court approval.

c. Probate documents are public records. Accordingly, anyone may examine these records to determine what assets are owned by the decedent at the time of death.

On the other hand, a living trust is usually not a public record. If secrecy is desired, a living trust would usually achieve this goal.

2. To protect your property in the event of incompetence (that is, diminished mental ability without a judicial declaration of legal incompetence).

a. There are many reported instances in which a trusted employee or relative takes advantage of one's incompetence. The other person has the incompetent sign over property to him or her. If it can be proven that such an act took place when a person was incompetent, the court will require that the property be returned.

However, it is difficult and costly to prove incompetence. If someone creates a living trust and appoints another person as trustee, the trustee will protect the property from being transferred.

b. An incompetent individual sometimes does foolish things with his or her property. One may make unwise investments or uncalled-for gifts. For example, assume I am the trustee of a trust created by you. You have retained the right to revoke the trust. Should you suddenly decide to give your housekeeper the gift of a substantial portion of your property, owned by me as trustee, I would investigate any such transfer that you wished to make.

If I felt that someone was trying to take advantage of you, I would present all the facts to an appropriate court before I would make any transfer. This would have the effect of protecting your assets. As trustee, I could even decline to make the requested transfer and put the burden of establishing entitlement to

your property on the third person. Before any transfer is made, you would have the protection of the trustee and the courts.

3. To dispose of your property as you initially direct, thereby lessening the right of members of your family to claim that undue influence was exercised or that you were incompetent at the time you made your will.

Here is an example of the use of undue influence. Assume I am unmarried (whether widowed or divorced) and have two children named John and Mary. I am estranged from John. I have not seen or heard from him for the past 10 years. During these 10 years, I have lived happily in Mary's home, baby-sat for her children (my grandchildren), and gone on many trips with Mary and her family. It is my wish that Mary shall inherit all my property to the exclusion of John.

If I leave all my property to Mary by will, John (who must be given notice of the probate of my will) can claim that the will was executed in favor of Mary because Mary exercised undue influence on me. The legal theory of "undue influence" in this case is that Mary exercised duress on me to leave all my property to her.

Stated another way, the wishes expressed in my will do not in reality express my wishes but are Mary's wishes, imposed on me by Mary as a result of her wrongful influence. If Mary did exercise such wrongful influence on me, then the contents of my will do not result from my voluntary act and should be declared invalid.

The reader should here remember that when my will is offered for probate (that is, for acceptance by the court), I am no longer alive and the burden is placed on Mary to disprove something of which she was not guilty—namely, of taking advantage of her close relationship with me to substitute her wishes or judgment for mine.

While no one can prevent one person from bringing a frivolous lawsuit against another, having a living trust in this situation would strengthen Mary's defense against John's unfounded claims. Assume that you were on the jury hearing this case and learned that I had created the trust five years ago. I had approved or signed income tax returns for the trust all these years, made bank deposits and withdrawals, communicated periodically with my attorney about the disposition of my property, and perhaps made periodic modest gifts to Mary from the trust funds; in other words, over a period of several years I showed my involvement in trust affairs. Because of this history, it is likely that you, the jury, would more readily reject John's claim that Mary exercised undue influence on me to prefer her to John.

This example should not be interpreted by the reader to mean that if I left all my property to Mary by will, without creating a living trust, my wishes would not be respected. All it suggests is that based on this example, a living trust would make a stronger case for Mary's position.

The reader should also be aware that when a will is offered for probate, all persons who would inherit from the decedent, if there were no will, may have to be given notice of the attempt to have the will probated. This is not necessary in the case of trusts. In the case just discussed, if I had created a living trust, John might never have learned of the disposition of my property to Mary.

4. To limit the amount that the surviving spouse may take of the decedent-spouse's assets. (Assume the surviving spouse is the wife.)

In most states, state law gives a wife (or a husband if he is the surviving spouse) the right to receive a certain percentage of a deceased husband's assets. The percentage is fixed by state law. If the wife exercises this right, usually known as the *right of election,* she takes the stated percentage in place of any property left to her by her husband by will.

The question that arises is whether the percentage includes only probate assets (that is, assets passing under the terms of the will) or whether the percentage includes other assets as well, such as assets that are in revocable trusts. By way of illustration, assume the state's laws give the wife the right to receive a minimum of one-third of the husband's assets. Assume, too, that the husband died owning in his own name $450,000, and that at the time of his death, there was in existence a revocable trust, created by him, with assets worth $150,000. Is the wife's share one-third of $450,000 or one-third of $600,000 ($450,000 plus $150,000)?

In many states, the spouse's right of election includes other assets (such as assets contained in a living trust) in addition to probate assets. This is known as the *augmented estate.* In the example just given, if the wife's right of election applies to the augmented estate, she would be entitled to $200,000 (one-third of $600,000). If her right of election only includes probate assets, she would be entitled to $150,000 (one-third of $450,000).

In those states where the right of election is limited to probate assets only, the decedent spouse may create a living trust for the purpose of limiting the surviving spouse's rights.

I note that you stated in the prior answer (at 1.b.) that the trustee *could* distribute the property. Is there any reason why you were not more positive?

Yes there is. There is absolutely no difference in estate or inheritance taxes (collectively known as *death taxes*) when property is transferred at death using a living trust or a will.

Assume there will be a federal estate tax. If the trustee distributes assets from the trust without withholding enough assets to pay such taxes, the trustee could become personally liable for such taxes. The same personal liability exists for any state death taxes.

Depending on all the facts, while the trustee has the lawful authority immediately to distribute trust assets, the trustee should not do so until all taxes are first determined and paid.

Assume too that the settlor-decedent owed income taxes and perhaps had as a creditor the state of residence. For example, the settlor-decedent may owe the state a substantial amount for medical care rendered to the spouse. In such case, the trustee could be liable for such items if the trustee does not withhold sufficient trust assets to pay same.

Note: When property passes under the terms of a will, the required legal advertising for creditors imposes a shortened time limit on such creditors to present claims. Where property passes under the terms of a living trust, the time limit for creditors to establish their entitlement to be paid is the usual period under state law. This is known as a *statute of limitations*. For trusts, this latter period is usually longer than the period set forth in the case of transfers under a will. For this reason, many lawyers suggest to their clients that they do not utilize living trusts.

You also stated, at 1.c., that a living trust would *usually* achieve the goal of secrecy. Is there any reason why you were not more positive?

Yes there is. When a will is probated, the court file is a public record and available to anyone for examination. When property is transferred by trust, there is usually no public record. However, there are some exceptions where secrecy might not be available. They are:

1. When litigation is instituted either to construe its terms, modify the same, set it aside, or for any other reason.

2. Seventeen states have an inheritance tax and seven additional states impose an estate tax, even if there is no federal estate tax. In these states, a petition is filed to fix the state death taxes. In some states, this petition becomes a public record and available for inspection by anyone.

3. When the estate is required to pay a federal estate tax, there is a credit for taxes paid to a state. To the extent of this credit, each state imposes an estate tax. This tax is known as a "pickup" tax. (This subject is discussed in Death Taxes.)

You should discuss with your lawyer or accountant whether or not the documents filed in connection with determining the amount of the pickup tax become a public record in your state.

4. Even when virtually all your assets become part of a living trust, the overwhelming majority of lawyers would advise you to have a will in addition. This will enable you to dispose of property that, at the time of your death, is owned by you individually. It would be a fair assumption to state that a substantial number of these wills have a *pour-over clause* (also referred to as a *pour-over will*). A pour-over will provides that the property subject to the terms of the will shall be added (poured-over) to the terms of the trust and be disposed of as therein provided.

Whether because of custom, fixing state taxes, state law, and especially where real property is involved, the trust instrument would then be filed with the probate court and thereby usually become a public record.

I have read that costs of probate are prohibitively expensive and that is why you should always avoid probate by creating trusts during lifetime. Would you please comment.

There are three important costs in administering an estate. They are commissions of the estate's personal representative, death taxes, and legal fees.

Commissions In most states, commissions are a percentage of probate assets. This is the biggest estate expense of the three items mentioned.

If you designate as personal representative a bank or an individual who is unrelated to you by blood or marriage, the maximum allowable commission will surely be asked (and probably granted).

It is recommended that you appoint your spouse, a child, or grandchild as personal representative. A waiver of entitlement to a commission should be filed. The personal representative would then hire a lawyer, at estate expense, to perform the necessary services. Hiring a lawyer is usually more economical than having the lawyer, or a third party, receive personal representative commissions.

When creating a living trust, you, your spouse, and children would also undoubtedly be the trustees or successor trustees. Each would also serve without commission. Thus, there is no difference in cost as to this item.

However, if you create a living trust to avoid probate and appoint a bank as trustee during your lifetime, it would certainly charge trustee's commissions. If the trust is in existence for several years before your death, these charges could exceed a personal representative's commissions.

Death Taxes   The same death taxes are incurred when property is transferred on death whether it is done by a living trust or a will. In other words, there is no difference in death taxes whether you use a living trust or will.

Legal Fees   The legal fees of most attorneys are based on their hourly charges and not the value of the property being transferred.

With a will, court documents are required that are not needed with a trust. However, with a trust the retitling of assets frequently requires additional legal services and recording costs (when real estate is involved). With a trust, time is devoted to the initial transfer to the trustee, who is usually the settlor, and when the settlor-trustee dies, additional time is then devoted to retitling the trust assets to show the name of the new trustee.

There are other considerations that are usually not of major importance. With probate, there are court filing fees, while with a trust, the opportunity of deferring income taxes or of equalizing the tax brackets of the trust and beneficiaries (by timing distributions) is lost.

I am concerned about proper management of my property in the event of my having a stroke or sustaining other physical or mental disability. I am aware of the benefits of creating a trust to take care of this problem. Nonetheless, I am uncomfortable with the idea of a trust and do not wish to create one. Do you have any other suggestions?

Yes. The laws of all states permit you to give someone a power of attorney. This enables the person who holds the power to act for you (sometimes called the attorney in fact or agent), on your behalf, as your legal representative. Consideration should be given to naming one or more successor attorneys in fact.

Several years ago, if a person became incompetent, the power of attorney given to someone else was automatically revoked. This rule caused any such power to have limited practical value. Today, the laws of every state provide that a power of attorney may contain appropriate language so that, even in the event of one's disability, the holder of the power may continue to act on behalf of the person who granted the power. A power of attorney that contains this language is known as a *durable power of attorney.*

A power of attorney may be revoked by the grantor of the power so long as that person is competent to act. On the death of the grantor of the power, the power is automatically revoked.

A grant of power may be effective immediately or it may become effective upon a later disability. Whichever power is used, on death of the grantor of the power, the power is considered withdrawn and may not be used thereafter.

How can a trust be used by an aging person?

The following situations can and do occur:

1. A parent has two children. One lives near the parent and the other child lives on the other side of the continent (or even in a foreign country).

The child who lives near the parent visits the parent regularly. The parent has all bank accounts titled in both names (that of the parent and of the child living nearby) with the child having right of survivorship. This form of titling was done at the suggestion of the child. When the parent dies, the child, whose name is on the bank account, claims ownership of the balance remaining in the bank accounts to the exclusion of the other child.

2. The child who lives near the parent "suggests" that a new will be drawn leaving everything to that child.

3. A nursing companion is engaged for a relative. The companion rapidly becomes dominant in the life of the patient. As a result of the companion's subtle threats to leave or do the patient bodily harm, the patient leaves a substantial bequest to the nursing companion.

4. A parent remarries. Since the parent, as well as the new spouse, each has independent financial means, they enter into a prenuptial agreement. The agreement provides that on the death of either, the survivor will have no legal claim to the assets of the first one to die. However, the agreement does not prevent either party from making gifts to the other or voluntarily leaving all or a substantial part of one's property to the other by will. The dominant spouse convinces the other to leave the survivor all of the assets at death.

Were the acts of the aging relatives free and voluntary, or were they induced by fraud, mistake, or undue influence of the one who benefits? Was the parent's act really the act of another imposed on the parent when the parent was weak by reason of age or illness?

The ultimate question is, How does one protect oneself from such situations? A possible solution is to place all of one's assets in a revocable living trust. Unless the trust is revoked or the assets are withdrawn, the assets cannot be disposed of by will. Also, since the trustee is the legal owner of the assets, the property cannot be retitled to make another the joint owner of the property.

However, if the trustee is the grantor (the one who funds the trust) and the trust is revocable, the grantor can readily withdraw all the assets. If the assets are withdrawn, they become subject to the problems mentioned earlier.

Another solution is to appoint someone else trustee. If someone else is trustee and you (as grantor) wish to withdraw assets, you must notify a third party (the trustee) of your wishes. Though the trustee cannot legally prevent you from doing what you wish, notification gives the trustee the opportunity and time to investigate the facts. If the trustee finds that you are being imposed upon, the trustee can notify members of the family or even seek the aid of the courts to protect your assets.

On the other hand, if the trustees are the children, they will learn of what is being attempted and will thereby be given an opportunity to intervene.

Making the trust irrevocable is the safest step to take to prevent dissipation of assets or fraudulent imposition. The trust will provide that you are entitled to the income for life plus such amounts of principal as the trustee determines are desirable for your health, maintenance, or support. You can even reserve the right to withdraw a percentage of the principal each and every year, at *your* discretion. The problem with an irrevocable trust is that you lose control over the assets because you cannot change your mind about them once the trust is in place, even if your circumstances change radically.

There are no absolutely right or wrong answers to these issues. This discussion is merely designed to give you some ideas to explore with your lawyer.

What are the duties of a trustee of a testamentary trust?

In addition to the same duties of a trustee of a living trust, discussed in the next several questions and answers, the trustee must see to it that the cash or property received from the estate's personal representative is what the trustee is entitled to. Therefore, the trustee should review

the stewardship of the personal representative in administering the estate, since the administration of the estate will affect the amount eventually distributed to the trustee.

What are the general duties of any trustee?

1. Once you accept appointment as trustee, you are under a duty to administer the trust (as long as you are a trustee). However, you have no legal obligation to accept appointment.

2. You have a duty to administer the trust solely in the interest of the beneficiaries. As an obvious example of this rule, assume you are a customer's representative in a stock brokerage firm and the sole trustee. You should not use your brokerage firm to buy or sell securities for the trust with the motive of generating more commissions for the firm and yourself.

3. You have a duty not to delegate to others the administration of the trust or the performance of acts that you ought to perform yourself. As an example of this rule, let's say you are a lawyer in general practice and the sole trustee. If the trust is running a business and gets involved in litigation that you normally handle, you should not refer the lawsuit to another lawyer.

This does not mean that you must personally perform every act that may be necessary or proper. You can permit others to perform acts that you cannot reasonably be required to perform personally.

4. You are under a duty to beneficiaries to keep clear and accurate accounts. These accounts should show what you received and what you spent; they should also show gains and losses. Further, the records should show what amounts are assigned to income and to principal.

5. You have a duty to the beneficiaries to give them complete and accurate information about the administration of the trust whenever they make a reasonable request.

6. You have a duty to administer the trust with the same care and skill as any person of caution would exercise in dealing with his or her own property; if you have special skills, you should use them on behalf of the trust.

For example, if you are a certified public accountant with substantial tax experience, you should analyze the trust's affairs with a view to reducing taxes.

7. You have a duty to take reasonable steps to take and keep control of the trust property.

8. You have a duty to use reasonable care and skill to preserve the trust property, to collect on claims, and to defend actions when appropriate.

9. You have a duty to keep the trust property separate from your own individual property and to see to it that the property is designated as property of the trust.

10. When making bank deposits, you should use care in selecting a bank. A bank deposit is considered a loan to a bank and, therefore, such deposits should be insured.

11. You have a duty to make the trust property productive. For example, you should not leave large sums in a checking account that does not pay interest unless you will be needing the money to pay current bills.

12. When a beneficiary is entitled to receive the income, you have a duty to pay it over at reasonable intervals.

13. When there are two or more beneficiaries, you are obligated to deal with them fairly and impartially. Two illustrations will help to clarify this:

a. Trusts frequently provide that on the death of the one who is entitled to the income for life or for a certain period of time, someone else is entitled to the trust property thereafter. The one who is later entitled to the property is referred to as the *remainderman*. Therefore, the trustee must, in these cases, not only invest the trust property to secure maximum income, but also must protect the remainderman. This entails meeting the needs of those entitled to income and also those eventually entitled to the trust property. This calls for making investments that produce income but also that have some growth potential to enhance the trust property that will eventually be distributed.

You will note that the interests of these beneficiaries are not necessarily identical. The income beneficiary is usually most interested in receiving the highest current income. The remainderman is usually most interested in having the trustee invest in assets that have the potential for the greatest appreciation.

b. When reading those portions of the will dealing with the trust, you and your lawyer must identify who the testator intended to benefit by creating the trust and how this is to be accomplished.

Let us assume that the trust was created to provide the decedent's sister, Mary, with income for her lifetime. Upon her death, the trust was to be divided between your two sons. Perhaps the testator (your husband) provided that part or all of the principal of the trust may be used for his sister's benefit, if needed for her health or support. (Another word for *principal* is *corpus*. Most wills that give the trustee authority to use principal will use the phrase "invade principal.")

So far, the important participants are as follows: There is a testator (your husband) who was the creator, or grantor, of the trust. You (the wife) are the trustee. Mary (your sister-in-law) is a beneficiary. Your children are also beneficiaries, but they will first derive benefit from the trust after Mary's death. Since your children will only be entitled to benefits from the trust after Mary's death, they are known as remaindermen beneficiaries or simply as remaindermen.

Your sister-in-law's interest as a beneficiary is as an income beneficiary. In view of the terms of the trust that require

that she is to receive income, it is your required or mandatory duty as trustee to see that income is actually paid to her.

If Mary is in need of further funds from principal for her health or support, it is within your discretionary power to pay these to her. This would be your second specific duty. As trustee, the more principal you pay to Mary, the less principal will be left for your children. Finally, when Mary dies you have a specific duty to pay over whatever is remaining in the trust to your two sons.

In determining how to deal with the beneficiaries fairly and impartially, it is essential for the trustee to study the terms of the will or trust to determine the intentions of the settlor or testator.

14. If there are several trustees, each trustee must participate in the administration of the trust.

15. When another party (not a trustee) is given certain powers, for example, the power to decide where to invest funds, you are under a duty to follow that party's instructions, unless this would violate the trust terms or violate your fiduciary duty.

What are some specific examples of my duties as a trustee?

1. If a trust is created by will, you should apply to the Internal Revenue Service for a federal identification number as soon as the trust is funded. This is done by filing Form SS-4. The instructions to this form will tell you where to file it.

When the grantor is also the trustee or cotrustee of a living trust and the trust is revocable, use the Social Security number of the grantor. Every other trust requires a federal identification number. This should be applied for as soon as the trust is created.

2. Open a bank checking account in the name of the trust. If the trust is testamentary, the bank will require documents showing the authority of the trustee. In some states, such as New York, the court issues a document under its seal that is referred to as *letters of trusteeship*. In other states where there is no provision for issuing letters of trusteeship, such as Maryland, the bank will accept a letter from an attorney stating that a trust was created under a will and naming the trustee(s).

When the trust is a living trust, the bank will usually request a copy of the trust. If you comply with its request, bear in mind that the provisions for disposition of your property are no longer as secret as you would have liked.

The account should read approximately as follows:

Trust under the Will of (decedent's name). John Doe, Trustee.

This is frequently abbreviated as:

Trust U/W/O (decedent's name). John Doe, Trustee.

or

The John Doe Trust under agreement dated 11/15/93 for the benefit of John Doe. John Doe, Trustee.

This is frequently abbreviated as:

John Doe Trust U/A dtd. 11/15/93 F/B/O John Doe. John Doe, Trustee.

When substantial amounts remain in the account for any lengthy periods of time, you should see to it that the account is, at the very least, interest bearing. Consideration should be given to investing large sums for returns higher than are available from an interest checking account.

All cash receipts and disbursements should be deposited to and withdrawn from this account. This will help you keep track of all receipts and expenditures.

3. Any brokerage accounts should have the same title as the bank accounts. The stockbroker will request documents similar to those requested by banks.

The broker, as well as the bank, may require an affidavit of domicile (for testamentary trusts) in addition to the usual signature cards and federal identification number.

4. If the trust property includes any jewelry, coin or stamp collections, art objects, or household furnishings, see to it that there is adequate fire and theft insurance. You may wish to rent a bank safe-deposit box for storing jewelry or coin or stamp collections.

You will have to consider whether these trust assets must be sold to realize current income. If a sale is necessary, you must then decide when to make the sale, to whom the assets should be sold to realize the greatest return, as well as all the details of the sale.

5. For real property, a deed should be recorded showing the owner to be the trustee. The recorded owner should be shown somewhat as follows:

John Doe, Trustee of a Trust U/W of (decedent's name).

or

John Doe, Trustee of John Doe Trust U/A dtd. 11/15/93 F/B/O John Doe.

The tax collector should be notified of the trustee's address. If the property is improved, the improvements should be adequately insured for fire, theft, and malicious mischief. Improved and unimproved property should have liability insurance coverage.

The trustee usually has authority to make improvements to the property, mortgage it, or lease it. Unless the trust provides otherwise, the property should be made productive. A sale thereof may be required.

6. If the trust is the owner of a going business, you will first have to determine whether the business must be sold or maintained as a going business. To determine this, you should study the trust terms. State law may also have provisions dealing with this matter. If it is to be maintained, you will need the services of a lawyer and accountant. It will then be necessary to determine what steps should be taken, if any, to identify the trust as the owner for purposes of bank relationships, insurance, tax authorities, licensing authorities, utility companies, vendors, suppliers, etc.

Do I, as trustee, have the authority to sell stock of a closely held corporation that the testator bequeathed to me as trustee?

You must look to the trust instrument to see its instructions. The instructions must be followed unless they violate some law or public policy. If the trust instrument does not contain any instructions, then you must look at state law to see what authority you have.

In general, you have broad powers to do whatever is necessary or appropriate to carry out the purposes of the trust. This would include incurring expenses; selling, leasing, and mortgaging property; voting shares of stock; and compromising, arbitrating, abandoning, and pursuing claims.

What investments may I, as trustee, make?

Once again, study the trust instrument to see what it says, if anything. Any instructions that it contains must be followed unless an instruction violates some law or public policy.

In the absence of specific instructions in the trust instrument, in most states the trustee is given a free hand as to what investments may be made. Though the trustee has broad discretion, the trustee does have a duty to invest as a prudent person would. This standard of investment was set forth many years ago in a Massachusetts court decision that most states now follow. The court stated that a trustee must observe how people of prudence, discretion, and intelligence manage their own affairs, not in regard to speculation but in regard to the permanent disposition of their funds, considering the probable income as well as the probable safety of the capital to be invested.

The laws of your state may limit the types of authorized investments or have other requirements. You should consult the laws of your state, preferably with your lawyer, for guidance.

I am the income beneficiary. The trustee has invested all of the trust assets in non-income-producing land that has excellent prospects for future growth. The remaindermen are happy with this investment but I am not. What can I do about this?

The trustee has a duty to deal impartially with the respective beneficiaries, and, therefore, the trustee has a duty to administer the trust to preserve a fair balance among them. In this case, the trustee is apparently sacrificing income while attempting to increase the value of the principal. While the trustee has discretion in administering the trust, this discretion is subject to the supervisory authority of the courts. As income beneficiary, you can file suit asking the court for an order to compel the trustee to invest the trust principal in an appropriate manner so that you will receive income from the property.

Will I, as trustee, be required to file any tax returns during the administration of the trust?

A trust is considered to be a separate taxpayer, and federal law requires the trustee to file an income tax return on Form 1041 when the trust has any taxable income, has gross income of $600 or more, or when any beneficiary of the trust is a nonresident alien. You should also check your state's laws to determine when a state income tax return must be filed for the trust.

I have heard of *sprinkling trusts*. What are they and when are they used?

A sprinkling trust allows the trustee to use his or her discretion to distribute the income of the trust equally or unequally among a certain class of beneficiaries. (Remember, a trustee is the one who holds property for the benefit of another; the one for whose benefit the property is held is called the beneficiary.) This type of trust is usually used in two situations. First, when one or more of your loved ones have a greater need; second, when there may be an income tax saving.

Here is an example of the first situation. You have three children, aged 26, 18, and 12. You have already paid for the education of the oldest child, and there may be greater need for income for the two younger children. Instead of distributing all your property equally among your three children on the death of you and your spouse, you provide that the property shall be held in trust until the youngest child reaches 22. While the property is held in trust, the trustee has discretion to favor one child over another, based on need and your hopes for the educational achievements of each. Then, much like a parent, the trustee could spend more of the income on the two youngest children, since the older child has already received his or her education during your lifetime. The trustee would therefore "sprinkle" more of the income toward the younger children.

Here is an example of the second situation. Your three children are aged 35, 33, and 29. The oldest child is now happily employed as a schoolteacher. He has a wife, who is a homemaker, and three young children aged five, two, and one. Your middle child is an unmarried rock concert promoter earning approximately $160,000 annually, and your youngest child is also unmarried, a gifted physician who has a private practice and is on the faculty of a major medical school. The physician is earning approximately $120,000 per year.

If the income of the trust were equally divided among the three children, income taxes would take away a disproportionate part of the income distributed to the two younger children. And they do not need the extra trust income. By being able to "sprinkle" the income, the trustee could benefit the oldest child at least until his children are older.

The distribution of the trust would be based on the needs of your children without your showing less affection for any of them.

What is meant by an accumulation trust and when should it be used?

When you leave property in trust under your will, you may provide that income shall be accumulated and not paid out until a certain date or event occurs.

For example, your spouse may be in the highest income tax bracket. If income is paid to your spouse following your death, most of the income may very well be reduced by high income taxes imposed on all your spouse's income. You could then provide that all trust income be "accumulated" until your spouse's income falls below a certain amount. Or if it never falls below this level, the accumulated income can then be paid to your children, who, we assume, are in the lowest income tax bracket.

What is a *Totten Trust*?

It is the name given to a revocable bank account trust, named after a famous New York case. If I deposit my funds in an account with a bank and have the account read: "Alex J. Soled in Trust for Ingrid H. Soled," this account is considered a Totten Trust in many states.

The features of a Totten Trust are:

1. The depositor has complete control of the account during lifetime.
2. The depositor has the absolute right to revoke same during lifetime.
3. If the named beneficiary dies before the depositor, the trust is revoked.
4. If the will of the depositor *specifically*

refers to the bank account, the trust can be revoked.

5. On death of the depositor, the account belongs to the named beneficiary, assuming it has not been revoked as noted earlier.

References to Totten Trusts keep appearing in newspaper and magazine articles. What is the importance of this type of trust?

Primarily, it creates certainty in most states as to the legal consequences of this type of trust. That is, on death of the depositor, the account will belong to the surviving named beneficiary.

As pointed out earlier, leaving property at death is not a constitutional or inherent right. It is a right granted by state law. The principal way this is accomplished is by will. Our laws are patterned after an English law commonly known as the *Statute of Wills*. A will usually requires a written document, and its execution with certain formality by the testator and at least two witnesses.

Over the years, other devices have been utilized to accomplish the transfer of property at death. Some of these devices are well recognized in the law, and some are considered violative of the principles of the Statute of Wills and therefore fail.

The well-recognized devices are joint ownership of real estate and securities, life insurance, IRAs, partnership agreements, contracts, living trusts, and pension and profit-sharing plans, among others. Although all of these devices are testamentary substitutes, they are not considered to violate the principles of the Statute of Wills.

However, when bank accounts are utilized as will substitutes, they do create legal problems of establishing ultimate ownership of the property. Without reflecting all arguments or the laws of every state, it can be stated:

1. When a bank account is registered in trust form, there is no violation of the laws relating to wills. Accordingly, there is a strong presumption that the survivor becomes the sole owner *unless* it can be shown that the account was created for convenience purposes. The convenience feature enables the beneficiary to make withdrawals for the benefit of the original depositor. Where the decedent's estate can establish that the trust account was a convenience account, the named surviving beneficiary will not become the owner of the account. Instead, the estate will become the owner. However, in states that accept the Totten Trust concept, the survivor will become the absolute owner of the entire account.

2. When a bank account is registered in joint names with another, the results have varied. The courts variously conclude:

a. The opening of the account is evidence that a gift was then made. Therefore, there was no need to satisfy the law as to wills, and the surviving joint owner becomes the owner of the account.

b. Even when the opening of the account is evidence of a gift, there could be overwhelming evidence to the contrary. In such a case, the law as to wills has not been satisfied, and on death of the depositor, the entire account belongs to the depositor's estate.

c. There is no gift at the time of the opening of the account. Nonetheless, the account belongs to the survivor *unless* it can be established that the account was a convenience account. If the account is proven to be a convenience account, on death of the original depositor, the account belongs to his or her estate.

Further uncertainties arise when the account is registered in the names of A and B (two people) in trust for C (where A is the sole depositor). This chaotic state of affairs exists in many states, and also applies to payable on death (P.O.D.) accounts.

You should not utilize joint accounts, trust accounts, or P.O.D. accounts as will substitutes without consulting your lawyer. If your bank clerk orally professes to assure you of the certainty of the legal effect of joint, trust, or P.O.D. accounts, you should ask for a letter from the bank substantiating any such advice.

What is an insurance trust?

It is a living trust that is almost always irrevocable. The trust is funded with life insurance and is usually created to save death taxes. (For further information, see Death Taxes.)

The trust terms invariably duplicate the usual provisions set forth in a will. That is, it provides who the income ben-

eficiary is, as well as the remaindermen. When the trustee receives the life insurance proceeds following the death of the insured, the trustee will then invest the proceeds for the benefit of the beneficiaries.

My lawyer has recommended a marital-deduction trust for my will. What does that mean?

If your taxable estate exceeds a certain amount, it will be subject to federal estate taxes. The taxes can be substantial. However, when property is left to one's spouse, federal estate tax law allows the estate a deduction for the amount of the property that passes to the spouse if the bequest meets certain requirements. This deduction, called a *marital deduction,* is obviously desirable because it reduces or completely eliminates federal estate taxes.

In order to get the benefit of the marital deduction, you need not leave the property to your spouse outright. The property may be left in a trust that meets certain technical requirements of the federal estate tax law. There are two types of trusts that meet these technical requirements. One of these trusts is commonly referred to as a *marital deduction trust,* and the other type is a *QTIP* trust. (For a more detailed discussion, see Death Taxes.)

You should also be aware of the impact of the marital deduction on transfers made by using a living trust. If you transfer property to your spouse during your lifetime, you have made a taxable gift. However, any such transfer usually qualifies for a deduction equal to the value of the gift. This deduction is known as the *gift tax marital deduction*. If your spouse is not a U.S. citizen, the deduction is limited. To qualify for a marital deduction for gifts to a spouse who is a U.S. citizen, the same technical rules apply as for transfers made on death. (See Death Taxes.)

When a living trust is created and property is transferred thereto, in most cases there is no gift at that time. Why? Because living trusts are usually revocable and a gift is only made when the transfer is complete. Assume, however, that the trust is irrevocable when created. If you retain the income for life, there is no gift of your interest, since by definition, one cannot make a gift to oneself. However, there would be a gift of the remainder interest, that is, the value of the property after deducting your retained or income interest. If your spouse is the one who has the initial income interest in an irrevocable trust, then a gift will have been made, but the interest will usually qualify for the gift tax marital deduction. This deduction is subject to the technical rules dealing with the marital deduction in general.

Other Types of Trusts

Please explain the meaning of (1) *A/B trusts*, **(2)** *bypass trusts*, **(3)** *credit shelter trusts*, **(4)** *residuary trusts*, **(5)** *family trusts*, **(6)** *support trusts*, **(7)** *discretionary trusts*, **(8)** *pour-over trusts*, **and (9)** *charitable trusts*.

The explanation of each is as follows:

(1), (2), and (3). Each individual may transfer to anyone up to $600,000 free of gift or death taxes. When drafting wills, the most desirable tax planning is to postpone for as long as possible any transfer tax on this amount. This postponement is accomplished by leaving property in trust. When a decedent leaves the surviving spouse the entire estate in trust, tax planning suggests that the estate be divided into two parts. This type of property disposition is known as A/B trusts.

When the decedent leaves only part of his or her estate in trust, if that part consists of the $600,000 or less that is intended to postpone a transfer tax for as long as possible, such a trust is commonly referred to as a bypass or credit shelter trust.

The term *bypass* is used because the trust postpones or defers the transfer tax for as long as possible by bypassing its taxation in the legatee's estate. The term *credit shelter* is used because the tax credit that is available to every individual equals the tax generated by a transfer of $600,000. Thus, if a transfer of up to $600,000 is left in trust by a decedent, the maximum tax on $600,000 is $192,800. The credit against this tax is also $192,800. The credit therefore also shelters the trust assets from taxation in the legatee's estate—hence, the name credit shelter.

(4). A residuary trust takes its name from the dictionary meaning of *residue*. That is, the remainder or something that remains after a portion is first subtracted. Accordingly, if I leave bequests of $200,000 to my brother and charity and leave the balance in trust for my wife, the balance is commonly referred to as a residuary trust. Sometimes it is referred to as the rest, residue, and remainder of my estate (which is left in trust).

(5). A family trust describes who the beneficiaries are. If my entire estate is left in trust for the benefit of my wife, children, and grandchildren, this type of trust would commonly be referred to as a family trust. You can also create a family trust during your lifetime by creating a living trust.

(6). When I create a trust during my lifetime or by will and instruct the trustee to use whatever proceeds may be necessary or advisable for the support of my mother, or other beneficiary, this trust would be called a support trust.

(7). When I create a trust during my lifetime or by will and instruct the trustee to use whatever proceeds may be advisable or desirable for any of my blood relatives at my trustee's sole and absolute discretion, this trust would be called a discretionary trust.

(8). When I provide by will that all my assets shall be poured over to, that is, added to and made part of, a living trust created by me on January 10, 1980, the 1980 trust is called a pour over trust when I die and my will is probated.

(9). When I create a trust during my lifetime or by will and instruct the trustee to use the proceeds for charitable purposes, this trust would be called a charitable trust.

If I provide in my will that my wife shall receive an annuity for life and upon her death the remainder of the trust property shall be paid over to a specified charity, this is known as a *charitable remainder trust*. If this trust meets certain technical requirements of the Internal Revenue Code, then my estate would receive a charitable deduction for the portion of my estate that will pass to the charity.

When does a trust end?

The terms of the trust provide for this. The trust may end on a certain date or it may end on the happening or nonhappening of a certain event.

For example, the trust instrument may provide that the trust ends (*terminates* is the word usually used) on October 1, 1996, or it may provide that it terminates on the death or remarriage of the income beneficiary. It may also provide that if my son fails to receive his medical degree by July 1, 2000, the trust shall then terminate.

When the trust is a living (inter vivos) trust, the settlor may have reserved the right to terminate the trust at any time merely by notifying the trustee of this desire. In such a case, the trust would terminate when the settlor so notifies the trustee.

In many states, if the settlor and all the beneficiaries, both present and future, desire to terminate a living trust, that desire will be sufficient to terminate the trust.

When the trust terminates, what am I to do with the trust property?

Turn the trust property over to the person or persons entitled to it. You should account for all assets and receive a receipt and release from the person or persons entitled to the property.

Please discuss what I should take into account in appointing a trustee.

In general, your trustee should have integrity, intelligence, experience, an interest in serving, good health to enable him or her to carry out the duties, and especially where a disabled child is involved, compassion.

A trustee is entitled to a commission for serving. (See Appendix F for the amount of the commission allowed in each state.)

A bank serving as trustee has the advantages of permanence and safety. Unfortunately, they are all too often inflexible when any discretionary payments are called for and in their investment philosophies. There is usually a good deal of turnover in the personnel of trust departments, and most recently, there are even more turnovers in trust personnel caused by mergers among banks. Dealing with different personnel each time can diminish the comfort level of beneficiaries and create confusion.

On the other hand, where an individual is appointed trustee, the individual is frequently ill-equipped to manage trust property. There is also the possibility of embezzlement, disinterest, neglect, poor record keeping, and the necessity to substitute trustees when the trustee dies.

For a living trust, you can be the sole trustee. As a successor trustee you can appoint your wife and as successors to her one or more of your children. As suc-

cessors to them, or as successor trustees under your will, consideration should be given to appointing a bank to serve as cotrustee with an individual. One or more successors to the individual should also be named.

Give the individual the right to replace the bank with another bank as cotrustee. When the trust terms give the trustees discretion to favor one beneficiary over another, consider giving this authority to the individual trustee.

By having this arrangement, you would have the benefit of the bank's permanence, investment experience, and record keeping. You would also have the peace of mind that your assets are not lost through theft or embezzlement, yet there would be the personal touch offered by the individual. If the bank became so difficult to deal with, or nonresponsive, then the individual could seek the services of another bank as cotrustee.

What happens if there is no trustee serving as such? Does the trust terminate?

No. The court will appoint a successor trustee. The problem with having an individual as sole trustee is that the trustee could die before the trust terminates. For this reason, name one or more individual successor trustees. When a bank is a trustee or cotrustee, a vacancy by reason of death is not possible. (If the bank fails, the successor bank takes over, and if there is no successor, the court [upon petition] will appoint a successor trustee.)

DEATH TAXES

Estate

and

Inheritance

(Including Gift Taxes)

General Information

What are *death taxes*?

Death taxes are those taxes imposed on the property that is transferred to another upon the death of an individual. The federal estate tax and state inheritance and estate taxes are referred to as death taxes. There are three basic death taxes, one federal and two state. In addition, there is a federal gift tax on the transfer of property by gift during lifetime. (Some states also impose a gift tax.)

1. The most important death tax is the federal estate tax. This tax is imposed on the *transfer* of property by reason of the death of a decedent who was a citizen or a resident of the United States at the time of his or her death. The tax is imposed on the total value of (a) property owned by the decedent at the time of death, (b) "other property" that the decedent either owned at one time or over which the decedent retained or had certain rights, and (c) taxable gifts made *after* December

31, 1976. (The technical name given to such gifts is *adjusted taxable gifts*.)

2. An inheritance tax is another form of death tax. Many states impose this tax. The inheritance tax is imposed upon the privilege of *receiving* property from a decedent at death. An inheritance tax is not imposed by federal law.

The right to impose an inheritance tax and the rate of tax is determined by the state where the decedent was domiciled (the place of principal residence) and not the state where the beneficiary resides.

There is a difference between an estate tax and an inheritance tax. The estate tax is imposed on the privilege of transferring property at death, whereas the inheritance tax is imposed on the privilege of *receiving* property. For example, I die in 1994 with a taxable estate of $650,000. The federal estate tax, after the unified credit, is $18,500 and is imposed on the privilege of transferring the $650,000 (which will be reduced by the $18,500 tax). Since I then lived in Maryland, if I leave $50,000 of that $650,000 to my cousin, Maryland would impose an inheritance tax on my cousin's privilege of receiving the $50,000 at the rate of 10 percent, or $5,000.

If at the time of my death, my cousin had his principal residence in Nevada (where there is no inheritance tax) or New Hampshire (where the inheritance tax is 18 percent), the tax would still be $5,000. This is so because the imposition of this tax and the rate is determined by Maryland (the state where I was domiciled at the time of my death) and not the state where my cousin has his or her principal residence.

3. Most states also impose an estate tax on the taxable estates of their residents or on real and tangible personal property located within their borders, whether the real or tangible personal property is owned by a resident or a nonresident.

The states that impose the estate tax may do so in addition to the state inheritance tax.

Please give me an overview of how the federal estate tax is calculated.

Individually owned property *plus* other types of property *equal* **gross estate**

minus

expenses, debts, and income taxes

losses from fires, casualties, thefts, storms, shipwrecks

bequests to or for charities and public uses

bequests to, or for the benefit of, the surviving spouse (the marital deduction)

equal
taxable estate

Federal estate tax (using rate schedule) applied to taxable estate *plus* adjusted taxable gifts *minus* gift taxes paid for gifts made after 1976 (except for gifts made within three years of death) *equal* **tentative estate tax**

minus

unified credit

credit for state death taxes paid

other credits

equals
net estate tax

Note: The estate may also be liable for two additional taxes. The first one is a 55 percent generation-skipping transfer tax. (See pages 199–201.) The second tax, at the rate of 15 percent, is imposed on excess accumulations from qualified plans. (See pages 201–202.) Thus, the total of (1) the net estate tax, (2) the generation-skipping transfer tax, and (3) the tax on excess accumulations from qualified plans constitutes the total transfer taxes due the federal government.

What is the unified credit?

The unified credit represents a mandatory dollar-for-dollar offset, or credit, against the estate tax. Between 1981 and 1987 it increased each year from $47,000 (in 1981) as follows:

Year of death or transfer	Amount of credit
1982	$ 62,800
1983	79,300
1984	96,300
1985	121,800
1986	155,800
1987 and thereafter	192,800

As of 1994, the credit is $192,800.

What is the amount of the federal estate tax?

The amount is determined by the Unified Rate Schedule set forth in Appendix A.

In general, if your taxable estate plus adjusted taxable gifts are not more than the amounts that are shown below, there will be no federal estate tax. (However, as noted earlier, there may be a 55 percent generation-skipping transfer tax and a 15 percent tax on excess accumulations from qualified plans.)

The amounts are

Year of death	Amount transferred without any tax
1982	$225,000
1983	275,000
1984	325,000
1985	400,000
1986	500,000
1987 and thereafter	600,000

There will not be a federal estate tax on the amount shown, for the years shown, because the credit eliminates the tax. For example, in 1993 the tax on $600,000 is exactly $192,800. Since the amount of the credit in 1993 is $192,800, the tax will be completely eliminated if death occurs in 1993.

What are the amounts of the estate and inheritance taxes for each state?

This information is in Appendix C. In general, the amounts vary from 1 percent to a spouse (in Maryland) to as high as 32 percent for property passing to a nonrelative (in Montana).

Who or what determines what my federal taxable estate consists of?

The Internal Revenue Code of 1986 does so. This is a compilation of all currently applicable tax laws enacted by Congress. The Internal Revenue Service, which is a division of the U.S. Treasury Department, is charged with the duty of applying, interpreting, and enforcing the tax laws. State laws usually follow federal law as to what assets are includable in a taxable estate and what their values are.

What does my taxable estate consist of?

Under federal law, it is your gross estate minus certain deductions.

What does my gross estate consist of?

Your gross estate for tax purposes includes property that you own in your own name at the time of your death, and "other property."

Property individually owned by you at the time of your death is the kind of property that you transfer by will at the time of your death. This property is known as part of your probate estate. Individually owned property could include cash on hand; an automobile; stocks and bonds; real estate; jewelry; a stamp, coin, or rifle collection; and debts owed to you. (This is not a complete list, but is given by way of illustration.)

For example, assume your father left some property in trust for your mother for her lifetime and provided that on her death the property would belong to you as outright owner, whether or not you were then living. If you die at age 55 before your mother, who is then age 75, is any part of the property part of your gross estate? Yes.

Why? Because while you are not there to receive the property when your mother dies, your estate will eventually receive it. Even though you are then dead, your interest in the property is fixed. Your will can dispose of it. Even though the one you leave it to may have to wait some years (for your mother's death) before enjoying the property, the interest is yours and is a property right just like any individually owned property. (Technically, when someone has fixed property interests, these rights are referred to as being "vested.")

The value of your interest in the property left in trust by your father is not 100 percent of the value of the entire property. After all, your mother has a right to use and enjoy the property during her lifetime before you or your estate receive it. Apart from valuing your interest in the property at something less than 100 percent of the whole, the law is clear that since you have a vested interest in the property, this interest is part of your gross estate too.

(Where someone has a vested, or fixed, property interest that will come into possession after someone else's interest lapses, this interest is known as a "remainder" interest.)

Instead of your father giving your mother an interest in the property before you, let us reverse the situation. Your father died in 1970 and by his will left an office building in a trust, from which you receive the income for your lifetime. His will then provides that if your mother is still alive when you die, she will receive the income for *her* lifetime. On the death of the last one of you and your mother, the building will be paid over to your father's then-surviving issue, *per stirpes*. (*Issue* means descendants—children, grandchildren, great-grandchildren, and so on; per stirpes means "by the root," and a parent takes the property to the exclusion of the succeeding generation; the phrase *his then-surviving issue* refers to the persons living at some particular point of time.)

By stating that the property will eventually belong to your father's then-surviving issue, the property will go to your children (and perhaps grandchildren), if any, and to your brothers and sisters, if any. In this case, at the moment of your death, you have no property interest in the office building. Your will cannot direct who shall inherit it after your death. The income interest you had in the office building ceased at your death. Therefore, no part of the building's value would be included in your gross estate.

If, at the time of your death, a tenant owes $4,000 for past due rent and this amount is paid over to the trustees, who then pay it to your estate after your death, the $4,000 will be included in your gross estate.

What about your Social Security benefits payable to your surviving spouse? Are they part of your gross estate? No, they are not.

You have loaned your daughter $10,000 to enable her to buy a house. She gave you a note to evidence the loan. When you die, you provide in your will that the debt is forgiven and canceled. Is the $10,000 included in your gross estate? Of course. The debt is a property right owned by you at the time of your death, even though you canceled it. ("Other property" is explained beginning on pages 143–144.)

Would rights to income be considered individually owned?

They could. For example, assume you are an insurance agent and are entitled to commissions on renewals of insurance you originally sold. Your rights to these renewals are considered property. Had you lived when they were paid, they would have been income. These renewals are rights to income. The value of these commissions would be part of your gross estate. While the value of the commissions is certainly difficult to estimate, the commissions must nevertheless be included in your gross estate.

If you were in an individually owned business or were a professional and had accounts receivable, these would also be included in your gross estate. Additionally, you would have to include in your estate any accrued rents, interest on savings, or debts owed you.

Are taxable gifts made after December 31, 1976, part of the gross estate?

Technically the answer is no. However, even though they are not part of the gross estate (and therefore cannot be part of the taxable estate), the amount of such gifts is subject to the federal estate tax. The reason for this is that federal law unifies taxable gifts (made after December 31, 1976, and called adjusted taxable gifts) with the taxable estate. The federal estate tax is imposed on the total of these two amounts. This is known as the unified system of taxation.

How does the unified system work?

The unified system imposes the estate tax on the total of the taxable lifetime transfers made after December 31, 1976, and taxable death-time transfers. Thus, the rate of tax, just as for income taxes, becomes progressively higher for the value of property or cash transferred whether transferred by gift or by death.

A simple example will clarify this. Let

us say that you are a widow, you make a cash gift of $235,000 to your son in 1982, and you die in 1989 possessing another $475,000. You will not have to pay any gift tax on the 1982 gift of $235,000 because the law allows a transfer of this amount before a tax is imposed. However, when you die, the tax imposed will be calculated *as though you died owning $700,000*—the $235,000 you gave away (less $10,000, which will be explained in the next question and answer) and the $475,000 you own on the date of your death. The rate of tax will be based on $700,000 and not on the total of two

lower rates imposed on the $225,000 gift and the $475,000.

Based on these facts, the following is a comparison of what happens when gifts are made during lifetime and when gifts are not made in advance but are owned until the date of death. Because the tax rates changed January 1, 1977, the comparison is shown under the old law (which applied when death occurred before 1977) as well as under the new law (which applies when death occurs after 1981). In both cases, we will assume that you never made any gifts before those shown.

OLD LAW
(before 1977)

	GIFTS MADE DURING LIFETIME		NO GIFTS MADE DURING LIFETIME	
Gift made in 1972	$235,000		-0-	
Less: Annual exclusion	(3,000)		-0-	
Lifetime exemption	(30,000)		-0-	
Amount subject to gift tax	$202,000		-0-	
Gift tax		$ 38,475		-0-
Taxable estate (before the $60,000 exemption)	475,000		$710,000	
Estate tax		118,500		$198,200
Total taxes		$156,975		$198,200

NEW LAW
(after 1978)

	GIFTS MADE DURING LIFETIME	NO GIFTS MADE DURING LIFETIME
Gift made in 1982	$235,000	-0-
Less: Annual exclusion	(10,000)	-0-
Amount subject to gift tax	$225,000	-0-
Gift tax	-0-	-0-
Taxable estate (1989)	$475,000	$710,000
Plus: Taxable gifts	225,000	-0-
Amount subject to estate tax	$700,000	$710,000
Estate tax (less the unified credit of $192,800)	$37,000	$40,700
Total taxes	$37,000	$40,700

Under the old law (before 1977), by making the gift the tax savings would have been $41,225, whereas under the new law, there is only a saving of $3,700. Under the old law, the taxpayer not only received the benefit of the annual gift exclusion (of $3,000) and the lifetime exemption (of $30,000), but also the benefit of having the gift tax and the estate tax split into two lower brackets.

Under the new law, the major change is the exclusion from taxation of the first $10,000 of the gift. The next question and answer will explain why this $10,000 is not taxed.

You previously mentioned exceptions in regard to gifts. What are they? Also, please explain the phrase *taxable gifts*.

Taxable gifts means the total gifts made in any year less the annual $10,000 exclusion and deductions for property gifted to charity and a spouse. Property that is transferred to one's spouse qualifies for a gift tax marital deduction. The rules for the marital deduction are similar to those for estates. (See pages 171–72.) In general, all property, without limit, that one transfers to his or her spouse receives a marital deduction that reduces the amount of gifts considered taxable gifts.

The most important exception states that when you make a gift, the first $10,000 of such a gift made to each person in any calendar year is excluded from the amount of taxable gifts. Stated differently, a taxable gift is that part of a gift greater than $10,000 made in any calendar year to any person. (The person who receives these gifts is called the *donee*. The one who makes the gifts is called the *donor*.)

For example, I make a gift to you of $8,500 this year, and this is my only gift to you. Since the first $10,000 of gifts made this year is excluded for federal purposes, I have not made any taxable gift to you. If the gift is $10,500, then I have made a taxable gift of $500 ($10,500 less the $10,000 exclusion).

You can make gifts of $10,000 to each of your 10 grandchildren every year, and the total of $100,000 given each year will *not* be taxable. There will be zero taxable gifts. Also, the amount given away will not be subject to estate tax. (Why won't this amount be subject to an estate tax? Because the estate tax is levied on the total of the taxable estate *and taxable gifts*.

Here the *taxable gifts* are zero because of the $10,000 exclusion. In the previous question and answer, you will note that the taxable gift to your son was reduced by $10,000.)

Another example: You make gifts of $12,000 to each of your 10 grandchildren in 1993. The first $10,000 of each gift will be excluded and only the balance of $2,000 to each grandchild will be considered taxable gifts. This totals $20,000. Therefore, you gave away a total of $120,000, and because of the annual exclusion of $10,000 for each grandchild, you will be considered to have made taxable gifts of only $20,000. In connection with this exception:

1. The $10,000 per year exclusion applies to anyone as the donee, except where the donee is a noncitizen spouse. The donee does not have to be related to the giver of the gift (the donor) but can be.

You can make $10,000 gifts each and every year of your life to each of your five closest friends without any part of the gifts being considered taxable. These amounts will not be subject to federal gift tax nor will they increase your federal estate tax.

Clearly then, if you have enough money and income, you can make such gifts to each of your children, grandchildren, friends, etc., without any gift or estate tax whatsoever.

2. In order to exclude the first $10,000 of gifts made each year to each donee, the gift may not be one that is a *future interest*. An example of a future interest would be when I make a cash gift to you but instead of turning it over to you now, I give it to your banker with the condition that no part of the money may be spent for one year. Then at the end of a year, the cash would be turned over to you. This gift is a completed one, but in the eyes of the tax law, it is a gift of a future interest because its use, possession, or enjoyment will begin at some future time.

A second exception can arise if you are married when you make a gift. If your spouse agrees to split the gift with you, then one-half of the amount of the gift will be considered made by you and one-half by your spouse.

The practical effect of this exception is that it reduces or can eliminate the total tax. As an example, assume you gave $20,000 to each of your three children in 1988 and only you filed a gift tax return. Were you to die in 1992, $30,000 would be added to your taxable estate. Therefore, the federal estate tax would be figured on your total taxable estate plus the $30,000. The $30,000 is arrived at as follows:

A gift of $20,000 to each of three children	$60,000
Three $10,000 exclusions	(30,000)
Taxable gifts	$30,000

On the other hand, if the split-gift treatment were elected, the result would be as follows:

GIFTS CONSIDERED MADE BY YOU		GIFTS CONSIDERED MADE BY YOUR SPOUSE	
Gift of $10,000 to each of 3 children	$30,000	Gift of $10,000 to each of 3 children	$30,000
Three $10,000 exclusions	(30,000)	Three $10,000 exclusions	(30,000)
Taxable gifts	$ -0-		$ -0-

In connection with this second exception, the following should be noted:

1. To take advantage of the split-gift treatment, both you and your spouse must be citizens or residents of the United States at the time of the gift. Also, your spouse must consent to the split gift, in writing, on a timely filed gift tax return (either yours or your spouse's).

2. In order to have benefited from a tax reduction or elimination for split gifts before the 1981 tax law change, you would have had to live more than three years from the date you made the gift. Now it is immaterial how much longer you live after the date of the gift.

3. You may take advantage of the split-gift treatment (but are not required to do so) even if all of the funds or property came from the individually owned assets of one of you.

A third exception states that the value of all taxable gifts made by you (after December 31, 1976) is the value on the dates when you made the gifts. For example, you made a gift of 50 acres of land to your son in 1982 when the value was $50,000. For gift tax purposes, the value is $50,000 (less the $10,000 annual exclusion). If the value of this land is $350,000 when you die, only the gift tax value (the $50,000 gift minus the $10,000 annual exclusion) will be used in figuring the estate tax. Therefore, for estate tax purposes, your estate will escape being taxed on the $300,000 increase in value of the land (plus the $10,000 that represents the annual exclusion).

A fourth exception provides that when a gift tax is paid for gifts made more than three years before death, the amount of the tax is not included in either your taxable estate or as part of your taxable gifts. You will therefore reduce the amount of estate taxes eventually paid by your estate to the extent of the gift tax paid.

Please explain what a gift is (for gift tax purposes).

A gift is any transfer of property that exceeds the value in money or money's worth of the consideration given by the recipient of the gift to the donor of the gift. Here are some examples:

1. I give my son $20,000 toward a down payment on a house based on his promise that he will stop smoking for one full year. He does so. What my son gave me in return was pleasure and satisfaction. While pleasure and satisfaction are valuable to me, they do not have money value. Therefore, the gift tax law states that I have made a gift to my son. (The amount of the taxable gift is $10,000—the first $10,000 is excluded.)

2. I give my fiancée an engagement present of a $15,000 ring. In return, I received her promise to marry me and she does. Have I made a gift to her? Of course—what I received in return was not consideration in money or money's worth. For gift tax purposes, I have made a taxable gift of $5,000 ($15,000 minus the $10,000 exclusion).

3. I perform legal services worth $15,000 for my brother and receive nothing in exchange. There is no gift subject to the gift tax law, because I did not transfer property to him. The giving of services is not considered the transfer of property.

You will note that the word *gift* is used. But if you sell something to someone, the general rule does not apply. Why? Because you have not made a gift. Instead, you have made a sale and substituted one type of property for another that is, in theory, of equal value.

For example, I sell you my house for $75,000. You pay me this sum in cash. If I die still owning the $75,000, my estate will include the $75,000 cash. If I own the house on my death, my estate will still include $75,000, only it would be represented by a house. From the point of view of estate taxation, it does not matter what the item is; all items are "translated" into U.S. dollar values.

Sometimes a transfer is both a gift and a sale. For example, if you sell your business to your son at any time after 1976 for $50,000, when it is really worth $100,000, what have you done? You have partly made a $50,000 gift and partly made a $50,000 sale. The $50,000 sale price is included in your gross estate because you received the $50,000 purchase price and presumably own it on your death. The balance of the $100,000, the $50,000 gift (less the annual exclusion of $10,000), is also included in your estate for tax purposes because of the rule that gifts made after 1976 to the extent they exceed the annual exclusion ($3,000 for years 1977 to 1981 and $10,000 thereafter) are part of your adjusted taxable gifts.

What are the recent principal changes in the law affecting taxation of gifts?

If you pay *any* amount as tuition for, or for medical care of, *any* individual, such amount is not considered a taxable gift. Such payments must be made *directly* to the educational institution or health care provider and not to the individual who will, in turn, make the required payments. Payments for books or room and board are not considered tuition.

Whereas there is an unlimited gift tax marital deduction for gifts to a spouse, this rule does not apply for gifts made after July 13, 1988, to a noncitizen spouse. If the (donee) spouse is not a U.S. citizen, the marital deduction is limited to $100,000 per year. For example, Mary makes a gift in 1993 to her spouse, Pierre. Pierre is a citizen of France. The gift consists of $500,000 cash. The taxable gift is $400,000 ($500,000 minus the marital deduction of $100,000). If Pierre were a U.S. citizen, the taxable gift would be zero ($500,000 minus the marital deduction of $500,000).

The annual gift tax marital deduction of $100,000 to a noncitizen spouse is *not* in addition to the annual $10,000 gift exclusion but is in place of it.

Note: Since several states now impose a gift tax too, the law of the state where the donor is domiciled should be considered as well.

Though it is now clear that the gross estate includes property individually owned on date of death, please explain what is meant by *other property* that is also to be included in the gross estate.

There are eight categories of such property:

1. Lifetime transfers where an interest is retained for life. (See pages 145 and 150–52.)

2. Lifetime transfers where the beneficiary can receive an interest only if he or she survives you and you retain certain rights to get the property back. (See pages 145–46 and 152–53.)

3. Lifetime transfers where you have the power at the time of your death to alter, amend, revoke, or terminate the enjoyment of the property transferred. (See pages 146–47 and 153–54.)

4. Annuities (under certain circumstances). (See page 155.)

5. Joint interests (under certain circumstances). (See pages 155–57.)

6. Property over which you have a general power of appointment at the time of death. (See pages 157–59.)

7. Life insurance (under certain circumstances). (See pages 159–68.)

8. Under very limited circumstances, certain property transferred within three years of death. (See pages 168–70.)

The first three categories are known as property that you have transferred, but to which there are "strings" attached. The following discussion of the first three categories is technical and detailed, and is divided into two parts, called Part A and Part B. Part A will give a broad overview, and Part B will explain the subject in greater detail with more illustrations.

Part A—Overview

1. Lifetime transfers where an interest is retained for life.

If you wish to make a gift of your house to your son, all that is necessary for you to do is sign a deed and record the deed with the clerk of the court having supervision over land records. The ownership interest transferred by a deed is known as the *fee simple* interest.

Let us suppose that you desire to leave your house to your son, but as long as you live you wish to live in the house. You then prepare a deed giving the house to your son on your death, but reserving the right for you to live in it until your death. This is known as *reserving a life estate*.

You will note that you gave away all of the property except for the value of what you kept. You will also note that the life interest you kept ends on the date of your death. Despite this, is the value of the entire property included in your gross estate? Yes. This is so because the law says that when you give something away but keep the right to the income or the right to the use and enjoyment of the property, you have kept a "string" on the property. Therefore, all of the property is included in your estate, even the part that you gave away.

Assume you create a trust and transfer all of your property to the trustee. You may make no changes in the terms of the trust, and it is irrevocable. On your death, all of the property will be transferred to your son. During your lifetime, you will receive all of the income from the trust. Is any part of the trust included in your gross estate? Yes, all of it. Since you retained the right to the income from the property during your lifetime, all of the property is included in your estate, even though you gave away the remainder interest (the part that remained after your death).

2. Lifetime transfers where the beneficiary can receive an interest only if he or she survives you and, in addition, you retain certain rights to get the property back.

Let us say you create an irrevocable trust and transfer to the trustee property worth $50,000. You provide that your mother shall receive the income for her lifetime, and on her death the trust property will be paid to your daughter if then living, and, if she is not then living, it will be paid to you if living.

No part of this property will be included in your gross estate because the income to be paid to your mother is not dependent on surviving you. That is, your mother is entitled to the income whether or not you are then living. Also, your daughter's interest is not dependent on surviving you. But if you provide that the trust income shall be paid to your mother for life if she survives you, then you will notice that here she *has* to survive you to enjoy the income. If the value of what you retained (the "string") is more than 5 percent of the value of the property, the law requires that the value of all of such property shall be included in your gross estate.

3. Lifetime transfers where you have the power at the time of your death to alter, amend, revoke, or terminate the enjoyment of the property transferred.

When a gift is made directly to a minor, the minor has no legal capacity to sell the property. The Uniform Transfers to Minors Act is a law that was passed as a means of permitting someone else, the custodian, to legally act for the minor. (This law is a revision of the law previously known as the Uniform Gifts to Minors Act.)

When you make a gift under this act, you transfer the property to an adult, usually the parent, who acts as custodian of the property for the minor. The cus-

todian can pay out the income or accumulate it, sell the property, exchange it for other property, and, in general, act as the owner of the property. The only limitation is that everything must be for the benefit of the minor.

When you make a gift under the act, the income from the property is not taxed to you even though you are the custodian. This is because the owner of the property is the minor.

However, if you are the custodian of property at the time of your death *and* you made a gift of the property you are holding as custodian, even though you are no longer the owner of the property, the property will be included in your gross estate. Why? Because the law says that although you originally made the transfer, as custodian you have the authority to affect the time when the income is paid out. This authority amounts to a power to alter the enjoyment of the property. When you have this power (a "string"), the law says the property is includable in your estate.

It does not matter that you may have first made your wife the custodian when you made the gifts. If she resigns as custodian, or dies, and you are the custodian at the time you die, all the property over which you are custodian and that you had transferred would be included in your gross estate.

In this connection, consider the following circumstances. You have five children, each one a year apart in age. The oldest is now 17. From the date each child was born and until 1982, you made yearly gifts of $3,000 worth of stock to yourself as custodian for each child.

When you die, the value of the property owned by *each* child, with yourself as custodian, ranges from $60,000 to $120,000.

If you die when you are custodian, close to $500,000 (the total value of all these custodial accounts) will be included as part of your gross estate. If someone else is the custodian, no part of these accounts will be included in your gross estate.

When you made a $3,000 gift to a donee in any year before 1982, no part of it was includable in your gross estate even if you died within three years of the date of the gift. But if at the time of your death you were the custodian of property that you gifted, the old three-year rule and the old $3,000-per-year-per-donee exclusion (now $10,000 per year per-donee) are both immaterial. The only material fact is that at the time of your death, you had the power to alter the enjoyment of property (the prohibited "string") that you had transferred. Under this rule, the amount that is included in your gross estate is the value of *all* the property of which you are custodian.

Part B—Details

What follows in this section is a more detailed analysis of the law dealing with property you have transferred and over which you have "strings" attached (the first three categories). The law states that when you transfer property during lifetime as a gift and retain *or* have certain rights at the time of your death, all or part of the property will be included in your gross estate.

Most transfers of this type require the creation or use of trusts. You will recall that a trust created under a will is called a *testamentary trust*. A trust that is created during lifetime is called a *living trust* or an *inter vivos* trust. Living trusts are either revocable or irrevocable. However, a trust that is created by will takes effect only some time after death. Therefore, such a trust is always irrevocable by the testator after the death of the creator of the trust (in this case, the testator).

If a trust is revocable, the one who creates the trust (who is usually called either the *settlor* or the *grantor*) may revoke the trust. Usually when a trust is created as a revocable trust, all that is necessary for the settlor to revoke the trust is to

send a written notice to the trustee saying so. For example, you have just retired from business and have decided to travel around the world. If you own stocks, someone should be able to collect the dividends, exercise stock options, sell the stock, and vote the stock in your absence. You create a trust with perhaps either a child, your attorney, or a bank as trustee. You transfer all the stock to the trustee, who collects the income and mails it to you periodically and watches the corporations' status. When you return from your trip, you might wish to revoke the trust and receive back all of the stock. Or you might like the arrangement so much that you decide to do nothing about the stock in the trust and let it continue. A revocable trust does not have any income or estate tax advantages.

An irrevocable trust is one that the settlor (the one who creates the trust) may not revoke. The settlor has given away property either absolutely or for the period of time specified in the trust instrument. An irrevocable trust frequently does have tax advantages, both in terms of income and estate tax.

Tax-Saving Suggestion

Instead of having the income from some of your savings taxed at your higher bracket, you can arrange your affairs so that some of the income will be taxed at your daughter's lower bracket. This can be accomplished without the expense of creating an irrevocable trust, or making taxable gifts.

How is this done? Assuming your daughter is over 14 years of age, you may make certain loans to her, and the income from the loaned property will be taxed to her and not to you. (If she is under 14 years of age, the income will be taxed at the parents' highest tax rate for that year.)

If the loan is interest-free and $10,000 or less, and if the recipient does not use the funds to purchase or maintain any income-producing assets, there is no income or gift tax disadvantage to the parent making the loan. The advantage is the obvious one of shifting the income tax on the income and having it taxed to the child at the child's lower income tax rate.

If the loan is interest-free and $100,000 or less and the funds are used to help a child buy a house or a business (and the child has no net investment income), then, as a practical matter, there is no income or gift tax disadvantage to the parent making the loan.

IRREVOCABLE TRUSTS

When you create an irrevocable trust, unless there are "strings" attached to the trust, no part of the trust will be included in your gross estate.

Before we review the "strings," you might ask about the advantages of an irrevocable trust. The principal ones are:

1. The property in the trust is no longer yours and therefore, on your death, would be transferred to your loved ones rapidly without the delays and administrative costs of probate.

2. If the property that is placed in trust is located in several states, then on your death the property can be transferred to your loved ones by the trustee without the necessity of going through some form of probate proceeding in each state. Accomplishing the transfer by using a trust can save substantial sums in comparison to the state-by-state probate method.

3. From the estate tax point of view, there would be savings because:

a. if the property increases in value after you transfer it to the trust, the increase in value will not be subject to any estate tax;

b. any tax you pay when you transfer the property to the trust will reduce the amount of your gross estate that will be subject to estate tax (assuming you die more than three years after the date of the gift); and

c. the amount of the taxable gift made to the trust will be reduced by the $10,000 annual exclusion for each donee and can be greater if the split-gift treatment is elected. (We are assuming that the gift is not one of a future interest.) Therefore, the $10,000 that is excluded from taxable gifts will not be subject to either a gift or an estate tax.

4. From the income tax point of view, there is usually a savings. When property is transferred, it is usually for the benefit of a member of the family whose income tax bracket is lower than yours. The difference between the tax brackets represents the savings.

There are some disadvantages in transferring property to an irrevocable trust. The principal ones are

1. If a bank, attorney, or third party is appointed the trustee, there will be trust commissions or fees to be paid every year.

2. If the property is sold after your death at a profit, income taxes will be higher than if you continued to own the property until death.

3. You will lose control of the asset. You may need the asset for your support or for investment in another business. When it is transferred to an irrevocable trust, the asset is forever lost to you.

4. A legal fee is incurred in preparing the trust instrument (also called a *trust agreement*).

The technical explanations that follow are patterned after the headings in Part A.

1. Lifetime transfers where an interest is retained for life.

An earlier illustration concerned creating an irrevocable trust whose income was to be paid to you for life. Even though you gave away the remainder interest (the balance remaining after your death), the value of the entire property was included in your gross estate. Why? Because by keeping the right to receive the income for your lifetime from all the property that you transferred to the trust, you have kept a prohibited "string," which causes all the trust property to be included in your gross estate.

What if you provide that for your lifetime you shall receive one-half the income from the trust property? In this case, the law provides that one-half of the value of the trust property will be included in your gross estate.

Let us change the facts slightly and provide that while you are entitled to the income from the trust property for your lifetime, income shall be paid to you four times a year. You will receive the income on March 31, June 30, September 30, and December 31 of each year, but if you die on any date other than these dates, the income for the period from the last payment date shall not be paid to your estate. For example, you die September 15. Since the pay date for income is September 30, the income from July 1 to September 15 will not be paid to your estate. Your estate representative could then argue that since you have not retained the income for your lifetime (because the last payment you received was on June 30), the property should not be included in your gross estate.

However, the law also says that property will be included in one's gross estate not only when income is retained for life, but also when income is retained for a period that cannot be determined except by reference to one's death. (The actual language of the law is "for a period not ascertainable without reference to his death.") In the example just given, the period for which you retained the income could be determined only by reference to your death, and therefore, the trust property must be included in your gross estate.

Let us change the facts once again. You now provide that the trust income will be paid to you for 20 years, and you die after 15 years. The rule just stated (retaining income for life or for a period that cannot be determined except by reference to your death) does not apply here. However, once again, the law covers this situation. It provides that if income is retained from property that is transferred for a period that does not actually end before the settlor's death, all of the trust property from which the income is derived is included in the gross estate. Since you retained the right to receive the income from the trust property for a period that did not actually end before your death, the trust property is included in your gross estate.

The technical requirement of the law goes one step further. It says that where the settlor of a trust reserves the right (either alone or with another) to determine who shall possess or enjoy the trust property or the income from the trust property, and the settlor dies having this right, the trust property will be included in the gross estate. It does not matter that the settlor personally cannot enjoy the property or the income. The prohibited "string" is the power to determine who may enjoy the trust property or the income from the trust property.

Some examples will help you understand this rule.

a. You create a trust during your lifetime in which the income from the trust property is to be paid to your wife for life, and on her death the trust will terminate and be paid over to your children. When you create the trust, you retain the right to have principal of the trust paid over to your mother, but only if needed. Because of this right, you are considered to have a prohibited "string" to the property transferred. The trust property will therefore be included in your gross estate.

b. You create a trust during your lifetime in which the income from the trust property is to be paid to your children, Ann and Robert, in equal shares, during their lifetimes, or all to the survivor of Ann and Robert. On the deaths of both, the trust will terminate and be paid over to your daughter, Susan. When you create the trust, you retain the right to give more income to one of the children and less to the other, but Ann and Robert must *consent* to any such unequal distribution. Even though you must receive someone's consent, the law says that you have retained the right to determine who shall possess or enjoy the property. This retained right is a prohibited "string" to the property transferred. Therefore, the trust property will be included in your gross estate.

c. You create a trust in which the trust income is to be paid to your sister for life, and on her death the trust will terminate and be paid over to your nieces and nephews. You retain the right to accumulate income and add it to the principal of the trust. Because of this power, you have really retained the right to determine who shall enjoy the income. This retained right is a prohibited "string" to the property transferred. Thus, the trust property will be included in your gross estate.

Each of these examples illustrates a situation in which you have retained the right to determine who shall enjoy the property. This right is, in each case, a prohibited "string." The law seems to say that this is the same as your enjoying the property yourself, and therefore, the property over which you have this power is included in your gross estate.

2. Lifetime transfers where the beneficiary can receive an interest only if he or she survives you and, in addition, you retain certain rights to get the property back.

Review of some definitions: The one who transfers property is called the donor or *transferor*. The one who receives the property is called the donee or *transferee*. The trustee of a trust is also the transferee. The settlor of a trust is also usually the *transferor*. Why "usually"? Be-

cause you may create a trust and transfer to it $1,000. Later, your son may add property to the trust, and he becomes the transferor of such (added) property. A *beneficiary* is the one who receives benefits from property.

If you, as transferor, provide that the property you gave be returned to you, this is known as retaining a *reversionary interest* (in other words, the property reverts, or is returned, to you). For example, you give certain property in trust for the benefit of your mother for her lifetime and provide that on her death the property be paid over to your children who survive her; however, if there are none, the property must be returned to you. This is known as retaining a reversionary interest. Of course, it is not certain whether you will actually outlive your mother and receive the return of the property.

The law says that if the value of your reversionary interest is greater than 5 percent of the value of the property the moment prior to your death, and when possession or enjoyment can be obtained *only* by surviving you, the property will be included in your gross estate.

In the prior example, you left property in trust, and your mother was to receive the income for her lifetime. She was entitled to receive the income whether or not you were then living. Since her possession or enjoyment of the income was not conditional upon surviving you, no part of the trust would be included in your estate by reason of this provision, even though you retained a reversionary interest. However, suppose you provided in the trust that your mother was to receive income from the trust *only* if she survives you. You will note that here your mother's enjoyment of the trust property is dependent on her surviving you. In this case, if your reversionary interest was greater than 5 percent of the value of the property the moment prior to your death, the trust property would be included in your gross estate.

How is the 5 percent calculated? This is done by checking the tables prepared by the Internal Revenue Service, published as part of the Treasury Regulations issued in connection with the Internal Revenue Code. The purpose of this rule is to tax property when there has not been a completed lifetime transfer. If the transfer is such that there is a prohibited "string" attached, then it is as though it is a transfer at death, and transfers at death are taxed as part of the gross estate.

3. Lifetime transfers where you have the power at the time of your death to alter, amend, revoke, or terminate the enjoyment of the property transferred.

In the two preceding categories, the property would be included in your gross estate only if you *retained* certain powers when you transferred the property. In this category, it is not necessary that you have retained the prohibited "string." It is only necessary that you have the prohibited power at the time of your death. In such a case, the property involved will be included in your gross estate.

For example, suppose you transfer property to your cousin, Robert, as trustee and provide that the income from the property shall be paid to your daughters, Ann and Susan, in equal shares, during their lifetimes; on the death of one of them, all the income shall be paid to the survivor for her lifetime. You also provide that the trustee may, at his discretion, use the principal of the trust for the benefit of any of your sons and any of your grandchildren. Five years later, Robert resigns as trustee, and you are appointed trustee. You die while serving as trustee.

In this case, you have the power to alter or terminate Ann's and Susan's enjoyment of the income. Why? Because you can distribute all of the principal to others, and this will either reduce or eliminate the amount of income available to Ann and Susan. Even if you can distribute only part of the principal to others, the amount of income available to Ann and Susan will also be reduced.

If the power you have to use principal could be exercised only with the consent of Ann, the property would still be included in your gross estate. The argument against inclusion is that if Ann approved your proposed action, that would be contrary to her financial interests. In other words, she is an *adverse party*. However, the law makes no distinction in this situation. Since you have the power to invade principal, even though the power is available only with the approval of an adverse party, the property is includable in your gross estate.

The law further states that it does not matter that you cannot take back the property for your own benefit. As long as at the time of your death, you have the power to alter, amend, revoke, or terminate the trust, any one of these powers will be sufficient to cause the property to be included in your estate.

Suppose you create a trust and retain some of the prohibited powers; however, four years before you die, you are declared to be incompetent. By reason of this declaration, you are legally incapable of exercising any of the powers. Is the property includable in your gross estate? Yes. The rule is that since you have the power, even though you could not do anything about it, the property is includable.

EXCEPTION TO ALL THREE CATEGORIES

It should now be reasonably clear that when a person has given away property but retains certain "strings," the situation is similar to that person's owning the property on the date of death.

That is, it is as though the decedent disposed of the property at death rather than during lifetime. It is equally clear that when an individual disposes of property at death, this type of transfer is subject to the estate taxes that are imposed on property being transferred at death.

When property is transferred in exchange for a cash payment made to the transferor, the transferor's estate is not artificially reduced. For example, if the transferor receives cash of $200,000 in exchange for property worth $200,000, the $200,000 cash is still part of the estate and will be subject to estate tax.

The law provides that if any of the transfers referred to in the prior three categories is made, the property that is included is only the amount, if any, that is greater than any cash or other property received in exchange for the transfer. The law refers to this important exception as a transfer made for an adequate and full consideration in money or money's worth.

For example, you transfer $200,000 to a trustee to be held in trust and you retain the income from the property so transferred for your life. On your death, the trust will terminate and will then be paid over to your son John, if then living, and if not then living, to his estate. When you made the transfer, your son paid you $150,000 to make the transfer.

Since you retained the income from the property for life, you have kept one of the prohibited "strings" that would cause the property to be included in your gross estate. If not for the exception that was just explained, your estate would include not only the $200,000 you transferred to the trust, but also the $150,000 your son transferred to you in exchange. To include $350,000 in your gross estate is obviously unfair. Therefore, the law states that of the $200,000 you transferred to the trust, only $50,000 of it (the amount by which the transfer is greater than the amount that was transferred to *you*) will be included in your estate.

In this case, your gross estate will include the $150,000 you received from your son (assuming you still have it on the date of your death) plus the $50,000 of the trust property. This is the $200,000 you had originally.

We have now concluded the technical discussion of the first three categories (Part B); what follows is a discussion of the remaining five categories.

4. Your gross estate includes annuities.

Simply stated, the word *annuity,* as used in the law, means the right to receive one or more payments extending over any period of time. The payments may be made on a regular basis, infrequently, or irregularly. Also, the payments do not have to be in equal sums.

The law includes an annuity in a decedent's gross estate, but only if (a) the decedent is entitled to receive payments and, *in addition,* a beneficiary is entitled to receive benefits under it *after* the decedent's death; and (b) the annuity is paid under any form of contract or agreement. The annuity is included in the gross estate only to the extent that its value is caused by contributions made by the decedent or his or her employer. For example, I buy an annuity from an insurance company that entitles me to receive $1,000 a month for my lifetime. I die. Is any part of the annuity included in my estate? No. Why not? Because there is no beneficiary under this annuity contract after my death.

Assume, though, that I buy an annuity that entitles me to receive $1,000 a month for my lifetime, and on my death my wife shall be entitled to receive $1,000 a month for *her* lifetime. If my wife outlives me, the value of her payments will be included in my gross estate for tax purposes.

When one thinks of an "annuity," one usually associates this with an insurance company. But annuities can be paid under other types of arrangements, too.

For example, you enter into a contract with your employer to pay you a retirement benefit of $1,000 a month for

life and provide that if you are survived by your wife, Joan, she is to receive a benefit of $750 a month for her lifetime. It has been determined that this arrangement is really an annuity that is included in your gross estate.

Benefits paid under any form of *qualified* plan are fully included in the gross estate, with limitations depending on the date of decedent's separation from employment. (This represents a change from prior law.) Such benefits include any trust or fund forming part of a pension, annuity, retirement, bonus, or profit-sharing plan, as well as individual retirement accounts (IRAs).

5. Your gross estate includes joint interests.

If I died today and my name appeared as joint owner of any property with someone who is *not* my spouse, federal estate tax law provides that the value of the *entire* property must be included in my gross estate. However, if my personal representative or my joint owner can establish that part of the property originated with him or her, then *that* part will not be included in my gross estate. For this purpose, when property is acquired by gift, bequest, devise, or inheritance by decedent and another as joint owners, only one-half of each jointly acquired property is included in the decedent's gross estate.

Tax law now provides that if the property is owned as tenants by the entirety or jointly owned by husband and wife and the surviving spouse is a U.S. citizen, then, regardless of who paid for the property, only one-half of the value of such property is included in the estate of the first one to die. If the surviving spouse is not a U.S. citizen, the rule set forth in the preceding paragraph applies.

What is the difference between property that is owned by two people as (a) joint owners, (b) tenants by the entireties, and (c) tenants in common?

---

a. Joint owners—On the death of one, the survivor owns all the property. (This is known as *right of survivorship;* that is, the survivor will own it all.) During lifetime, either joint owner can sever (break up) the joint ownership either by sale or other transfer. In such a case, each party is entitled to receive one-half of the property. (If there are more than two joint owners, each joint owner is entitled to receive the same proportion of the property as there are owners. That is, three owners and each is entitled to one-third; four owners and each is entitled to one-quarter; and so on.)

b. Tenants by the entireties—This is a joint ownership between husband and wife in which the survivor becomes the sole owner of the property on the death of the other. Neither party can break up the joint ownership without the other's consent. On divorce of the parties, the law provides that ownership changes from tenants by the entireties to tenants in common.

c. Tenants in common—Each party owns one-half of the property. On the death of one, that party's one-half interest passes as he or she provides by will or, if there is no will, as provided by state law. (If there are more than two tenants

in common, each tenant is entitled to receive the same proportion of the property as there are tenants.)

When we celebrated our silver wedding anniversary, I gave my husband a gift of $10,000. We are both U.S. citizens. He used the money to buy stock. The stock is registered in our joint names. If I die first, will the stock be part of my gross estate?

No, only one-half will be part of your gross estate. Since the stock is jointly owned, and you are one of the owners at the time of your death, the law provides that if you die in 1982 or thereafter, only one-half will be included in your gross estate. It is immaterial where the money came from or how the property was first registered or titled. What is important is how the property is owned (titled) at death.

My husband and I own the house we live in as joint tenants. The house was a gift to us both under the will of my uncle. If I die first and the house is then worth $90,000, what amount will be included in my gross estate?

Since it is owned jointly, the amount will be $45,000.

I have read that I can save taxes by titling property in joint names with my wife (or husband). Is this correct?

In general, no. In a few situations, such as when the total value of the property owned by you and your spouse is worth less than $600,000 (in which case, because of the unified credit, there will be no federal estate tax if death occurs in 1987 or later), titling property in joint names may save a little money. The savings here would take place because in some states there is no state death tax for property inherited on the death of one spouse by a surviving spouse, or for property owned by the husband and wife as tenants by the entireties. In the usual situation, titling property this way would cause substantially higher taxes because some property would be taxed twice, as shown by the following example.

Assume you own property worth $325,000, your wife owns property worth $525,000, and you title all *your* property (the $325,000) as joint tenants with your wife. You die first. There will be no federal estate tax or state death tax in your estate. (This could vary according to state law.) When your wife dies, her gross estate will be $850,000. The federal estate tax, before the unified credit, will be $287,300. The unified credit of $192,800 will reduce the net tax to $94,500. This amount ($94,500) *could* have been saved by your leaving $325,000 in trust for your wife.

When everything you own is in joint names with your spouse, at the moment of your death, the spouse becomes the owner of all such property. Therefore, regardless of what your will says, you have no power to leave anything in trust for your wife.

It is, of course, appropriate to note that when property is titled in joint names, such property would not be subject to the jurisdiction of the courts; in other words, it would not be probate property. This may save commissions and legal fees to some extent. On the other hand, whatever legal fees are paid could be an income tax deduction to your spouse. (In any event, commissions can be saved by designating your spouse as the personal representative.)

6. Your gross estate includes property over which you have a general power of appointment at the time of death.

When one has a general power of appointment over property at the time of death or, under certain circumstances has exercised or released this power, the value of the property is included in that person's gross estate and is therefore subject to estate tax.

To understand this rule, we must first understand what is meant by a *general power of appointment* as well as a *special power of appointment*.

A *power of appointment* (either *general* or *special*) is a right given to someone to dispose of property. The one who has this right does not own the property but has control over it to a certain extent (that is, to the extent of determining who shall eventually own it). The one who has this right is called the donee of the power and sometimes the *holder* of the power. The one who gives the right to the donee is called the donor of the power. When the donee exercises the power, the law provides that the eventual owner acquires ownership from the original owner, the donor of the power, and not from the donee of the power.

For example, by your will you give your wife the power to designate who shall own your (former) house on her death. Under your will, you did not leave her ownership of the house. She had a right to live in it for her lifetime. She does not own the house but she certainly has a lot of control over it—she has the right to determine who shall own it after her death. This right to give it away is called a *power of appointment*.

There are two kinds of powers of appointment—general and special. A general power is one in which the holder of the power (the donee) could give away (appoint) the property to anyone. "Anyone" includes even the holder of the power. In 1954, Congress decided that a general power of appointment should be included in the gross estate of the one who had this power, even though that person was not the owner. Congress felt that having this ability to give ownership of the property to anyone, including the holder of the power, was the equivalent of ownership.

A special power of appointment is one that limits the person or persons to whom property may be given. For example, by your will you give your wife the power to designate who shall own your (former) house on her death. However, you limit her power so that she may pick the owner from among only certain relatives of yours (normally children). Because of this limitation, this power is considered to be a special power. While the economic control over the property is a pretty broad one, it is not quite the same control as when someone has a general power. (A special power of appointment is sometimes called a *limited power of appointment*).

Congress decided that when someone has only a special power of appointment,

the property over which the power is held should *not* be included as part of that person's estate for tax purposes. When someone is given a power, they can exercise it, let it lapse, release it, or renounce or disclaim it.

To *exercise* the power means to act upon it. For example, if I give you the power to designate who among my children shall own my automobile next year and you give ownership to my daughter Jane, you have exercised the power. If you do nothing about the power, you have let it *lapse*. However, if you give up the power, that is, you voluntarily waive any right to exercise the power, you have *released* it.

The law also permits you to refuse to accept the power I have given you. This is known as a *renunciation* or *disclaimer*. If you renounce or disclaim the power shortly after learning of the power I have given you, it is as though you never had it, and it causes no tax problems.

The general rule is that when a person dies who has a general power of appointment over property, the value of that property is included in the person's gross estate. In addition, if the decedent had income rights in the property or kept certain "strings" and at any time before death had exercised, let lapse, or released a general power of appointment, the value of the property is included in the decedent's gross estate.

EXCEPTIONS TO THESE RULES

The two principal exceptions to the above rules are highlighted by the next two questions.

In his will, my late father created a trust for the benefit of my mother for her lifetime. The trustee is a bank that is required to pay her all the income. On her death, the property is to be paid over to me. Each year my mother has the right to receive $5,000 or 5 percent of the trust if she requests it. The trust is now and has always been worth $350,000. My mother owns another $450,000. From what you have said, since my mother could have received most of the trust over all these years but did not, she had a general power of appointment that she let lapse. Do you mean that the $350,000 will be part of her taxable estate?

Your question illustrates an exception to the general rule. The will permits your mother to request $5,000 or 5 percent of the trust, and this power on her part is a general power of appointment. In any year in which she does not take it, she has let it lapse. When she lets it lapse, she still enjoys the income from the $5,000 or 5 percent she could have received, but that remains part of the trust. The general rule says that when a person has a general power of appointment, allows it to lapse, and still enjoys the income from it, the property will be taxed as part of that person's estate.

The exception to this rule is that when there is a lapse, the first $5,000 or 5 percent of property, whichever is greater, is exempt from death or gift taxes. In your mother's case, she could have taken either $5,000 or $17,500 (5 percent of $350,000) each year, neither

of which she took. Any year in which she did not take the income, there was a lapse. However, because of the exception, the property that she did not take (that lapsed) will not be included in her gross estate.

Assume the same facts as in the previous question except that my mother was the trustee. The trustee could pay over to herself any amount of the principal of the trust if she found it necessary for her health, education, maintenance, or support. Am I to assume that since she can take whatever she needs for her support, this is the equivalent of a general power of appointment and, therefore, the entire trust property will be included in her gross estate?

No. This question illustrates another exception to the general rule. Here, your mother's power is limited to satisfying her needs for her health, education, maintenance, or support. Because of these limitations, the law states that the power she has is *not* considered the equivalent of a *general* power of appointment. Therefore, the property over which she had this control will not be included in her gross estate.

7. Your gross estate includes proceeds of life insurance under certain circumstances.

While the proceeds of life insurance are usually not subject to income tax, they can be the cause for substantial estate taxes.

Before explaining the basic rules, a

simple example of how life insurance can cause high and unexpected estate taxes is appropriate. Assume that all my possessions (house, car, cash, and miscellaneous) are worth $225,000, and that when I die I am married. If I leave everything to my wife, there will be no federal estate taxes on my death. When my wife dies owning the $225,000 (assuming she has no other assets), there would be no federal estate tax in her estate either. But assume I also own term life insurance on my life that pays my wife $600,000 on my death. In this case, the federal estate tax could be substantial.

On my death, there will be no estate tax, but on my wife's death, the tax will be $84,750. This tax can be saved, but before explaining how, let's discuss the basic rules. Simply stated, they are as follows:

a. When proceeds of life insurance are received by the estate of the insured, the amount received will be included in the gross estate of the decedent (and therefore subject to estate taxes), even if the insurance is not owned by the decedent.

b. When proceeds of life insurance are received by any beneficiary of the insured decedent, if the decedent owned any incidents of ownership (see page 16–62) in the insurance policy or policies on the date of death, then the proceeds of the life insurance insuring the decedent's life will be included in the gross estate of the decedent (and therefore subject to estate taxes), even if the insurance is not owned by the decedent.

If proceeds of life insurance on my life are not paid to my estate and I have no incidents of ownership in the policy, did I understand correctly that the proceeds will not be included in my estate for tax purposes?

Yes. However, when the proceeds are payable to another, if that person is under a legally binding obligation to pay debts of the estate, it is *as though* the proceeds were paid to your estate. In this situation, the proceeds of insurance would be included in your estate for tax purposes to the extent of such obligation.

Tell me what you mean by life insurance.

Life insurance is a contract in which there is a risk involving someone's life, and the risk of a loss is shifted from an individual to a group. For example, you and I enter into a contract. You agree to pay me $100 per month for life. On your death, I agree to pay $10,000 to whomever you name. I am taking a risk that by the time you die, the total amount paid over to me by you, together with the interest on the money, will be greater than the $10,000.

This type of arrangement is *not* considered life insurance for federal estate tax purposes because the risk I am taking involves only me, an individual.

However, if you enter into this same type of arrangement with an insurance company, the risk is spread among a large group of people, and this arrangement would be life insurance.

There are two broad types of life insurance policies: *term* and *ordinary*. (Ordinary is also called *whole life* or *universal life insurance*.) Term life insurance is the name given to that type of policy that never has any cash value. If the insured dies when the policy is in effect, then the company will pay over the face amount of the insurance. Ordinary life insurance is the name given to another type of policy that, with the passage of time, acquires cash value. With this type of policy (even before the death of the insured, which is when the face amount will become due), the owner can always ask the company to pay over the cash value.

An annuity policy is not life insurance. When you buy an annuity policy from a life insurance company, the company agrees to pay you a certain agreed-upon sum of money for a certain period of time. This amount is usually paid to you during your lifetime. The cost of the annuity is based on the amount that the insurance company believes it can earn with the money you pay, less an amount for overhead and profit. Unlike life insurance, the amount of the annuity paid to you has no relationship to how many people of your age die at any particular time. In other words, the company undertakes no risk related to how many people live or die at any particular time.

What are some features of life insurance?

1. Life insurance is a contract, usually between you and an insurance company.

2. A policy may insure you and yet be owned by someone else. For example, I applied for a policy on my life many years ago. I transferred ownership of the policy to my daughter. The owner of the policy is my child. The one whose life is insured is called the *insured* and the owner of the policy is called the *owner*.

3. The one who receives the face amount of the policy on the death of the insured is called the beneficiary. The insured, the owner, and the beneficiary could be three separate people. A corporation could also be an owner or a beneficiary.

4. Someone other than the owner of the policy can have certain rights in the policy. For example, life insurance is issued on my life, but my wife is the owner and beneficiary of the policy. If I have the right to either borrow on the policy or change the beneficiary (even though I am not the owner), then I am the one who has certain rights in the policy. These rights are considered to be *incidents of ownership*.

Give me some examples of incidents of ownership.

1. The power to change the beneficiary.
2. The power to surrender or cancel the policy.
3. The power to transfer ownership of the policy.

4. The power to revoke an assignment of the ownership of the policy.
5. The power to pledge the policy for a loan.
6. The power to obtain from the insurer a loan against the surrender value of the policy.

At the suggestion of my lawyer, four years ago I transferred ownership of life insurance on my life to my wife. She died, and all her property was left in trust for the benefit of our children. I am the trustee. Will the insurance be taxed as part of my estate?

The answer depends on the type of control you have over the policy. If the incident of ownership that you have over the policy is to change the beneficiary so that you or your estate can become the beneficiary, then the policy will be taxed as part of your estate. This will be the result, even if at the time of your death you have not exercised this power.

Merely having the power is sufficient to produce this tax consequence. However, if the incident of ownership you have is not for your personal economic benefit, then no part of the policy will be included in your gross estate.

Why does the law treat life insurance differently from other property?

Because life insurance is by its nature property that benefits someone when there is a death. With other kinds of property, benefits are derived during lifetime. Although life insurance is singled out for special treatment, all the general rules for taxing property still apply to it.

Tell me how life insurance is taxed.

Though the premiums for term life insurance are initially lower than for other forms of life insurance, term insurance has no buildup in cash value. It only acquires value when there is a death, when the face amount becomes payable. During lifetime, the cash value of term insurance is zero, but on death its value is the face amount.

Were you to own a term policy on your life with a face value of $100,000, on your death your beneficiary would receive $100,000. For federal estate tax purposes, the amount that is taxed is not the cash value during lifetime (which, in the case of term insurance, is zero), but the face amount that is payable on death.

Many readers may have heard or read that when insurance proceeds of a policy owned by a decedent-insured are paid to one's husband or wife, there is no death tax. For state death tax purposes, this may be the case (depending on the laws of your state), but this is not the case for federal death (or estate) tax purposes. For example, assume the insured is a woman who owns the policy and she designates her husband as beneficiary. If she is a Maryland resident at the time of her death, Maryland imposes no inheritance tax on the proceeds of this policy. However, for federal estate tax purposes, the policy proceeds are considered to be part of the gross estate. As discussed on pages 126–27, 172, and 175–76, if the surviving spouse is a U.S. citizen, any proceeds of life insurance that are paid over to the spouse would qualify for the marital deduction. (Also, in most cases, proceeds of life insurance are not subject to income tax.)

The owner of a policy can be different from the one who is the insured. The beneficiary can even be a third person. Thus, there is an opportunity to save estate tax.

I am 70 years old and happily married to my first wife. We have two lovely children who will eventually inherit everything we own. I own stock worth $600,000 and my wife owns stock worth $600,000. I also own term life insurance with a face amount of $200,000. Is there any way I can arrange it so she can benefit from this property and minimize estate taxes?

Yes. But we should first look at what the taxes will be if you continue to own this property, you take advantage of planning so there is no tax on your death, and you die first. This will require you to leave part of your property in trust for the benefit of your wife.

On your death, the estate taxes will be as follows:

Gross estate (stock worth $600,000 plus life insurance of $200,000)	$800,000

Marital deduction for property transferred to wife		(200,000)
Taxable estate		$600,000
Tentative tax	$192,800	
Unified credit	(192,800)	
Net estate tax		$ -0-

On your wife's later death, the estate taxes of her estate will be as follows:

Her own assets		$600,000
Receivable from your estate		+ 200,000
Taxable estate		$800,000
Tentative tax	$267,800	
Unified credit	(192,800)	
Net estate tax		$ 75,000
Total taxes on both estates:		
Your estate		$ -0-
Wife's estate		+ 75,000
Total		$ 75,000

In this case, $600,000 of your property will be left in trust. Your wife will benefit from this $600,000 during her lifetime, but no part of it will be taxable in her estate.

Substantial taxes can be saved as follows: Transfer the life insurance to an irrevocable living trust. If you live more than three years after the transfer, the life insurance will not be subject to estate tax in either your estate or your wife's estate.

On your death, the estate taxes of your estate will be as follows:

Gross estate		$600,000
Marital deduction for property transferred to wife		(0)
Taxable estate		$600,000
Tentative tax	$192,800	
Unified credit	(192,800)	
Net estate tax		$ -0-

All of your property, or $600,000, will be added to the irrevocable trust. Following your death, the trust will consist of the $200,000 of the life insurance proceeds plus your entire estate, or $600,000. The total will therefore be $800,000.

The terms of the trust shall provide that your wife will receive all of the income for life plus whatever principal she will need for her health, maintenance, or support to maintain the same standard of living she had when you died. You can also give her the privilege to withdraw $5,000 or 5 percent from the principal of the trust every year, whichever is greater. In other words, she will have full enjoyment of the property in trust.

The trust will not be taxed in your wife's estate on her death after you. On your wife's later death, the estate taxes of her estate will be as follows:

Her own assets		$600,000
Received from your estate	+	-0-
Taxable estate		$600,000
Tentative tax	$192,800	
Unified credit	(192,800)	
Net estate tax		$ -0-

Total taxes of both estates:

Your estate		$ -0-
Wife's estate	+	-0-
Total		$ -0-

Total savings:

Total estate taxes when you keep ownership of the life insurance		$ 75,000
Total estate taxes when you transfer ownership of the life insurance to an irrevocable trust	+	-0-
Total savings		$ 75,000

Note: If the life insurance was ordinary life, and had cash value, any transfer of the policy would constitute a taxable gift. The taxable gift is equal to the cash value. The taxable gift would be added to your gross estate under the unified system. If your assets plus such gifts exceed $600,000, the excess would be taxed unless it qualified for the marital deduction.

What will happen if my wife dies before I do and either (1) I still own

life insurance on my death or (2) at least three years prior to my death, I turn over the life insurance to an irrevocable trust?

Under (1), on your wife's earlier death, the estate taxes of her estate will be as follows:

Her gross estate	$600,000
Marital deduction for property transferred to you	(-0-)
Taxable estate	$600,000
Tentative tax	$192,800
Unified credit (1987 or later)	(192,800)
Net estate tax	$ -0-

On your later death, the estate taxes of your estate will be as follows:

Gross estate (stock worth $600,000 plus life insurance of $200,000)		$800,000
Received from wife's estate	+	-0-
Taxable estate		$800,000
Tentative tax	$267,800	
Unified credit	(192,800)	
Net estate tax		$ 75,000

Total taxes of both estates:

Your wife's estate	$	-0-
Your estate	+	75,000
	$	75,000

In this case, we are assuming that $600,000 of your wife's individually owned assets will be left in trust for your benefit. No part of these trust assets will be taxable in your estate.

Under (2), on your wife's earlier death, the estate taxes of her estate will be as follows:

Her gross estate		$600,000
Marital deduction for property transferred to you		(0)
Taxable estate		$600,000
Tentative tax	$192,800	
Unified credit	(192,800)	
Net estate tax		$ -0-

On your later death, the estate taxes of your estate will be as follows:

Gross estate (stock only)		$600,000
Received from wife's estate	+	-0-
Taxable estate		600,000
Tentative tax	$192,800	
Unified credit	(192,800)	
Net estate tax		$ -0-

Total taxes:	(1)	(2)
Wife's estate	$ -0-	$ -0-
Husband's estate	+ 75,000	+ -0-
	$ 75,000	$ -0-

You will note that here, if your wife dies before you, you will save $75,000 (the difference between $75,000 and $0) when you transfer the life insurance to an irrevocable trust.

Transferring ownership of life insurance sounds too good to be true. What is the catch?

There are a few drawbacks, none of which is too serious. They are as follows:

1. When you give ownership of your life insurance to a trustee of a trust, you cannot later change your mind and get it back if you so wish. The transfer is a final one. You can, of course, give your spouse the right to return the insurance to you. Giving your spouse this right will not result in any adverse tax consequence.

2. When the proceeds of the insurance are collected, your spouse will not be the owner. While he or she will have virtually 100 percent of the economic benefits from the trust, your spouse will not be the absolute owner of the property.

When I pay premiums on this life insurance, won't I be making taxable gifts?

No, provided there is a properly drafted *Crummey clause.*

What is a Crummey clause and why would this clause be necessary?

When you pay premiums on life insurance that you have given away, you make gifts of these premiums. When a gift is a *present interest,* the first $10,000 of gifts made to any person is excluded from federal gift tax. The law provides that when premiums are paid on life insurance in an irrevocable trust, the gift is usually one of a *future interest,* and therefore, the first dollar of the gift is taxable. Since taxable gifts are included in the base against which the estate tax is calculated, it is obviously desirable to take advantage of the $10,000 exclusion if possible.

The Crummey clause is named after a 1968 court case entitled *Crummey v. Commissioner.* The court decided that when someone is given the right to withdraw from the trust each year the amount that is excluded from gift taxation (then $3,000 but now $10,000), since they can have the present use and enjoyment of amounts withdrawn, any annual premiums that are paid of $10,000 or less will indeed be gifts of a present interest. Hence, if you use a Crummey clause, the annual premium payments (of $10,000, or less) will not be taxable gifts and will not be subject to estate tax.

Why bother with a trust? I can just transfer ownership of the policy to my wife. Is this okay?

No. If you do this, the insurance proceeds will be taxed in your wife's estate. This can be demonstrated as follows, based on the last example given.

On your death, the estate taxes of your estate will be as follows:

Gross estate		$600,000
Marital deduction for property transferred to wife		(-0-)
Taxable estate		$600,000
Tentative tax	$192,800	
Unified credit	(192,800)	
Net estate tax		$ -0-

On your wife's later death, the estate taxes of her estate will be as follows:

Her own assets		$600,000
Life insurance proceeds received		200,000
Received from your estate		-0-
Taxable estate		$800,000
Tentative tax	$267,800	
Unified credit	(192,800)	
Net estate tax		$ 75,000

You will note that, from the tax point of view, this result is not desirable. Despite this, assume you still do not choose to transfer ownership of the life insurance to an irrevocable trust, but wish to transfer ownership to your wife. There will be a saving if your wife dies before you and if under her will, she transfers ownership of the life insurance directly to your children. The saving will be accomplished because on your later death, the proceeds of the life insurance will not be part of your taxable estate.

I am a widower and am not in very good health. I have one living daughter who will inherit everything I own. I do not have much and therefore want to be sure that taxes are minimized. I own a $50,000 whole life insurance policy insuring my life. It now has a cash value of $19,000. If I transfer the policy to my daughter as a gift and I die within three years, I understand that the entire $50,000 will be subject to estate tax in my estate. Instead, I intend to sell my daughter the policy for the $19,000 cash value. Is this advisable?

It depends on the total tax generated, figured on a case-by-case basis. The law now provides that proceeds of a life insurance policy are not subject to income taxes. However, when you sell a policy to someone, the policy proceeds are then subject to income tax. In this case, if you sell the policy to your daughter, she would have to report the amount she receives above her cost of $19,000 as ordinary income.

For example, assume that your taxable estate, including the life insurance, totals $630,000. If you give the entire policy to your daughter as a gift and survive more than three years thereafter, the estate tax of your estate will be zero. If you do nothing and die owning the policy, the estate tax will be approximately $11,000.

If you sell the policy to your daughter for $19,000, which is at least your cost, you would reduce your taxable estate by $31,000 (the $50,000 policy less the $19,000 you would receive for the policy). In this case, the estate tax of your estate will be zero. When your daughter receives the $50,000 life insurance proceeds, she will be required to report $31,000 as taxable income (the $50,000 policy proceeds less the $19,000 she paid for it).

Assume that your daughter has other income of $15,000 in the year in which she receives the $50,000 and that she is single. Her income tax without the life insurance proceeds will be approximately $2,250. Adding the $31,000 of income will cause the tax to be approximately $11,000, or an additional $8,750.

Thus, you saved $11,000 in estate taxes, but your daughter's income taxes were increased by $8,750 for a total tax dollar savings to your estate and your daughter of approximately $2,250. This result can, of course, vary depending upon your daughter's state income tax, if any (offset by a federal deduction for state income tax), and the amount of her other income.

My husband died this year. I am the beneficiary of a $50,000 insurance policy on his life. I read somewhere that there are advantages to leaving this money with the insurance company, which will pay it out to me over a period of years. Would you please tell me if this is true and give details?

With rare exceptions, proceeds of life insurance are not subject to income tax. In most cases, you should invest the $50,000. If your investment returns an annual rate of 6 percent, you would be receiving $3,000 in income each year. The income of $3,000 is subject to federal income tax.

Prior to October 22, 1986, if you left these funds on deposit with the insurance company, up to $1,000 of the interest that the company would pay would be excluded from being considered income for income tax purposes. For example, let us assume that your husband died in 1985 and you agreed to leave the monies on deposit with the company for a 10-year period. Usually, you would have the right to withdraw the balance at any time. Assume the company agrees to pay you $5,000 a year plus the interest on the balance they are holding. The rate of the interest they would agree to pay depends upon the rate they are paying at that time. Thus, the excess above the $5,000 of principal will be considered interest income, and the first $1,000 of this interest income will be excluded from being subject to federal income taxation.

However, this $1,000 exclusion has now been repealed and does not apply if your husband died after October 22, 1986 (the date the 1986 law was enacted).

8. Transfers within three years of death.

Earlier you stated that certain property transferred within three years of death was included in the gross estate. Please explain.

Before January 1, 1977, any gift made within three years of death was included in the gross estate only if it was made in "contemplation of death." The problem became one of having the Internal Revenue Service and sometimes the courts struggle with what was meant by the phrase "contemplation of death." Taxpayers tried to show that transfers were not made in contemplation of death. For example, taxpayers argued that motives included making a loved one financially independent, a desire to relieve oneself of responsibilities of managing assets, a desire to avoid possible claims of creditors, and similar motives.

Under the law effective from January 1, 1977, to December 31, 1981, the motive for making gifts is immaterial. The only question is whether the gift falls within the three-year period. If it does, and the gift exceeded the annual gift exclusion (then $3,000 but now $10,000), the entire gift (even the part that is otherwise excluded for gift tax purposes) may be included in the gross estate at its value on the date of death or its alternate value (discussed later on pages 176–79). If it does not, it may be excluded.

A change in the law, effective January 1, 1982, has eliminated even this three-year rule so that, with certain technical exceptions and with the exception of life insurance policies transferred and gift taxes paid within three years of death, *any* transfer will now be excluded from the gross estate.

If the gift exceeds $10,000 to any person in any year, the excess above $10,000 will be considered a taxable gift and will be added to the taxable estate for purposes of calculating estate taxes.

Please give me some illustrations of gifts made within three years of death using life insurance.

Suppose that one year before death, you transfer the following:

1. A $100,000 group term life insurance policy to your son Frank
2. A $20,000 whole life insurance policy to your son James
3. A $20,000 whole life insurance policy to your daughter Karen
4. A $2,000 whole life insurance policy to your daughter Anne

When you transferred the group term policy to Frank, it had a cash value of $0; the $20,000 policy transferred to James had a cash value of $2,500; the $20,000 policy transferred to Karen had a cash value of $5,000; and the policy to Anne had a cash value of $800.

At death, a life insurance policy pays the beneficiary the face amount of the policy, but before death, the policy may have a *cash value*. That is, the policy could be cashed in at any time for its cash value. Will the $100,000 policy with a cash value of $0 be included in your gross estate?

The answer is yes. The amount to be included in your estate will be the face amount of $100,000, even though the cash value at the time of the gift is less than $10,000. This same answer applies to the $20,000 policy with a cash value of $5,000.

What about the $2,000 policy with a cash value of $800? Even though the death value (the amount to be paid on death, in this case, $2,000) is under $10,000 (and even though the total of both the face value and cash value is under $10,000), the entire face amount of the policy, or $2,000, is still included in the gross estate. This same answer applies to the $20,000 policy with a cash value of $2,500.

Why is this so? Because the law says that any transfer of life insurance within three years of death must be included in the value of the gross estate.

Apart from insurance, how is property valued for federal estate tax purposes?

The general rule is that for estate and gift tax purposes, the value of property is its fair market value. The date when the value is determined for estate tax purposes is usually the date of death. However, under certain circumstances, the executor of the estate can choose to have the property valued on the alternate valuation date, which is usually six months after date of death. The date when the value is determined for gift tax purposes is the date of the gift.

Fair market value has been defined as:

the price at which the property would change hands between a willing buyer and a willing seller, neither being under any compulsion to buy or to sell and both having reasonable knowledge of relevant facts.

The value of property is essentially a factual one and has been the subject of much litigation. The reader should seek the advice and counsel of an attorney, accountant, or trust officer in connection with valuation of property.

What deductions are available to every estate?

As we pointed out earlier, the federal estate tax is based on the taxable estate plus adjusted taxable gifts. The taxable estate consists of the gross estate minus certain deductions, as follows:

1. Funeral expenses that are allowable by the laws of the state that has jurisdiction over the estate. This item includes the expenses for a tombstone, monument, mausoleum, burial lot perpetual care and maintenance, and even the cost of transportation of the person accompanying the body to the place of burial. When a Social Security death benefit is paid to the decedent's surviving spouse or children, such benefit does *not* reduce the allowable funeral expense.

2. Administration expenses that are allowable by the laws of the state that has jurisdiction over the estate. Here, the expenses are those related to the settlement of the estate and the transfer of the prop-

Tax-Saving Suggestion

Under the change in the law (effective January 1, 1982) that increased the annual exclusion for gifts from $3,000 to $10,000, there is a unique opportunity to save substantial sums in estate and gift taxes. If a parent is close to death but legally competent, a gift of $10,000 could be made to each child and grandchild in one year. The separate $10,000 gifts would completely escape federal estate and gift taxes.

A client of mine recently had her father make gifts of $10,000 to herself, her husband, her four children and each of their spouses, and two grandchildren. The total gifts in one year were $120,000. By eliminating $120,000 from her father's taxable estate, the estate tax was reduced by $44,400. The amount of the savings will, of course, depend upon the amount of the taxable estate. The minimum saving for any taxable estate is now at the rate of 37 percent.

erty of the estate to individual beneficiaries or to a trustee. This would include executor's commissions, attorney's and accountant's fees, court costs, and appraiser's fees. Also deductible would be expenses for selling property of the estate if the sale is necessary to pay the decedent's debts, taxes, and expenses of administration to preserve the estate or to effect distribution.

3. Claims against the estate that represent personal obligations of the decedent existing at the time of death, and interest on those obligations to the time of death. This would include income taxes on income received before death, mortgages on estate property, and alimony. However, where the claim is based on a promise or agreement, the deductibility of such an obligation is limited to the extent that the liability was undertaken as a bona fide transaction and for adequate consideration in money or money's worth. For example, if I promise to leave my cousin $50,000 at my death because of my affection for her, such a promise is not made for consideration in money or money's worth. Therefore, if I fail to leave her the promised $50,000, any claim she may file against my estate, even if allowed by the probate court, would not constitute a valid deduction for federal estate tax purposes.

4. Losses incurred during the settlement of the estate arising from fires, storms, shipwreck, or other casualties, or from theft, if the losses have not been reimbursed by insurance or otherwise.

5. Transfers to or for the United States or any state and transfers for charitable and religious purposes.

6. Transfers to a surviving spouse. This deduction is known as the marital deduction. While prior law limited the amount that could be deducted, present law allows an unlimited deduction (or 100 percent) for any property passing to a surviving spouse subject to the following conditions:

a. The decedent from whom the property is transferred must be a citizen or resident of the United States at death. The surviving spouse must also be a United States citizen.

If the surviving spouse is not a United States citizen, then the marital deduction has specific limitations and conditions. (See pages 175–76.)

b. The property interest that passes to the surviving spouse must be included in the decedent's gross estate, have no strings or conditions attached, or be left in a fashion that meets the requirements of paragraphs c or d (following).

Except for interests in property passing on death of the spouse *and* meeting the requirements of paragraphs c or d, the type of property must be such that no other interest in the same property can pass from the decedent to another person who can possess or enjoy the property. For example, assume the decedent leaves a house to his wife for life (called a *life estate*), with the house going to his children upon her death. Since the property interest will end on the wife's death and the children will possess or enjoy the property (the house) after her death, the value of the property will not qualify for the marital deduction. This type of property interest is called a "terminable interest," because it will terminate on the death of the wife.

A terminable interest in property is nondeductible only when someone other than the spouse may enjoy or possess the property after the termination of the spouse's interest.

c. The interest in the property may be left to the surviving spouse either for life or in trust and must meet *all* the following conditions:
aa. The surviving spouse must be entitled for life to all the income from the property or to a specific portion of the income.
bb. The income from the property must be payable to the surviving spouse annually or more often.
cc. The surviving spouse must have the power to appoint the entire interest or the specific portion to either herself or her estate.
dd. The power in the surviving spouse to appoint the property must be exercisable by him or her alone and must be exercisable in all events.
ee. No person, other than the surviving spouse, may have a power to appoint any part of the interest in the property.

d. The interest in the property must be left to the surviving spouse either for life or in trust and must meet *all* the following conditions:
aa. The surviving spouse must be entitled for life to all the income from the property or to a specific portion of the income.
bb. There must be no power in any person (including the spouse) to appoint any part of the property to any person other than the spouse during the spouse's lifetime. In other words, the trustee may invade principal (corpus) of the trust for the benefit of the spouse only.

cc. The executor (personal representative) of the estate must elect, on the estate tax return, to treat the property as *qualified terminable interest property* (or *QTIP*, as the profession now refers to it).

What is the importance of qualified terminable interest property (QTIP), and in what ways is it different from the traditional trust described in paragraph c of the previous question?

In the traditional trust, the surviving spouse *must* be given the right to designate who shall own the property on his or her death. Thus, a second husband (or wife) of the surviving spouse can become the eventual owner of the trust property. With QTIP, the decedent can determine who shall own the property after the survivor's death.

For example, assume John and Mary are married and both are U.S. citizens. John has two children by a first marriage and Mary has one child by a previous marriage. If John dies in 1994, owns property worth $875,000, and leaves all this property to Mary outright, there will be no estate tax on his death. (Why? Because his estate receives a marital deduction for the $875,000 that Mary inherits.) However, the property can end up being owned by Mary's children and not by John's children.

Under current law, John can direct that the property be left in trust for Mary's benefit for her life, and on her death that the ownership of the property pass to *his* children. If John directs his executor to elect that part of the property

be treated as QTIP, there will be no estate tax on John's death because QTIP entitles John's estate to receive a marital deduction for the value of such property.

When Mary dies after John, the value of the QTIP as of her date of death (or alternate valuation, if elected) is added to the value of Mary's assets. If the total value on Mary's assets plus the QTIP is less than $600,000, there would be no estate tax on her estate. If such total value is over $600,000, then an estate tax will be imposed based on such higher total value.

What happens if the election is not made to treat such property as QTIP?

The property will still be disposed of as John directs, but there will be no marital deduction in John's estate, and the estate tax will be $104,250.

The QTIP device sounds great. My estate gets a marital deduction for property I eventually control. Since I direct who owns the property, on my spouse's death, will the property be taxed as part of my spouse's estate?

Yes. While you do control the disposition of QTIP after your spouse's death, the property will be added to your spouse's gross estate and taxed accordingly.

Where will the funds come from to pay the tax on my spouse's death,

since my spouse will have no control over the QTIP?

The law provides that the additional taxes generated by the QTIP shall be paid for *from* the QTIP unless the surviving spouse directs otherwise.

For example, assume your spouse dies after you. He then owns $150,000, and you had created a QTIP worth $600,000. The QTIP is included in his gross estate. Adding the $600,000 to the $150,000 will cause his gross estate to be $750,000. Assuming no deductions (just to simplify this discussion), his taxable estate of $750,000 will create a tax liability of $55,500. If the QTIP were not added to his gross estate, his estate's tax liability would have been zero. Therefore, the $55,500 in tax will become a legal liability of those who will inherit the QTIP worth $600,000; in other words, those beneficiaries must pay the $55,500. The $150,000 can then be left by your husband to whomever he designates, unreduced by taxes.

Is there any advice you can give me concerning the tax caused by a QTIP?

Yes. While the law provides that the tax is to be paid from the QTIP itself, this provision of the law shall not apply "if the decedent otherwise directs by will."

In the past, wills traditionally have used boilerplate language that directed that all death taxes shall be paid from the rest, residue, and remainder of one's estate. If this boilerplate language is used, it may very well designate the source for the payment of death taxes. Using the facts from the prior example, the tax of $55,500 may be required to be paid from the husband's own $150,000—undoubtedly an unintended result.

I have a joint will with my spouse. On the death of the last of us to die, all our property will go to our children. Will the property that my husband receives from me qualify for the marital deduction?

One of the conditions that must be fulfilled to qualify for the marital deduction for property left in trust (unless the trust is a QTIP) is that your husband *must* have the sole right to determine who shall receive the property on his death; that is, he must have the complete freedom to give it to anyone. In many states, a joint will has been considered by the courts to be a contract to leave the property as agreed upon by the two parties to the will. In such a case, your husband will not have the complete freedom to give it to anyone he wishes. Therefore, the property interest he receives will not qualify for the marital deduction.

I left all my property in trust. The trustee must give the income from this property to my wife for life. Upon her death, she has the right to have the trustee give the property to whomever she specifies. To protect my wife and children, I have given my trustee the discretion to give whatever principal my trustee determines to be necessary

to either my wife or children to meet their emergency needs for health or support. Since my trustee can give principal to my children only in emergency situations, will the trust property qualify for the marital deduction?

No. The law requires that your wife be entitled to and receive all of the income from the trust property you left to her at the time of your death. Since the trustee has the discretion to pay over principal to the children, even though the trustee may never actually exercise this power and it can only be exercised for emergency needs, your wife *may* not receive all of the income from all the property. Also, the law requires that no part of the trust property may be given to anyone else (even if it is for a good cause). Therefore, no part of the trust property will qualify for the marital deduction.

However, if the discretion were limited to paying out principal to your wife (and *only* your wife), this would be permissible, since no one but your wife would be possessing or enjoying the property.

I would like the proceeds of life insurance on my life to be paid out by the insurance company to my wife on my death. Could this be done in such a way that my estate receives the marital deduction?

Yes. You should consult with your attorney and insurance agent to be sure that the terms of the contract with the insur-ance company comply with all the requirements of Section 2056(b)(6) of the Internal Revenue Code.

Please explain the law affecting the marital deduction when the surviving spouse is not a United States citizen. Also, tell me why the law was enacted.

Answering the second question first will help to clarify and understand the law. Congress's reasons, as expressed by the House tax-writing committee, which introduced the legislation, are as follows:

> *The marital deduction defers the estate tax on the assumption that the deductible property if not consumed will ultimately be includable in the surviving spouse's estate. . . . Property passing to an alien surviving spouse [may not be includable in the spouse's estate] since to avoid [U.S.] taxation on the worldwide estate, the spouse need only give up U.S. residence.*

Accordingly, the committee believes that no marital deduction should be allowed for such property. With respect to the estate tax marital deduction, for property passing to a non-U.S. citizen, there is no longer a marital deduction.

Following are the exceptions:

1. If the surviving spouse becomes a U.S. citizen before the estate tax return due date (unless an extension of time is granted, nine months after date of death) *and* the surviving spouse was a resident of the U.S. at all times prior to the due date, the unlimited marital deduction will be allowed.

This allowance of the marital deduction is subject to all the usual rules applicable where both parties are U.S. citizens.

2. An unlimited marital deduction will also be allowed if the property the (non-citizen) surviving spouse has an interest in is left in the form of a "qualified domestic trust" (referred to as a QDOT). To become a QDOT, the executor of the decedent's estate must make an affirmative election to treat the trust as a QDOT. Also, the trust must meet certain technical requirements of the law already enacted (and Treasury regulations to be issued).

Because of the limited applicability of this new law, and the technical nature of its provisions, this discussion is necessarily limited. The reader is urged to consult with his or her attorney to ensure compliance with the provisions of this law.

I understand that the usual rule for valuing estates is to value the property as of the date of death. I understand that I may choose *alternate valuation*. Please tell me what alternate valuation is, why I should choose it, how I choose it, and its details.

Alternate valuation permits the executor of an estate to value the estate at a date other than date of death.

Why is it important? Selecting alternate valuation permits the estate to reduce its estate taxes. For example, on the decedent's date of death in 1993, all the assets are valued at $1.1 million. These assets consist of a house worth $100,000, life insurance of $100,000, and stock of a closely held corporation (which we will call X Corporation) worth $900,000. If the decedent dies without a surviving spouse and without ever having made any taxable gifts, the net estate tax in 1993 (after applying the unified credit of $192,800) will be $194,000.

If within six months of death X Corporation goes into bankruptcy without any assets, then if there were no such thing as alternate valuation, the estate would still be valued as of date of death, namely, $1.1 million, and the estate tax would remain at $194,000. In this case, practically all of the other assets would have to be paid over to the government. Even the house would have to be sold in order to pay the taxes.

With alternate valuation, the estate representatives could elect to have the estate valued at the "alternate valuation date," which would be six months after death. If they do so, the estate would have a value of only $200,000, and the estate tax would be zero. The importance of alternate valuation, therefore, is to reduce estate taxes.

What is the alternate valuation date? With respect to property distributed, sold, exchanged, or otherwise disposed of within six months after death, the property is valued as of the date of distribution, sale, exchange, or other disposition; with respect to property not so distributed, sold, etc., the property is valued as of six months after decedent's death.

How is alternate valuation elected? By indicating this on the federal estate tax return. While this election is available even if the return is filed late (not more than one year late, however), if the election is not made on the first filed return, it is lost forever. Also, once the election is made, it cannot be changed.

When would I not elect alternate valuation? When to do so would cause the beneficiaries of the estate to have higher income taxes. The determination as to when this would occur depends on comparing the estate tax liability with the potential income taxes.

An example will clarify this. Let us assume the decedent dies with a gross estate valued at $660,000. No alternate valuation is elected. He was domiciled in Maryland, where there is an estate tax that is a pickup tax (tax credit) and a direct inheritance tax of 1 percent.

His estate has no deductions and the entire value is represented by securities. He has no wife and leaves his entire estate to his daughter. The taxable estate is $660,000 (gross estate minus zero deductions). The net tax after the unified credit and credit for state death taxes is calculated as follows:

Taxable estate	$660,000
Tentative estate tax:	
First $500,000	$155,800
37% × $160,000	59,200
	$215,000
Minus: Unified credit	192,800

Credit for state death taxes paid	16,400
Other credits	-0-
Net federal estate tax	$ 5,800

If alternate valuation is elected and the fair market value is then $500,000, a comparison of the death taxes, *without considering income taxes*, would look like this:

	DATE OF DEATH VALUATION OF ASSETS	ALTERNATE VALUATION OF ASSETS
Federal death taxes	$ 5,800	$ -0-
State death taxes— where there is a federal estate tax	16,400	-0-
Without a federal estate tax	-0-	6,600
	$22,200	$6,600

You will tentatively conclude that you should elect alternate valuation. After all, it will now save $15,600 in estate taxes. However, by electing alternate valuation, the income tax basis of the securities inherited by your daughter will be $500,000 instead of $660,000. If she sells the securities for $660,000, there will be a gain, which will be the difference between the basis of $500,000 and the selling price of $660,000. The gain of $160,000 will cause your daughter to pay

Tax-Saving Suggestion

When my widowed mother died, she owned approximately $5,000 of face value United States Series E Savings Bonds. The bonds have been accumulating interest for the past 30 years. I am the executor of my mother's estate as well as her only child and will be inheriting these bonds from her estate. My husband has a good income. What advice can you give me with respect to these bonds?

The increase in value of the bonds is usually not reported as income during the time they are owned. If your mother held these bonds for the last 30 years, then the present value of the bonds will be approximately two and one-half times their original cost. If the original total face amount of the bonds is $5,000, they cost $3,750. Their present value is approximately $9,375. The difference between their cost and present value is $5,625. The law states that this amount of $5,625 constitutes taxable income.

As executor, you can determine which person shall report this amount as income. The income may be reported on your mother's final income tax return, on the estate's income tax return, or on your personal income tax return. If you choose the third option, you may report the income in the year in which you receive the bonds, any later year, or when you surrender or dispose of the bonds. You should therefore compare the income tax brackets of your mother, the estate, and yourself (assuming you file a joint return with your husband) to see which result would be most favorable to you.

---

additional income taxes of $44,800 at the present (1993) capital gain rate of 28 percent. (No account has been taken of the fact that whatever amount your daughter inherits will be reduced by the death taxes.) Should the estate (realistically your daughter) save $15,600 now versus an eventual *income tax* of $44,800?

Your daughter's plans for the securities must be known in order to make the best decision. If she intended to sell them immediately for $660,000, it would not be wise to elect alternate valuation. If she intended to hold them for several years, reduce taxes now by electing alternate valuation.

In this connection, it is important to remember that if you do choose to value estate property on the alternate valuation date, then all the property owned by the estate, not just one or two items, must be valued on the alternate valuation date.

Is alternate valuation available to every estate? No, it is available only where both the total value of the gross estate and the amount of the estate tax liability are reduced as a result of the election. Accordingly, if no estate tax is due, alternate valuation cannot be elected.

In the past, it was permissible to make the election to increase the gross estate. If the total estate and (eventual) income taxes were thereby reduced, it made sense to make this election. Now the election can be made only under the circumstances specified in the preceding paragraph.

Why would we have to report the increase in value of the bonds as income? I thought you said that when a person dies, all of the property owned by that person's estate gets a stepped-up basis equal to the estate tax value of the property in the estate (usually date-of-death values or alternate valuation values if so elected).

That is the usual rule but the exception involves property known as *income in respect of a decedent*. The increase in the value of the bonds is considered to be income in respect of a decedent, and the law says that this type of property does not get a stepped-up basis but must be considered as ordinary income to the person eventually receiving it. Essentially, any income that the decedent had a right to receive, and could have received had death not occurred, is income in respect of a decedent.

For example, assume that at the time of my death, I was a practicing lawyer and unpaid bills owed me for legal services totaled $10,000. Had I lived and received payment of these bills, they would have represented income to me. Thus, when these outstanding bills are received by my estate, the estate will have to pay an income tax on the money. This will be required even though the right to the $10,000 may be valued in my estate at $10,000 (*without* the right to take into account that it is really worth less because of the obligation to pay income taxes thereon), and even though it will also be subject to estate tax. U.S. Series E Bonds income falls into this income category.

The law gives those who receive or report this type of income a deduction for the estate tax generated by the income. This is known as a Section 691 deduction (named after Section 691 of the Internal Revenue Code of 1986).

My husband died this year. He designated me as the sole beneficiary of his interest in his employer's qualified pension plan. As of the date of his death, his interest was valued at $500,000. Since the total value of his assets including the value of the pension plan was $900,000 and I inherited it all, are there any taxes to pay?

There are no federal estate taxes, but federal income tax will have to be paid. As mentioned earlier (on pages 171–73), your late husband's estate receives an unlimited marital deduction for property bequeathed to you. However, the proceeds of the pension plan would have been subject to the federal income tax had he lived to receive it. Therefore, the proceeds are subject to federal income tax when you receive it. (It is beyond the scope of this book to discuss your ability to defer receipt of the proceeds, except to call this possibility to your attention.)

This type of asset is another illustration of income in respect of a decedent. You should be aware of the possible availability for this asset of a $5,000 death benefit exclusion for income tax purposes.

My wife and I own a house as joint tenants. It is worth $90,000. I own life insurance policies that will pay my wife $250,000 on my death. I also own stocks and bonds worth $410,000. I wish to save the costs of having my estate administered. Therefore, I will have the stocks and bonds retitled to show my wife as joint owner with right of survivorship. On my death, all this property will automatically be owned by my wife. Is this a good idea?

No. You may have saved pennies on probate costs, but you have just cost your wife's estate an extra $53,215 in estate taxes. (When the estate is administered under court supervision, the personal representative is entitled to a fee. Since your wife will become the sole owner of all the assets, we will assume you will appoint her the personal representative. She will serve without a fee.)

To demonstrate the prior statement:

	COSTS AND FEES	
	WHEN NO PROBATE COURT SUPERVISION	WHEN THERE IS PROBATE COURT SUPERVISION
Total value of assets: $750,000 Additional costs to date compared with joint ownership of all assets	$ -0-	$ -0-
Approximate additional costs of filing fees of court, advertising, etc. (when there is probate) compared with joint ownership of all assets (when there is no probate)	-0-	700

	COSTS AND FEES	
	WHEN NO PROBATE COURT SUPERVISION	WHEN THERE IS PROBATE COURT SUPERVISION
Approximate legal fees by reason of work performed to probate will, file accountings in court, transfer title to stock to personal representative and eventually to wife	$ -0-	$2,000
Note: Federal and state estate tax returns will be required whether everything is disposed of as you suggest or by will. Therefore, the fee does not take this cost into account.		
Cost of husband's simple will to dispose of assets, if any, that might have been overlooked (approximation)	125	-0-
Cost of husband's complex will with residuary trust (approximation)	-0-	500
Gift taxes when you, the husband, retitle stocks in joint names	-0-	-0-
Cost of retitling stocks, assuming you do this work yourself	-0-	-0-

| | COSTS AND FEES | |
	WHEN NO PROBATE COURT SUPERVISION	WHEN THERE IS PROBATE COURT SUPERVISION
Federal estate taxes on your death, whether leaving property as you suggested or by complex will	$ -0-	$ -0-
Stock ownership passing to wife on husband's death, after registration during lifetime as joint owners with right of survivorship. Maryland inheritance tax. (*Note:* Because of the variation in state death tax laws, the Maryland tax rate and law have been used as an example. Under Maryland law, there is no inheritance tax in this situation.)	-0-	-0-
State inheritance tax when transfer is under will ($100,000 is exempt)	-0-	3,100
	$125	$6,300
Additional total expenses, fees, and taxes when property is left to wife under will as compared with leaving all property outside of will ($6,300 minus $125)		$6,175

When your wife dies (assuming there is no change in values of these assets—they could go up as well as down), her estate's federal estate taxes will be calculated as follows:

Property acquired on husband's death	$750,000
Less expenses, fees, and taxes (approximate)	(6,175)
Taxable estate	$743,825

(This assumes that there will be no legal fees, etc., on your wife's death. While there will obviously be some, which would reduce the amount subject to tax, this simplifies the illustration.)

Tentative tax	$246,015	
Less unified credit	(192,800)	
Net tax		$53,215

A properly prepared will could save this $53,215. How can this be done? Your will should provide that $425,000 of your estate is left to your wife outright, including the house and insurance proceeds, and the balance (or $325,000) is left in trust for her benefit during her lifetime.

The $325,000 that your trustees hold in trust for your wife will *not* be subject to estate tax on her later death. However, in order to accomplish this, it is necessary that some of your assets not be jointly owned with your wife. Remember that when a person owns jointly owned property, on the death of the first joint owner, he or she cannot dispose of it under his or her will. On such death, the surviving joint owner will automatically become the sole owner.

On your death, your wife will automatically become the sole owner of the house, and the executor (or personal representative) of your estate (who will be your wife) will distribute to your wife $335,000 worth of stock. The trustee (who could be your wife) under your will shall receive the insurance proceeds plus $75,000 of the stock.

The terms of the trust will provide that your wife receive all of the income from the trust property (here, $325,000) for life, *plus* whatever she will need for her health, education, maintenance, or support, *plus* an additional $5,000 per year (or 5 percent of the value of the trust, if higher) if she so desires it. Your wife will have virtually 100 percent economic control of this trust.

This trust is known as a *residuary trust* (*residue* means what is left over). This trust will *not* be subject to federal or state estate taxes on your wife's death. Also, in this case, because of the value of property she individually owns, there will be no federal estate tax on your wife's estate.

A summary of all this is as follows:

	WHEN ALL PROPERTY IS JOINTLY OWNED	WHEN APPROXIMATELY ONE-HALF OF YOUR PROPERTY IS LEFT IN A RESIDUARY TRUST UNDER YOUR WILL
Expenses, fees, and taxes on husband's death	$ 125	$6,175
Estate taxes on wife's death	53,215	-0-
	$53,340	$6,175

The total loss by having all your property owned jointly will therefore be $47,165 ($53,340 minus $6,175).

I am a citizen of Spain. My employer in Spain sent me on a short-term assignment to the United States to conduct business. I now live in New York. If I die while living in New York, will my property be subject to the federal estate tax law?

It depends on whether or not you are really a resident of the United States. A person establishes a residence in a certain place by living there, even for a short period of time, with no present intention of moving away.

In your case, you probably have a visa that permits you to remain in the United States for a short time. Considering this fact and the fact that you were sent to the United States by your employer for a short-term assignment, you are probably not a resident of New York or the United States.

Even if you are a resident of the United States, special rules apply to citizens of certain countries because of treaties entered into between the United States and these countries. The countries are Australia, Austria, Canada, Denmark, Finland, France, Germany, Greece, Ireland, Italy, Japan, Netherlands, Norway, South Africa, Sweden, Switzerland, and the United Kingdom.

Please explain the difference between estate tax deductions and estate tax credits.

Tax-Saving Suggestion

At the time of my husband's death last year, he was the sole owner of a 150-acre farm. My husband farmed the land for the last 20 years. Ten years ago, a shopping center was built next to this farm. When he died, I became the farm's sole owner. The farmland is now worth $5,000 an acre, or $750,000. Both my children and I wish to continue to farm this land. To pay the estate taxes on my death, we would be forced to sell the land to raise the cash to pay estate taxes. I am heartbroken about this. Can you suggest anything?

Under present federal law, Congress has given every estate the option to value the land not on the basis of its fair market value (in this case, $5,000 an acre), but at its value as a farm for farming purposes. As farmland, the value of this 150-acre tract would be $1,000 per acre, or $150,000.

When you die, your estate can elect to value the land as farmland. The law further provides that when reducing the value of farmland, the value may not be reduced by more than $750,000. By taking advantage of the provisions of this law, you can eliminate or substantially reduce all estate taxes on your death, thereby enabling your children to farm the land without having to sell off any land to pay estate taxes.

This rule enables one to secure a lower valuation of property, and is also available for any real property located in the United States that is used in a trade or business. The provisions of this section are highly technical and require professional help in applying them. For example, special rules apply for nonresident U.S. citizens. It should be noted, though, that the law applies to any decedent who, at the time of death, is either a citizen or a resident of the United States.

Assume you die owning $800,000 in bank accounts, with your daughter named as the one who will receive the account balances on your death. The only expenses when you die are funeral expenses of $3,500, legal and accounting fees of $3,300, and debts you owed of $186,000. These items, totaling $192,800, are deductions from the $800,000, and your taxable estate will therefore be $607,200. (Note that deductions are made from your gross estate to arrive at the estate that is subject to estate tax; the estate subject to estate tax is called the taxable estate.) The tax on a taxable estate of $607,200 is $195,464 (without the credit).

If there were no deductions, the taxable estate would be $800,000. The estate tax on this amount, after the unified tax credit of $192,800, would be $75,000.

The deductions and credit are deliberately equal in this example. You will also note two things. First, deductions are subtractions from the gross estate to arrive at the amount that is subject to the estate tax. Second, a credit is a dollar-for-dollar offset of, or subtraction from, the tax that is due.

Comparing the estate tax of $195,464 (using deductions of $192,800) with the estate tax of $75,000 (using a credit of $192,800) demonstrates that a credit is far more valuable to a taxpayer than a deduction.

What are the most important estate tax credits?

1. The unified credit is $192,800 in 1987 and thereafter. This credit is available to all estates of citizens or residents of the United States. The exact amount of the credit for earlier years is shown in Appendix A.

2. A credit is given for death taxes paid to a state. In a few states, the state death taxes are higher than the amount of the credit allowed under federal law. In such cases, the credit is limited by federal law to the amount allowed by federal law.

3. A credit is given for the federal estate tax paid with respect to the transfer of property when a decedent dies prior to the decedent whose estate is being taxed now. For example, John's sister Mary dies in 1988 with an estate of $750,000. She leaves John her entire estate. The estate tax on her death is $55,500. John dies in 1989 with an estate of $850,000. John's estate will receive a credit of $55,500, the amount of estate tax generated by Mary's estate, because of the property transferred to John. If Mary dies more than two but less than four years before John, the credit will be reduced by 20 percent; for every additional two-year period, the credit will be reduced by an additional 20 percent until the credit disappears. If Mary dies more than 10 years before John, the credit will be zero.

4. A credit is given for death taxes paid to other countries. When a U.S. citizen or resident dies owning property in a foreign country, the U.S. federal estate tax is applied to all the property owned by the decedent—even to property in a foreign country. Most foreign countries will tax the property found within their territory. In this situation, the property will be taxed twice: once by the U.S. and once by the foreign country.

To alleviate the problem of having the same property taxed twice, our federal tax law allows a credit to estates of U.S. citizens or residents for any foreign death taxes paid.

Note: The foregoing rules contain certain restrictions, exceptions, and limitations that are beyond the scope of this book.

What are state death taxes?

In addition to the federal estate tax, every state imposes some form of death tax. The death tax is either an inheritance tax, an estate tax, or both.

The inheritance tax is imposed on the privilege of receiving property from a decedent at death, whereas an estate tax is imposed on the privilege of transferring property from a decedent at death. The practical differences between the two taxes are as follows:

Inheritance tax. The property subject to the tax is reduced by the state estate tax paid. Also, the rate of tax is based on the relationship of the heir to the decedent (a spouse or children pay the lowest rate).

Estate tax. The property subject to the tax is *not* reduced by the estate tax or the inheritance tax paid. Also, the rate of tax is based on the total amount subject to the tax and is not dependent on who inherits the property.

There are variations among the states (for this purpose, the District of Columbia is considered a state) as to what is taxed, the rate of tax, exemptions, and exclusions. What follows is therefore a general and broad overview of this subject.

The general rule is that a state imposes a death tax on all property, whether of a resident or nonresident, that is located in the state on the date of decedent's death and that passes to another on the death of a decedent. The technical legal way to describe the status of such property is to say that it has a *taxable situs* in the state.

Clearly, real estate (also called *real property*) is located in the state where the real estate exists. Accordingly, the taxable situs of real estate is always the state where the real estate is located. The rule with respect to personal property is more complicated and needs some explanation.

Personal property means property that is movable. There are two kinds of personal property, *tangible* and *intangible*. Personal property that can be felt or touched is tangible personal property. Jewelry, clothing, a stamp collection, automobiles, and paintings are examples of tangible personal property.

Tangible personal property would, in general, be subject to the death taxes of the state in which it is located. This is so because the taxable situs of tangible personal property is the place where the property is physically located at the time of decedent's death. However, this rule has some exceptions. For example, assume you were a Maryland resident and in connection with a six-week vacation trip abroad, you stayed at a Washington, D.C., hotel. You left all your jewelry with the hotel for safekeeping until your return—clearly a temporary arrangement. Were you to die abroad, the jewelry should not be taxed by the D.C. authorities, even though it was physically in the District of Columbia at the time of your death, but rather by Maryland.

Intangible personal property is property that cannot be felt or touched. Stock certificates, bonds, and promissory notes are considered to be intangible personal property. Though each asset is usually represented by a piece of paper and the paper can, of course, be felt, the paper is only evidence of a property interest. In the case of the stock certificate, the certificate is evidence of an ownership interest in a corporation.

Intangible personal property is considered to be located—to have a taxable situs—in the state where the decedent was a resident at the time of death. If a decedent was a resident of Maryland and owned a promissory note that was physically held for safekeeping by the decedent's Connecticut attorney, the value of the promissory note would be subject to death tax in Maryland. This is because the taxable situs of the note is considered to be in Maryland.

What is meant by the term *residence?* For most legal purposes, including death taxes, a residence is that place where a person is domiciled, and *domicile* is that place where one resides with the intent to make a fixed and permanent home. A person can have several residences but only one domicile. For example, you may have a residence in Florida (for the winter), a residence in northern Michigan (for the summer), and a residence in Pennsylvania. If your fixed and permanent home is in Pennsylvania, then Pennsylvania is your domicile, and for tax purposes that is your residence.

Sometimes it is not clear where a person's domicile is, and this is something the taxing authorities frequently have to determine. They may inquire where the decedent voted, where the automobiles were registered, where a safe-deposit box was maintained, where the children went to school, where checking and savings accounts were maintained, what state the decedent declared to be his or her residence in a will, and so on. In other words, they will look to see where the decedent's "roots" are.

Some states maintain that certain intangible property has a taxable situs and therefore should be taxed in their states, even when the decedent was a resident of another state. This could happen when the nonresident of the taxing state owns stock of a corporation that is incorporated in the state. For example, Utah exercises the power of taxation in this situation on the theory that because the corporation has incorporated there, the state has extended its legal protection over the corporation and therefore the property of the nonresident decedent has a taxable situs in Utah.

The same result occurs when a trust is created in a state by a nonresident with a trustee who is a resident of that state. In this situation, the state claims that the intangible property of a nonresident decedent should be taxed by it because the property has acquired a taxable situs in its state.

Even when a state has legal authority to impose a death tax upon intangible property of nonresidents because such property has acquired a taxable situs in its jurisdiction, its laws may exempt intangible personal property from taxation. This happens when the laws of the state that can impose a tax on the nonresident decedent's intangible personal property has a reciprocal exemption with the other state. As an example, Maryland law states that it will not tax such property of a resident of another state if the laws of the other state similarly exempt intangible personal property of Maryland residents.

When the laws of another state do tax intangible personal property of a non-resident decedent, there is really nothing the decedent's estate can do about it. Be aware of this possibility and that if the tax laws of another state do apply, it may be necessary for the estate's local attorney to seek the assistance of an attorney in the other state. Certainly, extra tax returns will be required and there may be delays and increased costs before property is transferred to the decedent's loved ones.

What is a state inheritance tax?

This tax is imposed on the privilege of receiving property from a decedent. Property can be "received" from a decedent even though the decedent did not own it at the time of his or her death. There are two broad categories of property that can be "received" from a decedent and that can be subject to inheritance tax.

Property owned by the decedent at the moment of death. For example, I own 100 shares of common stock (considered probate property) at the time of my death. I die and leave it to you by my will or I die without a will (intestate), and state law provides that you become the owner of this stock. In either of these cases, you

will have received the stock from me (the decedent).

Property that is not *owned by the decedent at the moment of death.* In this second category, you will find the same type of property that is subject to the federal estate tax. This statement is of necessity a general one, since there are variations among state laws. Property that falls into this category includes the following:

1. property in which the decedent had an interest as a joint tenant;
2. property that the decedent had transferred to someone in contemplation of death, or within one to three years before death (although federal law did away with the concept of gifts or transfers made in "contemplation of death," many states still adhere to that principle);
3. property the decedent controls or draws income from during lifetime, even after having transferred ownership;
4. property that the decedent transferred during lifetime while retaining the power to revoke the transfer; and
5. property over which the decedent had a general power of appointment (whether or not the decedent owned it at one time).

The power of the states to tax property for inheritance tax purposes is limited to property that has acquired a taxable situs in the state. This usually means real property (real estate) located in the state, tangible personal property physically located in the state, and intangible personal property of a resident of the state.

With respect to intangible personal property, the property's location does not matter, since the taxable situs of this type of property is the place where the decedent resides at the time of death. This does not mean that another state cannot tax such property when it finds that intangible personal property of a nonresident acquires a taxable situs in its state too.

Since inheritance taxes are imposed on the privilege of receiving property, the amount that is subject to tax is the net value of property actually received. Therefore, any debts to which the property is subject—estate taxes, mortgages, and costs of administering the property, such as commissions and legal and accounting fees—are subtracted from the gross value of such property.

Proceeds of life insurance that are paid to a named beneficiary other than the estate are exempted from inheritance taxes by most states. With rare exceptions, if a beneficiary of an insurance policy is not named, on the insured's death the insurance company will pay the proceeds to the estate of the insured. This will cause the insurance proceeds to be subject to an inheritance tax in many states.

Some states also exempt from an inheritance tax any type of property jointly owned by a husband and wife for which, on the death of the first one to die, the survivor becomes the sole owner. Property received by charitable and religious institutions is usually exempt, as is property received by a government agency.

The rate of tax that is applied depends on the relationship of the person who receives the property to the decedent. (Details of these variations are shown in Appendix C.) In general, the lowest rate is applied to the net amount received by a surviving spouse (husband or wife) of the decedent as well as by parents, grandparents, children, grandchildren, and more remote descendants. In some states, everyone else is taxed at the highest rates.

When a state imposes more than two rates, the next lowest rate is imposed on property received by brothers, sisters, nieces, nephews, and perhaps a spouse of any of them. The highest rate would be imposed on property received by all others.

What is a state estate tax?

The majority of states impose a state estate tax. This tax falls into two broad categories:

1. a state estate tax on "certain" property that also has a taxable situs in its state; in general, this "certain" property would be subject to state estate tax if federal law causes such property to be subject to federal estate tax; and
2. imposing a state estate tax only to the extent that any inheritance tax or state estate tax paid is less than the credit allowed by federal law for state death taxes paid; this type of tax is referred to as a *pickup tax*.

The first category needs no further comment. The second category can be explained by what follows. Under federal law, the estate tax is imposed on the total of the taxable estate and adjusted taxable gifts. When this figure is determined, the unified credit is then deducted from the total tax due. When the property subject to federal estate tax is $600,000 or less, the tentative tax is $192,800 or less. Because of the unified credit of $192,800 (since 1987), there will be no federal estate tax to pay.

However, where the federal estate tax is higher than $192,800, federal law gives each estate, in addition to the unified credit, an additional credit for death taxes paid to a state. The amount of the credit is set forth in a table provided by federal law. (This table is reproduced in Appendix B.)

In some states, it is possible for the amount of the inheritance or estate tax due the state to be less than the federal credit for death taxes paid to a state. When this occurs, every state imposes a state estate tax to make up the difference between its inheritance tax and this federal credit. In other words, the state estate tax becomes a "pickup" of the difference.

A simple illustration will explain this. Assume that while a resident of Maryland I die in 1993 owning a life insurance policy that pays $650,000. The beneficiary is my daughter, who receives this amount from the insurance company. Assume also that I never made any taxable gifts, I own cash (in bank accounts) totaling $30,000, and my debts amount to $30,000. For federal estate purposes, my taxable estate is:

Life insurance	$650,000
Cash	+30,000
	680,000

Less debts	(30,000)
Taxable estate	$650,000

Federal estate tax:

Tentative tax	$211,300	
Unified credit	(192,800)	
Federal estate tax		$ 18,500

My estate is also entitled to a credit for death taxes paid to Maryland. Federal law provides that this credit is $16,000. However, under Maryland law, my daughter will pay no inheritance tax on the $650,000 of life insurance proceeds she receives. This is because Maryland exempts from inheritance tax the life insurance proceeds she receives as a named beneficiary.

Since Maryland will now impose its estate tax based on the pickup rule, my estate will be required to pay a Maryland estate tax that is equal to the federal credit allowed my estate, or $16,000.

Had Maryland not imposed its estate tax, my estate would have had to pay the federal government $18,500. Because Maryland imposes the estate pickup tax, my estate will still pay only a total of $18,500, but instead of paying it all to the federal government, the payment will be as follows:

To the federal government	$ 2,500
To the Maryland government	+16,000
	$18,500

What difference does it make to you whether or not you save the inheritance tax, since there will be an estate tax and the actual payment of tax dollars will be the same? There *could* be a difference, as the following two examples will show.

First, assume you live in a state that has a death tax system similar to Maryland's, and the amount of your estate subject to federal estate tax is less than $650,000, say $550,000. Assume also that you die in 1994 and that the $550,000 represents proceeds of an insurance policy on your life.

If the policy proceeds are paid to your estate and your will leaves all your property to your niece, the $550,000 will be subject to inheritance tax. The inheritance tax on this property will be $55,000 (10 percent of $550,000). There will be no state estate tax, since there is no federal estate tax and no federal credit for state death taxes.

If the life insurance proceeds are paid directly to your niece, there will still be no federal estate tax and no inheritance tax (because state law exempts life insurance proceeds paid directly to a named beneficiary). There will be no state pickup estate tax because when there is no federal estate tax, no federal credit for state death tax is allowed or necessary.

Or, second, assume once again that you live in a state with a death tax system similar to Maryland's and that the amount of your taxable estate is $550,000. Assume this $550,000 represents proceeds of a life insurance policy on your life.

If the policy proceeds are paid to your estate and your will leaves all your property to your husband, the $550,000 will be subject to inheritance tax. The inheritance tax on this property will be $4,500 (1 percent of $550,000 minus an exemption to a spouse of $100,000). Assuming you die in 1994, under federal law your estate receives a marital deduction for the $545,500 ($550,000 minus $4,500) your husband inherits. There will be no federal estate tax and therefore no federal credit for state death taxes paid. In view of this, there will be no state pickup estate tax.

If the insurance proceeds are paid directly to your husband, there will still be no federal estate tax and no inheritance tax (because state law exempts life insurance proceeds paid directly to a named beneficiary). There will be no state pickup estate tax because when there is no federal estate tax, no federal credit for state death tax is allowed or necessary.

From these two examples, it is clear that it is sometimes advisable to avoid, if possible, being liable for the inheritance tax. In neither case was there a federal estate tax. In the first example, there was a state inheritance tax of $55,000 that could have been saved, and in the other case, there was a state inheritance tax of $4,500 that could have been saved.

Some states (e.g., New York) have a state estate tax that is patterned after federal law but that has lower rates. These states have an estate tax but not an inheritance tax. In five states, the state estate tax is payable regardless of any other death taxes that are due. These states also have a pickup estate tax. They also provide that if the regular state estate tax is less than the federal credit for state

Tax-Saving Suggestion

My husband died and left all of his property to me outright. I have more than enough assets owned by me in my own name plus enough income to support myself comfortably for the rest of my life. I understand that if I receive all of my husband's assets, that when I die his assets will be added to my assets and will be subject to a very high estate tax. Is it too late to do anything about this situation?

No. Under present federal law and the laws of most states, you have a right to disclaim all or part of your late husband's property (which is now owned by his estate).

Disclaim means that you forever give up an interest in this property. The act of disclaiming is sometimes called *renouncing*. Most states pattern their law on this subject after one of the Uniform laws known as the Uniform Disclaimer of Property Interests Acts.

What does this do? In the eyes of the law, disclaiming property is the same as dying before the other person. In this case, it is as though you died before your husband. Assume that your late husband's will provided that everything was to be left to you if you survived him, but that if you failed to survive him the

property would be left to those of your children who survived him. In this case, your children would inherit the property that you disclaimed. By your disclaiming, the situation is the same as if you did not survive your husband.

The advantages of disclaiming can be demonstrated by the following. Assume you own $550,000 and when your husband dies, he owns $150,000. For federal estate tax purposes, when your husband dies, there will be no estate tax at all.

If you inherit the $150,000, then on your death your total estate would amount to $700,000. The estate tax of an estate totaling $700,000 will be approximately $37,000. On the other hand, if you disclaim the entire $150,000 that you could have inherited under your husband's will, the estate tax on your death would be zero. As you can see, this will result in a savings of $37,000.

When you disclaim, you are essentially giving up any direct interest in the property that you are disclaiming. Therefore, you would usually lose the benefit of being able to use this money.

The law permitting you to disclaim (or renounce) an interest in property also allows you to enjoy the income from other property that you have not disclaimed. For example, assume that your husband's will left you an outright bequest of $125,000, and that he left the balance of his estate in trust. The trust provides that you are to receive the income from the trust for life. If you disclaim the $125,000, that is all you disclaim; you will still be entitled to the income from the trust. Also, the $125,000 may even be added to the trust property, depending, of course, on the language of the will. If the $125,000 is added to the trust property, you will be entitled to the income, even from the $125,000.

When a person disclaims an interest in another's property or estate, the law states that this act does not cause the property or estate to be considered a gift. (The one who disclaims never had any ownership interest in the property and, therefore, had nothing to give away.) Accordingly, it does not increase your gift or estate liability. For your disclaimer to be effective without causing any tax problems, the law says the disclaimer must be timely and must comply with certain other requirements of state and federal law.

In your case, federal law requires you to file your disclaimer within nine months of your husband's death. In addition, you must file the appropriate documents with the state court having jurisdiction over the estate. If these requirements are not strictly complied with, then the law says you acted as if you made a gift. If you make any taxable gifts, the amount of such gifts will be added to your taxable estate and will be subject to federal estate tax as though you owned the property in your own name. This is why it is important that there be strict compliance with the disclaimer rules.

death taxes, the difference between the state's regular estate tax and the amount of the credit allowed by federal law will still be imposed as a state pickup estate tax.

Note: Six states impose a gift tax. (See Appendix C.)

Please give me some examples of your experiences with disclaimers.

The examples are designed to highlight the possibilities, but you should be aware that this area of the law has many pitfalls.

Example 1   When the husband died, his wife and three children survived him. In his will, he left one-half of his estate to his wife as an outright bequest and the balance of his estate (the rest, residue, and remainder) was left in trust. The trust provided that his wife was to receive income for life plus whatever principal was needed for her health, support, and maintenance. Upon the wife's death, the trust was to be continued until the children attained certain specified ages.

Following the husband's death, it became apparent that his wife was already the owner of substantial assets. If she were to inherit one-half of her husband's estate (the part left to her outright), a substantial estate tax would be generated upon her death. The wife then disclaimed the bequest of one-half. What happened? Under the law, the wife was deemed to have died before the husband. Under the husband's will, since the wife did not survive him (as to the one-half—the disclaimed property), the disclaimed property was disposed of as part of the rest, residue, and remainder of his estate, and was left in trust. However, she did not disclaim any interest in the trust property. Accordingly, she was and is entitled to all the income from the trust property for her lifetime. In addition, if ever needed (an unlikely event), the trust principal could be invaded for her needs.

From the tax point of view, when the husband died his estate was required to pay a minor estate tax ($7,400). This tax was due because by disclaiming, there was no longer a marital deduction in his estate. When the wife disclaimed the one-half outright bequest to her, no gift or other transfer tax was occasioned by her. When the wife dies, the bequest she disclaimed (then valued at $310,000 and in 1993 valued at $720,000) will completely escape estate taxes. Had she not disclaimed, on her death the estate taxes on the disclaimed property would have been approximately $300,000.

There is really no substitute for outright ownership of property. You (the owner) are the boss and do not have to deal with trustees, lawyers, etc. However, when the taxable amount can be altered in your favor, as in this example, serious consideration should be given to the use of disclaimer.

Example 2 Under Maryland law, when an in-law inherits property there is a 10 percent inheritance tax to be paid. In this case, during her lifetime a woman had her lawyer prepare a new deed to her home. She wanted to avoid the probate process. The lawyer prepared a life estate deed giving her full power during her lifetime to sell, mortgage, or give away the property. However, if she still owned the property on her death, it was to be left to her daughter and son-in-law as joint tenants with right of survivorship.

When the woman died, the house was worth $150,000. The estate was modest in size and there was no federal estate tax. If disclaimer were not permitted, the Maryland inheritance tax would have been:

$75,000 (½ of $150,000) to daughter at 1% inheritance tax	$ 750
$75,000 (½ of $150,000) to son-in-law at 10% inheritance tax	+7,500
Total inheritance tax	$8,250

In this case, disclaimer was recommended. The son-in-law disclaimed his one-half interest. When he disclaimed, it was as though he died before his mother-in-law. Therefore, the daughter (his wife) inherited 100 percent of the house. Tax result:

$150,000 to daughter at 1% inheritance tax	$1,500

Net savings:

Without disclaimer	$8,250
With disclaimer	(1,500)
Total tax savings	$6,750

Shortly after filing and recording the disclaimer, the daughter had a new deed prepared showing the new owners to be herself and her husband as joint tenants with right of survivorship. The transfer by the daughter did not carry with it any transfer tax.

Example 3 The family consisted of husband, wife, and one son, mature but unmarried. Despite advice to the contrary, the husband's will left one-half of his estate to his wife as an outright bequest and the other one-half was left in the form of two equal trusts. The income from one trust was to be paid to the wife for life, and the income from the other trust was to be paid to the son for life. The son would receive principal from each trust upon his mother's death.

The problem was that because of the substantial size of the husband's estate (approximately $4 million), there would have been a present estate tax of approximately $153,000. The son disclaimed $400,000 of his interest in the trust. The disclaimed amount was inherited by his mother (the wife). The disclaimer increased the estate's marital deduction from $3 million to $3.4 million.

The transaction looks like this:

	WITHOUT DISCLAIMER	WITH DISCLAIMER
Gross estate	$4,000,000	$4,000,000
Marital deduction:		
one-half outright to wife	2,000,000	2,000,000
one-half in trust for wife (QTIP elected)	1,000,000	1,000,000
Property disclaimed by son and added to mother's bequest	-0-	400,000
	$3,000,000	$3,400,000
Taxable estate:		
Gross estate	$4,000,000	$4,000,000
Marital deduction	(3,000,000)	(3,400,000)
Taxable estate	$1,000,000	$ 600,000
Tentative tax	345,800	192,800

	WITHOUT DISCLAIMER	WITH DISCLAIMER
Unified credit	(192,800)	(192,800)
Net tax	$ 153,000	-0-

Did the son really give up and risk $400,000? No, because had he not disclaimed, his share of the trust would have borne the burden of the $153,000 tax. The son gave up $247,000.

In this estate, the relationship between mother and son was so good that as a practical matter the son really risked nothing. However, at worst, his economic loss could be $247,000. The time value of the disclaimer was that the mother has the use of the $153,000 for her lifetime. These examples, as well as the prior question, highlight the importance of *postmortem* estate planning and not just estate planning during lifetime. When and how you should disclaim are matters that should be discussed with your attorney.

What do you mean by postmortem estate planning?

The words *postmortem* mean after death. Accordingly, it is advisable for every estate to engage in postmortem tax and financial planning in light of the facts that are then evident. The use of disclaimers should then be considered in addition to a regular program of making gifts of cash and property, including life insurance. Consideration should also be given to retitling ownership of property, business interests, and partnerships, among other assets, to achieve the greatest transfer tax savings.

When my father died, he designated my brother and me as co–personal representatives of his estate. I am in the U.S. foreign service, do extensive travel, and am not readily available for consultation or for signing documents. Our lawyer suggested I renounce my right to serve as co–personal representative. In view of what you said about disclaimers and renunciation, I am reluctant to take our lawyer's advice. What do you think?

There is a substantial difference between renouncing your right to serve as co–personal representative and disclaiming (or renouncing) your right to inherit your share of your father's estate. If you renounce your right to serve as co–personal representative, it does not cause you to waive your right to your share of your father's estate. The only consequence of renouncing your right to serve is that your brother will serve as sole estate personal representative. Your right to inherit is *not* affected.

Bear in mind that if your brother does serve as sole personal representative, this will enable the estate to be administered more quickly and efficiently. Since the personal representative is entitled to a commission for serving as such, he should also sign a waiver of any entitlement to a commission, if you so desire. The personal representative also has the lawful authority to make decisions for the estate, such as selling or running a business, investing the estate funds, or selling or leasing estate assets. These additional factors should also be considered.

If you and your brother have a good relationship, renouncing your right to serve as co–personal representative seems advisable.

How would my inheritance be affected if I also disclaimed my property interest in my father's estate?

Assume your father's will left the bulk of his estate to "my issue surviving me, per stirpes." Your disclaimer will have the same legal effect as though you died a moment before your father. If you have children surviving your father and you, and you file a *qualified disclaimer,* your share of your father's estate will be inherited by your children, in equal shares.

If you have sufficient personal assets, you should consider filing a qualified disclaimer. If you do so, your children will inherit your share of your father's prop-

erty without the inheritance having any impact on your gift or estate taxes.

I notice that you used the phrase qualified disclaimer. Is there a difference between a qualified disclaimer and a disclaimer?

Yes. Virtually every state has enacted legislation that allows a legatee to disclaim his or her interest in an estate. As noted earlier, the effect is that the *disclaimant* (the person who disclaims) died a moment before the decedent whose property is to be distributed. Who inherits the property that is disclaimed depends on what state law provides. Unless the disclaimer is a *qualified* one, the legal tax effect is that the disclaimant has made a gift of the disclaimed property, and it could have an adverse tax effect on the donor (the disclaimant).

A qualified disclaimer is a disclaimer that complies with federal tax law. If the disclaimer is qualified, then the disclaimant will not have made a taxable gift. This is obviously desirable.

What is required in order to have a qualified disclaimer?

In general, and as required by Section 2518 of the Internal Revenue Code, an irrevocable and unqualified refusal to accept an interest in property but only if:

1. the refusal is in writing;
2. the writing is made (and delivered as required by law) within nine months of the later of the date when the trans-

fer creating the interest is made or when the disclaimant (the person who executes the disclaimer) attains age 21;

3. the disclaimant has not accepted the interest or any of its benefits; and

4. the property interest passes to someone other than the disclaimant without any direction on the part of the disclaimant.

What other advice do you have in connection with disclaimers?

1. Have your lawyer research the results of the disclaimer under your state's laws to find out who will receive the property that you have disclaimed. This will ensure that the property will benefit those closest and dearest to you.

The laws of your state may differ as to the availability of disclaimer under a will or disclaimer of intestate property. Also, your lawyer should consider if disclaimer must be of all or part of your potential inherited interest.

2. Ensure that the disclaimer is a qualified one. This is usually, but not always, the reason for disclaiming.

If you are not concerned with the tax effects of a disclaimer, then you could always do nothing initially, inherit your share, and later make gifts as you desire.

3. Ask your lawyer for a written opinion. The opinion should state:

1. that the disclaimer is effective under state law to accomplish the desired transfer;

2. who inherits the disclaimed property; and

3. the federal tax effects of your disclaimer (and state tax effects where they apply).

I have heard that Congress has imposed a tax called the *generation-skipping tax*. What is it?

Congress has stated that the purpose of federal estate and gift taxes is not only to raise revenue but to do so in a uniform manner, generation by generation. These policies, Congress stated, are frustrated when the imposition of transfer taxes (estate and gift) is deferred for very long intervals by the use of generation-skipping transfers, either outright or in trust.

To illustrate this, assume you are the parent, have no spouse, and have one son and two grandchildren. You bequeath your entire estate to a trust whose income is paid to your son for life and upon your son's death, the property left in trust is paid over to your grandchildren. Before the enactment of this federal tax imposing the generation-skipping (transfer) tax, the trust property would not be taxed as part of your son's estate.

Congress felt that this device was contrary to one of their policies of taxing transfers generation by generation. Though Congress felt that there are valid reasons to have trusts, from the tax point of view, the property that passes from one generation to successive generations in trust form is to be treated, for estate tax purposes, substantially the same as property that is transferred outright

Tax-Saving Suggestion

Because of the complexity and amount of the assets in my husband's estate, the legal, accounting, and appraisal fees and the other expenses of administering the estate amount to $15,000. Since these expenses are deductions from the gross estate, should the estate claim these deductions? Would this have the effect of reducing estate taxes?

Administration expenses can certainly reduce the amount of the gross estate and estate taxes. However, these expenses can be claimed as an estate income tax deduction instead of an estate tax deduction.

An estate is a separate taxpayer for income tax purposes. Therefore, when the estate has significant taxable income, to the extent it has available deductions offsetting such income, these deductions can be valuable. Beginning in 1988, the minimum estate tax rate for estates above $600,000 is 37 percent. For estates, any income below $5,500 is taxed at 31 percent or less; above $7,500 the rate is 39.6 percent. Therefore, when an estate is liable for a federal estate tax, it is important to claim any available deductions on the estate tax or estate income tax return, whichever will produce the lower total tax.

However, when the estate is not required to pay a federal estate tax, do not claim such deductions on the estate tax return. To do so is to waste them. While the general rule for individuals is that such deductions are only available to the extent that they exceed 2 percent of adjusted gross income, for estates there is no such limitation. Therefore, the full amount of these deductions would be available to offset estate income.

(Prior to the 1986 tax law changes, it would have been preferable to have claimed such expenses as income tax deductions even where a federal estate tax was imposed.)

from one generation to a successive generation.

The generation-skipping transfer tax imposes a tax on the property you left in trust for the benefit of your son (based on the prior illustration). This tax would be treated as though the property were owned by your son, taxed as part of his estate, and then transferred by your son to his children (your grandchildren). In other words, there would be a generation-by-generation tax on such property.

In addition, if you bypassed your son while he was still alive and left an outright bequest to one of his children (your grandchild), such a bequest is potentially also subject to the generation-skipping transfer tax.

The generation-skipping transfer tax is at a flat rate of 55 percent of the value of the property when transferred to the younger generation.

The tax is imposed in addition to any other taxes. However, there is available an exemption of up to $1 million for each person making generation-skipping transfers.

Be aware that a generation-skipping transfer only exists where there is a transfer to a beneficiary at least two generations younger than the transferor. Only transfers to grandchildren or younger generations are subject to tax. From a technical point of view, you should also be aware that there are only three events that trigger the tax—a taxable distribution, a taxable termination, or a direct skip. You are encouraged to discuss this matter with your lawyer.

Note: This tax must be paid from the property being transferred *unless* the will or trust provides otherwise. (The discussion of a similar rule applicable to QTIPs, on page 174, should be reviewed at this time.)

What is a tax on excess accumulations in qualified retirement plans?

It is a tax, imposed since 1987, that "increases" the estate tax. Even if there is no estate tax, this "increase" in estate tax is due. The tax is at the rate of 15 percent on any excess retirement accumulation. Excess retirement accumulation means:

The total value of the decedent's interest in retirement plans (qualified plans, IRAs, and tax-sheltered annuities)

minus

The present value of a single life annuity paying, each year, $150,000 or $112,500 indexed for inflation, whichever is higher. (As of 1993, the index brought the $112,500 figure to $144,551. For purposes of the following example, the $150,000 figure will be used.)

For example, I die owning an IRA worth $2.5 million. At the time of my death, I am 70 years of age. Assume that at the moment of my death, I had an annuity paying me $150,000 per year and the interest rate provided by federal law was then 8.6 percent.

The value of this hypothetical annuity would be $1,043,685. (This value is based on the federal tables, which take into account the theoretical life expectancy of a 70-year-old person—even though I am then dead. Thus, 6.9579 times $150,000 equals $1,043,685.)

The excess retirement accumulation and the "increase" in estate tax is:

1. My IRA valued at	$2,500,000
minus	
2. The value of the annuity	(1,043,685)
Excess accumulation	$1,456,315
Multiplied by the tax of	× 15%
Increase in estate tax	$ 218,447

You should be aware of two important features of this law. They are as follows:

1. If my wife is the beneficiary of the IRA, she may make an election so that my estate would not have to pay the 15 percent tax. If she does this, her estate would be considered as owning the IRA. Thus, taxes may be due from her estate. (Whether or not taxes would be due from her estate depends on the value of the IRA at the time of her death.)

2. If my estate pays the tax (the so-called increase in estate tax), this amount is considered a debt of my estate. As a debt, it is deductible from my gross estate to arrive at the calculation of my taxable estate.

If death taxes are due when I die, who is required to pay these taxes and what will be the source of the payment?

The law permits you to specify in your will or trust which of your assets shall bear the burden of death taxes. If you do not specify this or if you die without a will, then state and federal laws specify what is required.

Whatever the source of the funds, existing federal and state laws require that the executor or personal representative pay all taxes that are due from your assets before a beneficiary can receive any property from the estate. If there is no executor or personal representative, then such taxes must be paid by any trustee holding property subject to death taxes from such property; if there is no trustee, then any person in possession of prop-

erty subject to death taxes is required to pay the taxes from such property.

In the absence of specific directions in the will or trust, the majority of states provide as follows:

When a state imposes an inheritance tax, the amount of this tax comes directly from the property to be received by the beneficiary or legatee. For example, if I leave my daughter a bequest of $30,000 and the inheritance tax rate on this bequest in my state is 1 percent, then the $300 tax must be deducted from my daughter's $30,000. She will therefore receive $29,700.

Any federal and state estate taxes must be apportioned among all property subject to such tax (that is, in proportion to the benefits received). There is an exception to this rule. When property is left to someone who would be entitled to a deduction because of this bequest, then the property shall be exempt from having to share in paying the tax.

An example of this exception would be when property is left to a surviving spouse. Assume that the property subject to tax totals $800,000 and that the spouse is left $100,000. This $100,000 qualifies for a marital deduction, which will reduce the amount subject to estate tax to $700,000 ($800,000 minus $100,000). The net estate tax, after the unified credit, will be $37,000. But for this exception, the surviving spouse's share would have to pay one-eighth of the $37,000, or $4,625. Because of the exception, the entire $37,000 tax will have to be paid from the balance passing to others.

To illustrate the general rule, if the total amount subject to estate tax is

$886,665, the estate tax after the unified credit will be $108,800. Assume that the entire estate is left to three children, Abner, Bertha, and Charles. Abner and Bertha each are entitled to 40 percent and Charles to 20 percent. From each of Abner's and Bertha's shares, there shall be paid $43,520 (40 percent of $108,800) and from Charles's share $21,760 (20 percent of $108,800). The total tax will be paid as follows:

Abner's share	$ 43,520
Bertha's share	43,520
Charles's share	21,760
Total tax	$108,800

After taxes, each child will then inherit the following:

Abner ($354,666 minus $43,520)	$311,146
Bertha ($354,666 minus $43,520)	311,146
Charles ($177,333 minus $21,760)	155,573
Total inherited	$777,865
Total taxes paid	108,800
Total estate	$886,665

The following example is more complicated than the preceding one. In 1984, a father made a gift of $200,000 to one of his two sons. You will recall that in 1984 one could make gifts of up to $325,000 without causing any gift tax to occur, because the credit wiped out any tax. When the father died in 1989, he owned an additional $800,000. Since the gift tax is unified with the estate tax, the federal estate tax is computed as though the father died with $1 million. This results from adding the $800,000 the father owned at the time of his death to the $200,000 gift he made in 1984 (for this purpose, we are ignoring the annual exclusion of $10,000). The net tax on this estate would therefore be $153,000.

The apportionment rules (summarized on page 202) have been adopted in most of the states. The legislation is patterned after one of the uniform laws known as the Uniform Estate Tax Apportionment Act. This act provides that the estate tax is apportioned among all persons who inherit any interest in property included in the decedent's *taxable estate*. From a technical point of view, the taxable estate here is $800,000, even though the tax is applied against the entire $1 million. Assume that each son inherits one-half of the estate and the Apportionment Act applies because there is no tax clause in the will. Each share of the $800,000 will bear the burden of a tax of $76,500 (one-half of $153,000).

The result is that the $200,000 gift inherited by one son will not be reduced by any tax. This occurs because the entire burden of the tax is borne by the $800,000 taxable estate.

Note: The Apportionment Act does not deal with the situation illustrated above, simply because it does not address death taxes where gifts have been made. If a decedent wishes to vary the results illustrated above, this can be done by use of a tax-apportionment clause.

What is a tax-apportionment clause? Do you have any suggestions as to whether my will should contain one?

In the prior question and answer, it was noted that you may specify in your will or trust which assets shall bear the burden of death taxes. When you specifically provide the source for such payment, such direction is called a tax-apportionment clause.

If the father (in the last example of the prior question and answer) used a tax-apportionment clause, he could have varied the results shown. He could have provided for an allocation of the $153,000 tax in proportion to the amounts received by the children, whether at death or by gift. For example, the will could provide that the son who received $523,500 ($200,000 plus one-half of $800,000 minus one-half of $153,000) shall pay 61.8 percent of the tax of $153,000, or $94,554 ($523,500 divided by $847,000 [$1,000,000 minus $153,000] equals 61.8 percent).

Using a tax-apportionment clause where an inheritance tax is involved should also be considered. Such a clause may be desired by the decedent because the Apportionment Act also does not provide for apportionment of inheritance taxes (nor does it provide for apportionment of the generation-skipping transfer tax or the "increase" in estate tax by reason of excess accumulations in qualified plans).

The impact of a tax-apportionment clause in a state that has an inheritance tax may be demonstrated by the following example.

Assume a Maryland resident bequeaths the sum of $5,000 to her physician. Before he receives this $5,000, the applicable inheritance tax on this sum must be subtracted and paid over to the tax collector, because the theory of an inheritance tax is that the tax is imposed on the privilege of receiving the property. Thus, the one who bears the burden of this tax is the recipient. In Maryland, the tax rate on such a bequest to one who is not a spouse or descendant is at the rate of 10 percent. Therefore, the personal representative (executor) of the estate would have to withhold $500 from this bequest, and the physician would receive $4,500.

In many cases, the tax applicable to this $5,000 bequest would be paid by the estate. However, since the $500 tax that the estate will pay satisfies a legal obligation of the recipient, the $500 represents an additional bequest. Therefore, an additional 10 percent inheritance tax would be imposed on this $500. This tax is $50 (10 percent of $500). The tax on $50 is $5, the tax on $5 is $.50, and so on. If the typical tax clause were used, there would have to be set aside $5,555.55 for the beneficiary to receive $5,000. It is questionable whether the intent of the testator was to make a bequest not of $5,000 but of $5,555.55. You can see that this becomes a very complex matter; therefore, a tax-apportionment clause should only be used if you fully understand its effect.

In answer to your second question, the use of a tax clause is certainly appropriate where the client understands what the result will be. However, in the vast majority of cases, in the interests of simplicity and certainty, the matter should be left to state law.

I have put $15,000 in a bank account in my name as custodian under the Uniform Transfers to Minors Act. Have I made a gift, since I am the custodian as well as the donor?

Yes. A gift under the Uniform Transfers to Minors Act is a completed gift. The legal owner of the gifted property is the minor. The custodian is just that—a custodian.

The custodian manages the property for the benefit of the minor. If the donor dies while acting as custodian, the property will be included as part of the gross estate of the custodian.

To avoid having this property taxed as part of the gross estate, the spouse or other relative of the donor should serve as custodian.

I loaned my son $20,000 when he purchased a house. My son gave me a note due this year. I tore up the note and told him it was my Christmas gift to him. Have I made a gift subject to the gift tax?

Yes. Forgiveness of a debt is considered to be the making of a gift. The amount of the taxable gift will be $10,000, since the first $10,000 of a gift made to any person in any year is excluded. The $10,000 of taxable gifts will be added to your taxable estate for purposes of figuring the estate tax eventually due from your estate.

Is there something you can suggest to reduce the eventual estate tax in connection with the last transaction?

Yes. Assuming that you are married, you can forgive one-half of the debt at any time during the year, and immediately after the first of the year, you can forgive the other half. Also, you and your spouse can file split-gift tax returns. In this case, there will be no gift taxes to pay and no estate taxes to pay with respect to the $20,000 gift.

Why is this so? When you have forgiven one-half of the debt this year, you have made a gift of $10,000 (one-half of $20,000). However, since there is an annual exclusion of $10,000 per donee, the taxable gift will be zero. Forgiving the balance of the debt next year will also produce a taxable gift of zero next year.

In addition, the law provides that a husband and wife can elect to treat any gift made by one of them to a third party as though each made a gift of one-half the gift. This election is entirely optional. However, in order to do this, each spouse must be a U.S. citizen or resident, and a gift tax return must be filed showing that the split-gift treatment is desired (elected).

In the latter case, you and your husband should both file gift tax returns showing the split-gift treatment. When this is done, the gift of $20,000 will be treated as two $10,000 gifts. Each one of you will now be able to exclude the first $10,000 of gifts made to your son this year. Therefore, the taxable gifts for each of you will be zero. Next year you can repeat this procedure if you wish to transfer an additional $20,000.

My mother died in 1991. In her will she left my sister the family home, and she left my brother and me the balance of her estate. At the time she signed her will, the home was worth approximately $100,000 and the balance of her property was worth $200,000. About two years before my mother died, she sold the home for $100,000 and used the proceeds to live in a nursing home. She never changed her will. At the time of Mother's death, her estate was worth $240,000, which my brother and I are now legally entitled to. Our sister will receive nothing from Mother's estate. We feel this is unfair, and we wish to share the estate with our sister. Can we do so? Also, will we have made any gifts if we do so?

Your mother's wishes were that each of her three children would receive approximately $100,000 before taxes. However, because the house was sold and the will left property to two children, only you and your brother will inherit anything from your mother. Your sister will receive nothing.

Assuming that debts and administrative expenses would be approximately $30,000, this would leave $210,000 to be divided. You and your brother are each legally entitled to receive $105,000 (if we first deduct the estimated $30,000). If you choose to take less and divide the $210,000 three ways, thus providing $70,000 each, the law

says that you and your brother will each have made a taxable gift to your sister of $35,000.

What tax consequences are there if a taxable gift is made?

There are two consequences—one during lifetime and one at death. The lifetime consequence is that there may be gift taxes due when the gift is made; therefore, you lose the benefit of the use of these taxes during your lifetime. However, at death, the amount of the gift taxes as well as the taxable gifts usually reduce the eventual estate taxes. The reasons for this are explained in what follows.

Gift and estate taxes are unified. Even though you gave property away during your lifetime, the grand total of all taxable gifts made after 1976 (called *adjusted taxable gifts*) will be added to the amount of your taxable estate in figuring the estate tax. (Your taxable estate is your gross estate less deductions.) If the value of property rises, and if the gift were not made and the property were owned by the decedent as of date of death, the amount subject to tax would be the higher date-of-death value of the property still owned.

For example, assume I own a small parcel of land in Gainesville, Florida. I transfer it to my daughter as a gift at a time when the parcel is worth $100,000. With the $10,000 annual exclusion, I have made a taxable gift of $90,000. If, on the date of my death, I own another $500,000, the unified rate schedule (the estate tax) will be applied to a total of

$590,000. In addition, if the amount given away during lifetime causes gift taxes to be paid and if I live more than three years after making the gift, the gift taxes will reduce the amount of the gross estate, and this will therefore reduce the estate tax. Also, while gifts made during lifetime will be added to your taxable estate and on death be subject to tax, each annual gift will be reduced by the $10,000 annual exclusion.

On the other hand, assume I continue to own the parcel of land and on the date of my death it is worth $300,000. By adding this $300,000 to my other property worth $500,000, the total estate subject to the unified rate schedule (the estate tax) will be $800,000.

This example will demonstrate the savings when a gift has been made and when no gift has been made. Assume you are unmarried and have three children and one sister. In 1982 you made the following gifts:

To sister		$ 60,000
To each child, $80,000		+240,000
		$300,000
Less four annual exclusions		(40,000)
Taxable gifts		$260,000
Tentative tax	$74,200	
Unified credit (in 1982)	(62,800)	
Net gift tax		$ 11,400

Assume you die in 1993 and then own $488,600 ($500,000 less the gift tax of $11,400). On your death the estate tax will be as follows:

Taxable estate		$488,600
Adjusted taxable gifts		+260,000
Total amount subject to estate tax		$748,600
Tentative tax	$247,782	
Unified credit	(192,800)	
		$ 54,982
Less:		
Gift tax paid		(11,400)
Net estate tax		$ 43,582

Had you not made any gifts, the estate tax would be as follows:

Taxable estate		$800,000
Adjusted taxable gifts		-0-
Total amount subject to estate tax		$800,000
Tentative tax	$267,800	
Unified credit	(192,800)	
Net estate tax		$ 75,000

The total taxes paid are as follows:

	WHERE GIFTS MADE	WHERE NO GIFTS MADE
Gift tax	$11,400	$ -0-
Estate tax	+43,582	75,000
	$54,982	$75,000

The net tax saved is therefore $20,018. (In this case, you have lost the use of the $11,400 for the period between 1983—when the gift tax was due—and your death in 1993.)

After 1976, I gave my son $250,000 as a taxable gift. If this amount is added to my taxable estate for purposes of calculating the estate tax due, will it have the effect of taxing this property twice?

No. When the estate tax is calculated, the amount due is reduced by any gift taxes that have been paid. Therefore, there is no duplication of the gift and estate taxes. (This was demonstrated in the prior question and answer.)

I understand that when a person gives away a total of $610,000 or less to one person in 1987 or any year thereafter, and has never made previous taxable gifts, there will be no federal gift tax. Why is this so?

From $610,000 you are entitled to deduct $10,000, which is the amount of the annual exclusion. The balance of $600,000 is subject to the gift tax. The gift tax on $600,000 is $192,800. In 1987 and thereafter, the law allows every person a $192,800 credit against gift taxes. Since a tax credit is a dollar-for-dollar offset against the tax, when the tax is $192,800 and the credit is $192,800, there will be no gift tax due.

This credit became part of the law as of January 1, 1977. The amount of the credit has increased each year beginning in 1977, as follows:

YEAR	AMOUNT OF CREDIT	YEAR	AMOUNT OF CREDIT
1977	$30,000	1983	$ 79,300
1978	34,000	1984	96,300
1979	38,000	1985	121,800
1980	42,500	1986	155,800
1981	47,000	1987 and thereafter	
1982	62,800		192,800

Since several states impose a gift tax, you should consult with your accountant or lawyer as to the effect of such laws.

Is there a credit for estate tax purposes?

Yes, the credit is identical.

Since there are separate credits for gift and estate tax purposes, if I gave away, after 1976, gifts totaling $235,000 and I died in 1982 owning another $225,000, would there be gift or estate taxes to pay?

Yes. Though there is a separate credit for each type of tax, the mechanics of the interchange between the two taxes prevent your getting the practical effect of both credits.

For example, when a person dies in 1982 owning $225,000 (ignoring for this purpose any deductions), the taxable estate is $225,000. To this figure (the taxable estate of $225,000), add taxable gifts ($235,000 minus one $10,000 annual gift). Disregard the fact that because of the gift tax credit, there was no gift tax paid.

Total of taxable estate plus adjusted taxable gifts	$450,000
Tax on $450,000	$138,800

Estate tax credit (in 1982)	(62,800)
Net tax	$ 76,000

You will note that the amount subject to tax at death (the taxable estate) is added to the amount of adjusted taxable gifts (those made after 1976); that is, they are "unified" to arrive at the total amount against which the estate tax is calculated.

A friend of mine told me that he and his wife gave away $106,000 to their son in July 1976 and paid a total of $2,400 in gift taxes. If my friend dies before his wife, still owning the $650,000 he owns now, will there be estate taxes to pay either on his death or on the death of his wife?

You will note that your friends made the gift in July of 1976. At that time, the unified system of estate and gift taxation was not the law.

At that time, if a couple made no prior taxable gifts and agreed to split the gift, then each one made a gift of one-half. In your friends' case, each made a gift of $53,000. The law excluded the first $3,000 of each gift. In addition, the law permitted each person a lifetime specific exemption of $30,000. When you subtract $33,000 from the gift of $53,000 each of your friends made, then each one has made a taxable gift of $20,000. The tax on $20,000 made by each person was then $1,200, or a total of $2,400.

The present estate tax law does not unify gifts made *before* January 1, 1977, and therefore, when your friend dies owning $650,000, only those assets are relevant to see what the tax will be.

What happens if, on your friend's death in 1987 or later, he leaves $325,000 to his wife outright and leaves $325,000 in a trust whose assets will not be taxed on his wife's death? We start out with his gross estate, which will be $650,000. Since he will leave $325,000 to his wife outright, his estate will receive a marital deduction of $325,000. His taxable estate will therefore be the $325,000 left in trust.

The estate tax is figured on the total of the taxable estate (here $325,000) plus adjusted taxable gifts. Since adjusted taxable gifts only include such gifts made after December 31, 1976, such gifts here would be zero. The tax on $325,000 is $96,300. In 1987, the estate receives a credit of an amount equal to the tax but not to exceed $192,800. Since the credit is greater than the tax of $96,300, there will be no estate tax on his death.

When your friend's wife dies, the amount she receives outright, $325,000, is the only amount on which her estate will be taxed. Once again, the credit available to her estate is greater than the tax. Hence, there will be no tax due on her death.

The fact that one leaves property in trust does not always mean that the survivor's estate will not be taxed on it. Where, for example, the survivor has the right to invade principal, at the survivor's discretion, the trust property will be included in the survivor's taxable estate. It is clear, though, that if the only control your friend's wife had over the trust was the right to receive income, no part of the trust property would be taxed in her estate. Therefore, there will be no estate taxes to pay either by your friend's estate or by his wife's estate.

When and where must estate and gift tax returns be filed?

The answer to this question is found on the instructions to the estate tax return (Form 706) as well as on the instructions to the gift tax return (Form 709).

In general, an estate tax return must be filed when the gross estate (not taxable estate) plus adjusted taxable gifts exceeds the following:

YEAR OF DEATH	AMOUNT
1982	$225,000
1983	275,000
1984	325,000
1985	400,000
1986	500,000
1987 and thereafter	600,000

Also, in general, the gift tax return must be filed when the amount of the gift exceeds $10,000 in any year to any one person (even if no gift tax is due). (See also the discussion on pages 92–93 in Estates.)

What are the advantages and disadvantages of making gifts?

The disadvantages are as follows:

1. The one who makes the gift loses the benefit of having the use of the property that is transferred.
2. When a gift tax is paid, there is also a loss of use of the cash used to pay the tax.

The advantages are as follows:

1. The first $10,000 of gifts made to a donee each year is excluded from being considered part of the adjusted taxable gifts. Therefore, this amount will be subject neither to estate tax nor to gift tax.

For example, I make $10,000 gifts each year to each of my three children for 10 years and similar $10,000 gifts to each of my six grandchildren. I have then disposed of $90,000 each year ($10,000 times nine individuals) for 10 years, or a total of $900,000. If my wife agrees to split the gifts, I can double the amount of the gifts made each year. Thus, we have disposed of $1.8 million that will not be subject to gift tax or to estate tax.

2. The income generated by these gifts will belong to each donee (my children and grandchildren in the above example). The income tax on this income will presumably be taxed at a lower rate, since the income will be spread among a greater number of taxpayers. Also, since I can afford to make these gifts, I am presumably in a higher income tax bracket than the donees. Therefore, the total income tax impact on the family from the income generated by the gifted property will be less.

However, please note that under the Tax Reform Act of 1986, unearned income of a child under 14 years old will be taxed to the child at the parents' highest tax rate.

3. If I make a gift of land or stock, the value for gift tax purposes is the value of the property at the time I make the gift. If the property grows in value over the years, the growth in the property transferred by gift will not be subject to estate tax in my estate. For example, I own 10 acres of land now worth $12,000. If on the date of my death I still own the land and it is then worth $100,000, this $100,000 will be part of my taxable estate and taxed accordingly. However, if I have given the land to my son as a gift, even though the value of the land on the date of my death is $100,000, only the value of the land on the date of the gift, or $12,000, will be considered as an adjusted taxable gift. Therefore, only $12,000 will be added to my taxable estate for purposes of calculating the estate tax due on my death. (If I have made no other taxable gifts to my son that year, the $12,000 gift will, of course, be reduced by the annual $10,000 exclusion.)

Is it true that I can give away all my property during my lifetime and avoid the federal estate tax?

In general, no—but see the exception discussed in the last paragraph of this answer. Federal law states that if you make gifts of all your property, with certain exceptions, the value of the property will be subject to federal gift tax. The amount of the federal gift tax is equal to the federal estate tax. Therefore, with exceptions, the total tax will be the same whether one calls the tax an estate tax or a gift tax.

From the technical point of view, when you give away property during your lifetime (again with certain exceptions), the property is no longer part of your taxable estate. However, in calculating the estate tax, the taxable gifts made after December 31, 1976, are added to the taxable estate.

The exception occurs when gifts do not exceed $10,000 per donee per year (or $20,000 per donee per year where husband and wife file split-gift tax returns).

Please explain the basis for this exception.

By definition, any gifts (with a limited exception) totaling $10,000 or less to any person in any year are not considered part of your taxable gifts. Accordingly, they are simply not taxable gifts, and are not subject to gift tax nor are they added back to the gross estate for purposes of calculating the estate tax.

If what you say is correct, why do I have the impression that I can save on taxes by giving away property as gifts during my lifetime?

At one time your impression was correct. However, the change in the law that was made in 1976 changes that result. Before 1976, the law provided that the federal estate tax was imposed only on a taxable estate (plus some gifts made within three

years of death). Therefore, if you lived more than three years after making a gift, your taxable estate was reduced. The gift tax that was imposed was three-fourths of the estate tax rate—and even this was reduced by exempting from the gift tax the first $30,000 in gifts made by any person. At that time, you were able to accomplish an overall lowering of the tax by having, in effect, two taxpayers (one paying estate taxes and one paying gift taxes), and each tax was paid at the lowest brackets.

As of 1994, the law imposes the federal tax on the total of (1) your taxable estate, and (2) taxable gifts made after December 31, 1976 (taxable gifts made after December 31, 1976, are called adjusted taxable gifts).

Note: Even though you pay a gift tax now, you get credit toward the estate tax for the gift tax paid. The present system of taxation is known as the unified system of taxing estates and gifts.

I create an irrevocable trust. I retain the right to receive the income for life and provide that on my death the trust will be distributed to my two children. Have I made a gift?

Yes. Assuming you placed $100,000 in the trust, you have made a gift of what is left after your death. The value of the gift is based on tables published by the U.S. Treasury Department. These tables are incorporated as part of the regulations dealing with gift taxes.

Assuming you were age 60 when you transferred the money, the tables show the gift to be worth .27712 of the value of the property transferred. In this case, it would be $27,712. (Because you have retained the income for life, the entire property will also be includable in your gross estate.)

Note: Congress required that such valuations be based on a certain federal rate of interest. This rate is calculated monthly. The value shown in this illustration of .27712 is based on an assumed rate of 8.2 percent for the month when the gift has been made.

What if the trust provides that I may change the beneficiaries? Have I still made a gift?

No. The law states that when you reserve the right to change beneficiaries, the transfer is an incomplete one and there is no gift.

With my own money I purchased 2,000 shares of common stock, which cost $24,000. I have had the stock registered in my name and my son's name as joint tenants with right of survivorship. Have I made a gift?

Yes. Each joint tenant becomes the owner of one-half of the property, and as a joint tenant, you are the owner of $12,000 worth of stock. Therefore, you have made a gift of $12,000 (the cost of the stock, $24,000, less the amount you retain, $12,000). The taxable gift is therefore $2,000: $12,000 less the annual exclusion of $10,000.

What if the stock is purchased in my name and my husband's name as joint tenants with right of survivorship? Is there still a gift?

Yes, but, as in the case of the estate tax law, the gift tax law allows a marital deduction for all property one spouse transfers to his or her spouse as a gift. The deduction is the entire value of the gift.

As in the case of the estate tax marital deduction, the donor must be a U.S. citizen or resident to get the benefit of the gift tax marital deduction. If the donee spouse (the one to whom the gift is made) is not a U.S. citizen, there is no marital deduction. However, the annual exclusion is $100,000 (instead of $10,000).

Please summarize the rules about gifts made when title to property is taken as joint tenants (or tenants by the entirety).

A gift is made when any property is purchased and titled as joint tenants and when one party contributes more to the purchase price than a proportionate share of the ownership, except in the case of (1) property owned by husband and wife, both of whom are U.S. citizens; (2) bank accounts; and (3) U.S. Savings Bonds.

In general, you should bear in mind that when property is registered in joint names, the percentage of ownership of each joint owner is divided by the number of joint owners. For example, if there are two joint owners, then, as soon as stock is bought in two names, each person will own one-half.

If one of the new owners puts up $7,500 to buy stock and the other puts up $2,500 when the stock is registered in joint names, each will then end up owning $5,000 worth of stock. The one who put up the $7,500 made a gift of $2,500 to the other person.

Please explain the reason for the exceptions.

By definition, a gift will have been made for tax purposes only when the donor has given up the control and power to change the gift's disposition.

In the case of joint bank accounts, the donor can unilaterally regain the entire fund without the donee's consent. Therefore, there will be a gift, if at all, only when the noncontributing joint owner withdraws any money without the legal obligation to the other owner for the amounts withdrawn.

In the case of U.S. Savings Bonds, if ownership is registered as "A or B," the same principles apply as in the case of the joint bank account.

In the case of property owned by husband and wife, the explanation for U.S. citizens is that there is now (since January 1, 1982) an unlimited marital deduction. Any gifts made by wife to husband, or husband to wife, qualify for the marital deduction. Therefore, no gift tax will be due and no gift tax return will be required.

What is the rule for such property when the donee is not a U.S. citizen?

There is no taxable gift when the property involved is real property, but there would be a taxable gift when the property involved is personal property. The policy decision for this rule, effective June 30, 1989, is identical to that applicable to estate taxes, namely, the government is concerned about its ability to collect a transfer tax from a non–U.S. citizen donee spouse. Despite this concern, an exception was made in the case of real property.

For example, I purchase a house for $600,000 and the furnishings cost $250,000. My funds are used for both purchases, and there is no mortgage. I am a U.S. citizen. My wife is a citizen of France. Title to the house is in our names as tenants by the entireties. The contents are owned by us as joint tenants with right of survivorship.

What gifts have I made? From the nontax point of view, I have made a gift of one-half of $600,000, or $300,000, and one-half of $250,000, or $125,000. From the tax point of view, the gift of one-half of the real property, or $300,000, is not considered as a taxable gift simply because tax law so provides. The gift of one-half of the personal property, or $125,000, constitutes a taxable gift only to the extent of $25,000. Why? Because tax law provides for an exclusion of $100,000 per year. Since the total presumed gift is $125,000, deducting $100,000 leaves a balance of $25,000.

It has been argued that when the

transfer simply satisfies one's legal obligation of maintenance and support (considering the parties' standard of living), there has been no taxable gift at all. There is merit to this position.

In connection with gifts, one should also consider state law to determine what exceptions, exclusions, and variations from federal law they provide.

What do you consider the single most important aspect of estate planning?

The ability to convert estate assets into cash or cash equivalent for their true value with the least delay and cost.

Some case histories will help illustrate the importance of this matter. (All of these case histories are taken from actual cases but are disguised to protect the confidentiality of the clients.)

CASE HISTORY 1

This client conducted a stamp business from his home. The business was primarily mail order. Over the last 30 to 40 years, he accumulated a stamp inventory worth approximately $500,000 or more. When he died, his wife was appointed the executrix of his estate. Her problem was to convert the stamp collection into cash equal to its fair value. The husband earned a good living during his lifetime because he knew the stamp business. However, his wife had no idea of the true value of the collection. She did not know whether to auction off the collection or

sell it in one lot to one dealer; she did not even know what dealers or auctioneers to go to in order to realize the true value of the collection. Her husband had given no guidance whatsoever. He should have left detailed notes specifying names and addresses of dealers he trusted and suggesting how to sell the stamps (that is, in one lot, piecemeal, by auction, privately, by advertisement, etc.).

CASE HISTORY 2

Both husband and wife worked outside the home for the last several years of their life together. Each earned a good salary. They had surplus funds, which they had invested. The husband was the one who was active in purchasing securities for both of them. The titling of the securities varied; some were in his name, some in her name, and some in both names. All of the securities were purchased through discount brokers. The husband died first.

When an individual dies owning securities, the securities acquire a cost basis equal to the fair market value of the securities as of the decedent's date of death. However, with respect to securities owned individually by the wife, the basis of the securities for income tax purposes is their purchase price. With respect to jointly owned securities, only one-half of the securities acquire a new cost basis equal to their fair market value as of the decedent's date of death. The other half continues to have a cost basis equal to the purchase price.

The husband left few records showing the cost of the securities in the wife's name or of the jointly owned assets. There is a rule that when you can identify the securities by date, it is presumed that the cost of the securities is the price of the securities as of the date shown on the securities. Since the wife could not determine the historical cost, the problem became one of accurately identifying all the dates of dozens of securities. This effort consumed hours and hours of an attorney's time.

Obviously, the cost of this research was borne by the surviving wife. This cost and effort could have been avoided had the husband taken appropriate steps to identify the purchase price of each of the securities.

CASE HISTORY 3

The husband had developed a very successful construction business. Though he had a sizable staff, he had been primarily responsible for the financial success of the business. He died rather suddenly, leaving a wife who had very little knowledge of how the business should be run, not having worked in the business.

The husband had told her that the business was worth close to $1 million. However, when the husband died, she had absolutely no way of seeing to it that the business could be sold for its true potential. Perhaps the husband was exaggerating the value of the business. While the business kept operating with the help of one senior executive, for several years she did not receive any economic benefit from the business at all.

Considering the fact that the business was, according to the prior owner, worth somewhere in the neighborhood of $1 million, if the widow could have received the $1 million in cash and invested the funds, she would have had a yearly income of approximately $75,000 from the invested funds without touching principal.

The deceased husband could have helped to realize this potential for his wife and his family by leaving appropriate written instructions, including the value range of the business, the names and addresses of potential buyers, and information on how to go about selling the business, among other things.

CASE HISTORY 4

The deceased husband was in the restaurant business. The clientele of the restaurant was loyal, and the restaurant had an excellent reputation in the community. The restaurant was not one of the fancier downtown restaurants, but it attracted an areawide loyal following because of the quality of the food, the reasonable prices, the ambience and comfort, and so on.

The husband had advised his wife that the restaurant was worth in the neighborhood of $750,000. When he died, though the gross income of the restaurant dropped somewhat, it nonetheless maintained its pace. Fortunately, in this case, the wife knew something about the restaurant business and knew the sources of food and material supplies. She was able to keep the restaurant afloat. However, she was working practically for nothing, seven days a week, had bills to pay, a household to run, and was unable to realize the true economic benefit that could have come from selling the restaurant.

Why was this so? The husband had never advised the wife what she should do upon his death, who would be the broker to sell the business, and how she should go about selling it. In other words, the ability to realize the economic benefits from the restaurant was a secret that the husband took with him to the grave. Fortunately, in this case, the husband had appointed a close friend of the family as a coexecutor of the estate. This coexecutor was able to help, but not to the extent of getting the maximum value from the restaurant.

CASE HISTORY 5

A husband who died was survived by his wife and grown-up children. The husband was in the restaurant business with two of his brothers. He owned one-third of the stock of the corporation that owned the restaurant. The husband was able to earn a very good living for many years, since each of the brothers took one-third of the economic benefits from the business in the form of a salary. However, when this brother died, the surviving two brothers, who had never liked the surviving widow, brought in their children to take the place of the deceased brother, paying their salaries with what the brother had been receiving. The widow was shut out of the operation of the restaurant.

What could the surviving wife have done? If the husband had a contract that required the corporation or his two brothers to buy his stock, or if he made an agreement providing that the salary he was receiving at the time of his death would be paid to his wife for another 10 years, he would have protected his family and his economic interest in the restaurant. As it turns out, a lot of litigation ensued, all to the detriment of the surviving spouse.

CASE HISTORY 6

This decedent had purchased life insurance from a close friend and insurance broker many years earlier. The insurance broker had kept in touch with the decedent during his lifetime, and there was both a business and a social relationship between them. Shortly before the husband died, the insurance broker retired and moved to another state. The husband had a substantial amount of insurance and left his wife as the beneficiary. When the husband died, there was no one whom the wife trusted at the insurance agency or the insurance company to give the surviving spouse advice about what to do with the insurance policies.

Should she receive the proceeds in a lump sum? Where should she invest it? Should she leave the proceeds with the company and get interest from the policies? This situation was complicated by the fact that several of the policies were part of a qualified pension plan. Should the widow collect an annuity now from the policies or wait for several years? No one at the agency was receiving any economic incentive to help the widow, and no one did.

Had the husband prepared notes and advice to the widow, she would have known who to consult and how to get the best value from the policies.

Note: The asset update in Appendix G is designed to show you what is needed to ensure that your loved ones will receive the greatest economic potential from your assets.

All of these complex rules convince me that I should seek professional assistance. You have not indicated what a lawyer would charge to plan an estate or to counsel with respect to some of the items you mentioned. Would you please discuss this?

In general, fees vary from lawyer to lawyer and from region to region. In the Baltimore area, hourly fees (as of January 1994) ranged generally from $125 to $250 for the experienced lawyer. Obviously, there are those who charge less and those who charge more. You should always inquire about the charges.

If a client wishes a complex will with trust clauses, the time necessary to plan and draft the instrument will be greater than for the simple will. The time necessary for the lawyer to learn all the financial facts, the family history, and the wishes of the client may vary from one hour to five or more hours. The time necessary to prepare the simple will should be one hour or less.

Time will necessarily be spent reviewing other documents such as corporate records, pension plan provisions, insurance policies, land records or deeds, income tax returns, and registration of passbooks. It may be important to learn who supplied the cash to purchase jointly owned assets (a residence, land, a business, or stocks). The lawyer may want to review prior gift tax returns.

It may be appropriate for the lawyer to prepare additional documents such as a stockholder's agreement, partnership agreement, trust agreements, and memoranda of facts. It may be necessary to retitle property.

At the first meeting, after learning some of the facts, the lawyer can be in a position to give an estimate of the total cost. Frequently, the lawyer will also need to consult with one or more of the following: client's accountant, insurance agent, pension consultant, trust officer.

When a person has a potentially taxable estate, the portion of legal fees paid for estate planning that is allocable to tax advice and services is currently (1994) partially deductible for income tax purposes.

APPENDIX A

Unified Rate Schedule Imposed by Federal Law

(For persons dying January 1, 1977, and thereafter and for gifts made January 1, 1977, and thereafter)

CALCULATING THE NET FEDERAL ESTATE TAX

1. Figure total gross estate.
2. Deduct debts, expenses, and deductions.
3. Subtract item 2 from item 1 (the result is called the taxable estate).
4. Add adjusted taxable gifts (all taxable gifts made on or after January 1, 1977) to taxable estate.
5. Apply the Unified Rate Schedule to the sum total of item 4 (the taxable estate plus adjusted taxable gifts). The amount arrived at will be the tentative tax.
6. Subtract from the tentative tax any federal tax imposed by reason of gifts made after 1976 (using the current rate schedule). Then subtract (a) the unified credit, (b) the credit for state death taxes paid (see Appendix B), and (c) other credits (such as for foreign death taxes paid).

7. The net amount, after subtracting item 6 from item 5, will be the federal estate tax due.

Note: The estate may also be liable for two additional taxes. The first one is a generation-skipping transfer tax. (This tax is explained on pages 199–201.) The second tax is imposed on excess accumulations in qualified retirement plans, including IRAs. (This tax is explained on pages 201–202.) The total of (1) the net estate tax, (2) the generation-skipping transfer tax, and (3) the tax on excess accumulations in qualified retirement plans (including IRAs) constitutes the total transfer taxes due the federal government.

CALCULATING THE NET FEDERAL GIFT TAX

1. Figure total taxable gifts (those made since June 7, 1932), including gifts

made this year, by subtracting from gross gifts (a) the annual exclusion (now $10,000) and (b) the lifetime specific exemption where gifts were made prior to 1977.

2. Apply the Unified Rate Schedule to the total amount of item 1.
3. Apply the Unified Rate Schedule to the total taxable gifts, excluding gifts made this year.
4. Subtract the amount in item 3 from the amount in item 2. This amount will be the tentative tax.
5. Subtract from the unified credit any such credit used in prior years (since 1977) plus 20 percent of any lifetime specific exemption used for gifts made after September 8, 1976, and before January 1, 1977.
6. Subtract the amount in item 5 from the amount in item 4. This amount is the net federal gift tax due for this year.

Note: If a generation-skipping transfer has been made by an individual (donor) during donor's lifetime, donor must report the transfer on donor's gift tax return (Form 709). If the transfer is subject to the generation-skipping transfer tax, such tax must be paid by donor at the time the return is due.

UNIFIED CREDIT

YEAR OF DEATH OR TRANSFER	AMOUNT OF CREDIT
1977	$30,000
1978	34,000
1979	38,000
1980	42,500
1981	47,000
1982	62,800
1983	79,300
1984	96,300
1985	121,800
1986	155,800
1987 and thereafter	192,800

UNIFIED RATE SCHEDULE

A. TAXABLE AMOUNT OVER	B. TAXABLE AMOUNT NOT OVER	C. TAX ON AMOUNT IN COL. A	D. RATE OF TAX ON EXCESS OVER AMOUNT IN COL. A (%)
0	$ 10,000	0	18
$ 10,000	20,000	$ 1,800	20
20,000	40,000	3,800	22
40,000	60,000	8,200	24
60,000	80,000	13,000	26
80,000	100,000	18,200	28

UNIFIED RATE SCHEDULE (Cont.)

A. TAXABLE AMOUNT OVER	B. TAXABLE AMOUNT NOT OVER	C. TAX ON AMOUNT IN COL. A	D. RATE OF TAX ON EXCESS OVER AMOUNT IN COL. A (%)
100,000	150,000	23,800	30
150,000	250,000	38,800	32
250,000	500,000	70,800	34
500,000	750,000	155,800	37
750,000	1,000,000	248,300	39
1,000,000	1,250,000	345,800	41
1,250,000	1,500,000	448,300	43
1,500,000	2,000,000	555,800	45
2,000,000	2,500,000	780,800	49
2,500,000	3,000,000	1,025,800	53
3,000,000	—	1,290,800	55

Note: An additional 5 percent tax is imposed on taxable amounts of $10,000,001 to $21,040,000.

Appendix B

Credit for State Death Taxes

The credit is only available to the extent that state death taxes are actually paid to a state.

A. TAXABLE AMOUNT EQUAL TO OR OVER	B. TAXABLE AMOUNT NOT OVER	C. CREDIT ON AMOUNT IN COL. A	D. RATE OF CREDIT ON EXCESS OVER AMOUNT IN COL. A (%)
$ 100,000	$ 150,000	0	0.8
150,000	200,000	$ 400	1.6
200,000	300,000	1,200	2.4
300,000	500,000	3,600	3.2
500,000	700,000	10,000	4.0
700,000	900,000	18,000	4.8
900,000	1,100,000	27,600	5.6
1,100,000	1,600,000	38,800	6.4
1,600,000	2,100,000	70,800	7.2
2,100,000	2,600,000	106,800	8.0
2,600,000	3,100,000	146,800	8.8
3,100,000	3,600,000	190,800	9.6
3,600,000	4,100,000	238,800	10.4
4,100,000	5,100,000	290,800	11.2
5,100,000	6,100,000	402,800	12.0
6,100,000	7,100,000	522,800	12.8
7,100,000	8,100,000	650,800	13.6
8,100,000	9,100,000	786,800	14.4
9,100,000	10,100,000	930,800	15.2
10,100,000	—	1,082,800	16.0

Appendix C

Death Taxes Imposed, by State

The listings that follow are intended to serve as a guide only and are not intended to be a complete statement of the applicable tax laws. For example, the listings do not reflect all available deductions (for charities, marital deduction—except where noted—gift taxes paid), nor do they reflect exclusions or exempt property such as life insurance proceeds, government benefits, benefits from qualified plans, or community property laws. Some states also impose a generation-skipping tax.

Not all states define *child* in the same way. Some states include an adopted child, a stepchild, children of an adopted child, and so on, in their definition. The applicability of the tax to property of a nonresident decedent is also not shown in this table.

Note: The laws with respect to rates, exemptions, etc., may have changed since the date this list was compiled (January 1993).

ALABAMA

Inheritance Tax: None

Estate Tax: Equal to federal credit for state death taxes

Gift Tax: None

ALASKA

Inheritance Tax: None

Estate Tax: Equal to federal credit for state death taxes

Gift Tax: None

ARIZONA

Inheritance Tax: None

Estate Tax: Equal to federal credit for state death taxes

Gift Tax: None

ARKANSAS

Inheritance Tax: None

Estate Tax: Equal to federal credit for state death taxes

Gift Tax: None

CALIFORNIA

Inheritance Tax: None

Estate Tax: Equal to federal credit for state death taxes

Gift Tax: None

COLORADO

Inheritance Tax: None

Estate Tax: Equal to federal credit for state death taxes

Gift Tax: None

CONNECTICUT

Inheritance Tax (called Succession and Transfer Tax):
Class AA beneficiary: Spouse (all exempt)
Class A beneficiaries: Parent, grandparent, descendant
Class B beneficiaries: Spouse or surviving spouse of child, stepchild, brother and sister or their descendants
Class C beneficiaries: All others

AMOUNT RECEIVED BY EACH	CLASS A (%)	CLASS B (%)	CLASS C (%)
To $1,000	-0-	-0-	-0-
From $1,001 to $6,000	-0-	-0-	11.44
From $6,001 to $25,000	-0-	5.72	11.44
From $25,001 to $50,000	-0-	7.15	12.87
From $50,001 to $150,000	4.29	7.15	12.87
From $150,001 to $250,000	5.72	8.58	14.30
From $250,001 to $400,000	7.15	10.01	15.73
From $400,001 to $600,000	8.58	11.44	17.16
From $600,001 to $1,000,000	10.01	12.87	18.59
From $1,000,001 and over	11.44	14.30	20.02

(Exemptions are reflected in the tables and are available to the entire class and not to each beneficiary in each class.)

Estate Tax: Equal to federal credit for state death taxes. If an inheritance tax amounts to less than the maximum credit allowable under federal estate tax law, an additional tax is imposed by the state to make total death taxes collected by the state equal to the maximum allowable credit under federal estate tax law.

Gift Tax: Tax imposed

DELAWARE

Inheritance Tax:
Class A beneficiary: Spouse (if marital deduction not allowed)

Class B beneficiaries: Grandparent, parent, descendants, spouse or surviving spouse of child

Class C beneficiaries: Brother or sister or their descendants, aunt or uncle or their descendants

Class D beneficiaries: All others

AMOUNT RECEIVED BY EACH	CLASS A (%)	CLASS B (%)
To $25,000	-0-	-0-
From $25,001 to $50,000	-0-	2
From $50,001 to $70,000	-0-	3
From $70,001 to $75,000	2	3
From $75,001 to $100,000	2	4
From $100,001 to $200,000	3	5
From $200,001 and over	4	6

Note: A marital deduction, similar to federal law, is allowed for all property passing to a spouse.

AMOUNT RECEIVED BY EACH	CLASS C (%)	CLASS D (%)
To $1,000	-0-	-0-
From $1,001 to $5,000	-0-	10
From $5,001 to $25,000	5	10
From $25,001 to $50,000	6	12

AMOUNT RECEIVED BY EACH	CLASS C (%)	CLASS D (%)
From $50,001 to $100,000	7	14
From $100,001 to $150,000	8	16
From $150,001 to $200,000	9	16
From $200,001 and over	10	16

Estate Tax: Equal to federal credit for state death taxes. If an inheritance tax amounts to less than the maximum credit allowable under federal estate tax law, an additional tax is imposed by the state to make total death taxes collected by the state equal to the maximum allowable credit under federal estate tax law.

Gift Tax: Tax imposed

DISTRICT OF COLUMBIA

Inheritance Tax: None

Estate Tax: Equal to federal credit for state death taxes

Gift Tax: None

FLORIDA

Inheritance Tax: None

Estate Tax: Equal to federal credit for state death taxes

Gift Tax: None

GEORGIA

Inheritance Tax: None

Estate Tax: Equal to federal credit for state death taxes

Gift Tax: None

HAWAII

Inheritance Tax: None

Estate Tax: Equal to federal credit for state death taxes

Gift Tax: None

IDAHO

Inheritance Tax: None

Estate Tax: Equal to federal credit for state death taxes

Gift Tax: None

ILLINOIS

Inheritance Tax: None

Estate Tax: Equal to federal credit for state death taxes

Gift Tax: None

INDIANA

Inheritance Tax:
- Class A beneficiaries: Descendant and ancestor
- Class B beneficiaries: Brother and sister or their descendants, spouse, or surviving spouse of child

Class C beneficiaries: All others

AMOUNT RECEIVED BY EACH	CLASS A (%)
To $25,000	1
From $25,001 to $50,000	2
From $50,001 to $200,000	3
From $200,001 to $300,000	4
From $300,001 to $500,000	5
From $500,001 to $700,000	6
From $700,001 to $1,000,000	7
From $1,000,001 to $1,500,000	8
From $1,500,001 and over	10

	CLASS B (%)
To $100,000	7
From $100,001 to $500,000	10
From $500,001 to $1,000,000	12
From $1,000,001 and over	15

	CLASS C (%)
To $100,000	10
From $100,000 to $1,000,000	15
From $1,000,000 and over	20

(Exemptions: Spouse, all property; child, $5,000—but child under 21, $10,000; parent, $5,000; other lineals, $2,000; Class B beneficiaries, $500; Class C beneficiaries, $100. The rates shown are for amounts in excess of the exemptions.)

Estate Tax: Equal to federal credit for state death taxes. If an inheritance tax amounts to less than the maximum credit allowable under federal estate tax law, an additional tax is imposed by the state to make total death taxes collected by the state equal to the maximum allowable credit under federal estate tax law.

Gift Tax: None

IOWA

Inheritance Tax:

Class 1 beneficiaries: Spouse, parent, descendant

Class 2 beneficiaries: Brother and sister, spouse of child, stepchild

Class 3 beneficiaries: All others except those in classes 4–6

Class 4 beneficiaries: Societies, institutions, or associations of other states or countries for charitable, educational, religious, cemetery, or humane purposes; resident trustees for uses outside the state

Class 5 beneficiaries: Firm, corporation, or society organized for profit

Class 6 beneficiaries: Aliens or nonresidents of United States.

AMOUNT RECEIVED BY EACH	CLASS 1 (%)	CLASS 2 (%)	CLASS 3 (%)
To $5,000	1	5	10
From $5,001 to $12,500	2	5	10
From $12,501 to $25,000	3	6	10
From $25,001 to $50,000	4	7	10
From $50,001 to $75,000	5	7	12
From $75,001 to $100,000	6	8	12
From $100,001 to $150,000	7	9	15
From $150,001 and over	8	10	15

The tax on Class 4 beneficiaries is 10 percent; on Class 5 beneficiaries, 15 percent; on Class 6 beneficiaries, 20 percent, except if any are brothers and sisters or are within Class 1 (in which event the rate is 10 percent).

(Exemptions: Spouse, all property; child, $50,000; each parent, $15,000; lineal descendants other than child, $15,000. The rates shown are for amounts in excess of the exemptions.)

Estate Tax: Equal to federal credit for state death taxes. If an inheritance tax amounts to less than the maximum credit allowable under federal estate tax law, an additional tax is imposed by the state to make total death taxes collected by the state equal to the maximum allowable credit under federal estate tax law.

Gift Tax: None

KANSAS

Inheritance Tax:

Class B beneficiaries: Ancestor, descendant, stepparent and stepchild, surviving spouse of child

Class C beneficiaries: Brother and sister

Class D beneficiaries: All others

Note: The spouse was formerly the Class A beneficiary. There is no longer a Class A beneficiary, since all property passing to a spouse is exempt.

AMOUNT RECEIVED BY EACH	CLASS B (%)
To $30,000	-0-
From $30,001 to $55,000	1.0
From $55,001 to $80,000	2.0
From $80,001 to $130,000	3.0
From $130,001 to $530,000	4.0
From $530,001 and over	5.0
	CLASS C (%)
To $5,000	-0-
From $5,001 to $30,000	3.0
From $30,001 to $55,000	5.0
From $55,001 to $105,000	7.5
From $105,001 to $505,000	10.0
From $505,001 and over	12.5
	CLASS D (%)
To $100,000	10
From $100,001 to $200,000	12
From $200,001 and over	15

Estate Tax: Equal to federal credit for state death taxes. If an inheritance tax amounts to less than the maximum credit allowable under federal estate tax law, an additional tax is imposed by the state to make total death taxes collected by the state equal to the maximum allowable credit under federal estate tax law.

Gift Tax: None

KENTUCKY

Inheritance Tax:

Class A beneficiaries: Spouse, minor child or mentally disabled child, other children, stepchild, stepchild's child, grandchild, parent

Class B beneficiaries: Brother or sister, nephew or niece, aunt, uncle, spouse of child

Class C beneficiaries: All others

AMOUNT RECEIVED BY EACH	CLASS A (%)	CLASS B (%)	CLASS C (%)
To $10,000	2	4	6
From $10,001 to $20,000	2	5	8
From $20,001 to $30,000	3	6	10
From $30,001 to $45,000	4	8	12
From $45,001 to $60,000	5	10	14
From $60,001 to $100,000	6	12	16
From $100,001 to $200,000	7	14	16
From $200,001 to $500,000	8	16	16
From $500,001 and over	10	16	16

(Exemptions: Spouse, all property; minor or mentally disabled child, $20,000; all other Class A beneficiaries, $5,000; Class B beneficiaries, $1,000; Class C beneficiaries, $500. The rates shown are for amounts in excess of the exemptions.)

Estate Tax: Equal to federal credit for state death taxes. If an inheritance tax amounts to less than the maximum credit allowable under federal estate tax law, an additional tax is imposed by the state to make total death taxes collected by the state equal to the maximum allowable credit under federal estate tax law.

Gift Tax: None

LOUISIANA

Inheritance Tax:

Class 1 beneficiaries: Spouse, direct descendant by blood or affinity, and direct ascendant

Class 2 beneficiaries: Collateral relation, including brother, sister, nephew and niece by affinity

Class 3 beneficiaries: State of Louisiana or political subdivision

Class 4 beneficiaries: All others

AMOUNT RECEIVED BY EACH	CLASS 1 (%)	CLASS 2 (%)	CLASS 4 (%)
To $5,000	2	5	5
From $5,001 to $20,000	2	5	10
From $20,001 and over	3	7	10

(Exemptions: Spouse, all property; Class 1 beneficiary, $25,000; Class 2 beneficiary, $1,000; Class 3 beneficiary, all property; Class 4 beneficiary, $500. The rates shown are for amounts in excess of the exemptions.)

Estate Tax: Equal to federal credit for state death taxes. If an inheritance tax amounts to less than the maximum credit allowable under federal estate tax law, an additional tax is imposed by the state to make total death taxes collected by the state equal to the maximum allowable credit under federal estate tax law.

Gift Tax: Tax imposed

MAINE

Inheritance Tax: None

Estate Tax: Equal to federal credit for state death taxes

Gift Tax: None

MARYLAND

Inheritance Tax:

Class 1 beneficiaries: Parent, stepparent, spouse, child, stepchild, descendant

Class 2 beneficiaries: All others

AMOUNT RECEIVED BY EACH	CLASS 1 (%)	CLASS 2 (%)
Any amount	1	10

(Exemptions: Spouse, all jointly owned property plus all real property and $100,000 of other property; any share that does not exceed $150; spouse of descendant, first $2,000 of jointly owned savings accounts taxed at 1 percent; life insurance received by trust or named beneficiary.)

Estate Tax: Equal to federal credit for state death taxes. If an inheritance tax amounts to less than the maximum credit allowable under federal estate tax law, an additional tax is imposed by the state to make total death taxes collected by the state equal to the maximum allowable credit under federal estate tax law.

Gift Tax: None

MASSACHUSETTS

Inheritance Tax: None

Estate Tax:

AMOUNT OF TAXABLE ESTATE	RATE (%)
To $50,000	5
From $50,001 to $100,000	7
From $100,001 to $200,000	9
From $200,001 to $400,000	10
From $400,001 to $600,000	11
From $600,001 to $800,000	12
From $800,001 to $1,000,000	13
From $1,000,001 to $2,000,000	14
From $2,000,001 to $4,000,000	15
from $4,000,001 and over	16

If the estate tax amounts to less than the maximum credit allowable under federal estate tax law, the estate tax shall be increased to equal such maximum credit.

(Exemptions: If estate is $200,000 or less, no tax. If estate is greater than $200,000, credit is lesser of $1,500 or tax.)

Note: A marital deduction, similar to federal law, is allowed for property passing to a spouse, but not to exceed 50 percent of the Massachusetts adjusted gross estate. However, effective January 1, 1994, this limitation is removed; tax may not be greater than 20 percent of amount by which net estate exceeds $200,000. Effective January 1, 1997, the above-scheduled estate tax is repealed and replaced by an estate tax equal to the federal credit for state death taxes. Until then, the exemptions from the above schedule will be: effective January 1, 1993, $300,000; January 1, 1994, $400,000; January 1, 1995, $500,000; January 1, 1996, $600,000.

Gift Tax: None

MICHIGAN

Inheritance Tax:

　　Class 1 beneficiaries: Spouse, grandparent, parent, child, brother, sister, spouse of son or daughter, descendant

　　Class 2 beneficiaries: All others

AMOUNT RECEIVED BY EACH	CLASS 1 (%)	CLASS 2 (%)
To $50,000	2	12
From $50,001 to $250,000	4	14
From $250,001 to $500,000	7	14
From $500,001 to $750,000	8	17
From $750,001 and over	10	17

A tax of one-half of 1 percent is added to the inheritance tax and the estate tax if applicable.

(Exemptions: Spouse, all property; all other Class 1 beneficiaries, $10,000. The rates shown are for amounts in excess of the exemptions.)

Estate Tax: Equal to federal credit for state death taxes. If an inheritance tax amounts to less than the maximum credit allowable under federal estate tax law, an additional tax is imposed by the state to make total death taxes collected by the state equal to the maximum allowable credit under federal estate tax law.

Gift Tax: None

MINNESOTA

Inheritance Tax: None

Estate Tax: Equal to federal credit for state death taxes

Gift Tax: None

MISSISSIPPI

Inheritance Tax: None

Estate Tax:

AMOUNT OF TAXABLE ESTATE	RATE (%)
From $600,000 to $800,000	4.8
From $800,001 to $1,000,000	5.6
From $1,000,001 to $1,500,000	6.4
From $1,500,001 to $2,000,000	7.2
From $2,000,001 to $2,500,000	8.0
From $2,500,001 to $3,000,000	8.8

AMOUNT OF TAXABLE ESTATE	RATE (%)
From $3,000,001 to $3,500,000	9.6
From $3,500,001 to $4,000,000	10.4
From $4,000,001 to $5,000,000	11.2
From $5,000,001 to $6,000,000	12.0
From $6,000,001 to $7,000,000	12.8
From $7,000,001 to $8,000,000	13.6
From $8,000,001 to $9,000,000	14.4
From $9,000,001 to $10,000,000	15.2
From $10,000,001 and over	16.0

(Exemptions: Spouse, all property qualifying for federal marital deduction.)

If the estate tax amounts to less than the maximum credit allowable under federal estate tax law, the estate tax shall be increased to equal such maximum credit.

Gift Tax: None

MISSOURI

Inheritance Tax: None

Estate Tax: Equal to federal credit for state death taxes

Gift Tax: None

MONTANA

Inheritance Tax:

Class 1 beneficiaries: Spouse; child to whom decedent stood in mutually acknowledged relationship of parent or stepparent, provided relationship began on or before child's eighteenth birthday; ancestor; descendant

Class 2 beneficiaries: Brother and sister or their descendants, spouse of child

Class 3 beneficiaries: Uncle, aunt, and their children

Class 4 beneficiaries: All others

AMOUNT RECEIVED BY EACH	CLASS 1 (%)	CLASS 2 (%)	CLASS 3 (%)	CLASS 4 (%)
To $25,000	2	4	6	8
From $25,001 to $50,000	4	8	12	16
From $50,001 to $100,000	6	12	18	24
From $100,001 and over	8	16	24	32

(Exemptions: Spouse and descendants, all property; lineal ancestor, $7,000; Class 2 beneficiaries, $1,000. The rates shown are for amounts in excess of the exemptions.)

Estate Tax: Equal to federal credit for state death taxes. If an inheritance tax amounts to less than the maximum credit allowable under federal estate tax law, an additional tax is imposed by the state to make total death taxes collected by the state equal to the maximum allowable credit under federal estate tax law.

Gift Tax: None

NEBRASKA

Inheritance Tax:

Class 1 beneficiaries: Parent, child, brother, sister, spouse of daughter, spouse of son, descendant

Class 2 beneficiaries: Aunt, uncle, niece, nephew, or descendant of any of them

Class 3 beneficiaries: All others

AMOUNT RECEIVED BY EACH	CLASS 1 (%)	CLASS 2 (%)	CLASS 3 (%)
To $2,000	-0-	6	6
From $2,001 to $5,000	-0-	6	6
From $5,001 to $10,000	-0-	6	9
From $10,001 to $20,000	1	6	12
From $20,001 to $50,000	1	6	15
From $50,001 to $60,000	1	6	18
From $60,001 and over	1	9	18

(Exemptions: Spouse, all property; other Class 1 beneficiaries, $10,000; Class 2 beneficiaries, $2,000; Class 3 beneficiaries, $500.)

Estate Tax: Equal to federal credit for state death taxes. If an inheritance tax amounts to less than the maximum credit allowable under federal estate tax law, an additional tax is imposed by the state to make total death taxes collected by the state equal to the maximum allowable credit under federal estate tax law.

Gift Tax: None

NEVADA

Inheritance Tax: None

Estate Tax: Equal to federal credit for state death taxes

Gift Tax: None

NEW HAMPSHIRE

Inheritance Tax: All property received is subject to tax at the rate of 18 percent.

(Exemptions: Spouse, ancestor, descendant, spouse of ancestor or descendant—all property.)

Estate Tax: Equal to federal credit for state death taxes. If an inheritance tax amounts to less than the maximum credit allowable under federal estate tax law, an additional tax is imposed by the state to make total death taxes collected by the state equal to the maximum allowable credit under federal estate tax law.

Gift Tax: None

NEW JERSEY

Inheritance Tax:
  Class B beneficiaries: Brother, sister, spouse, or surviving spouse of child
  Class C beneficiaries: All others

AMOUNT RECEIVED BY EACH	CLASS B (%)	CLASS C (%)
To $700,000	11	15
From $700,001 to $1,100,000	11	16
From $1,100,001 to $1,400,000	13	16
From $1,400,001 to $1,700,000	14	16
From $1,700,001 and over	16	16

(Exemptions: Spouse, parent, grandparent, child, stepchild, descendants, all property; Class B beneficiaries, $25,000; Class C beneficiaries, $500 if share is less than this amount.)

Estate Tax: Equal to federal credit for state death taxes. If an inheritance tax amounts to less than the maximum credit allowable under federal estate tax law, an additional tax is imposed by the state to make total death taxes collected by the state equal to the maximum allowable credit under federal estate tax law.

Gift Tax: None

NEW MEXICO

Inheritance Tax: None

Estate Tax: Equal to federal credit for state death taxes

Gift Tax: None

NEW YORK

Inheritance Tax: None

Estate Tax:

AMOUNT OF TAXABLE ESTATE	RATE (%)
To $50,000	2
From $50,001 to $150,000	3
From $150,001 to $300,000	4
From $300,001 to $500,000	5
From $500,001 to $700,000	6
From $700,001 to $900,000	7
From $900,001 to $1,100,000	8
From $1,100,001 to $1,600,000	9
From $1,600,001 to $2,100,000	10
From $2,100,001 to $2,600,000	11
From $2,600,001 to $3,100,000	12
From $3,100,001 to $3,600,000	13
From $3,600,001 to $4,100,000	14
From $4,100,001 to $5,100,000	15
From $5,100,001 to $6,100,000	16
From $6,100,001 to $7,100,000	17
From $7,100,001 to $8,100,000	18
From $8,100,001 to $9,100,000	19
From $9,100,001 to $10,100,000	20
From $10,100,001 and over	21

(Exemptions: Spouse, all property. Credits: If tax is up to $2,750, then credit is for entire tax; if tax is $2,750 to $5,000, then credit is for difference between amount of tax and $5,500; if tax is $5,001 or more, then credit is $500.)

    If the estate tax amounts to less than the maximum credit allowable under federal estate tax law, the estate tax shall be increased to equal such maximum credit.

Gift Tax: Tax imposed

NORTH CAROLINA

Inheritance Tax:

    Class A beneficiaries: Issue, stepchild, ancestor, spouse of child where child is not entitled to property of deceased

    Class B beneficiaries: Brother or sister or their issue, aunt or uncle by blood

    Class C beneficiaries: All others

(Exemptions: Spouse, all property. For Class A beneficiaries, $26,150.)

AMOUNT RECEIVED BY EACH	CLASS A (%)	CLASS B (%)	CLASS C (%)
To $5,000	1	4	8
From $5,001 to $10,000	1	5	8
From $10,001 to $25,000	2	6	9
From $25,001 to $50,000	3	7	10
From $50,001 to $100,000	4	8	11
From $100,001 to $200,000	5	10	12
From $200,001 to $250,000	6	10	12
From $250,001 to $500,000	6	11	13

AMOUNT RECEIVED BY EACH	CLASS A (%)	CLASS B (%)	CLASS C (%)
From $500,001 to $1,000,000	7	12	14
From $1,000,001 to $1,500,000	8	13	15
From $1,500,001 to $2,000,000	9	14	16
From $2,000,001 to $2,500,000	10	15	16
From $2,500,001 to $3,000,000	11	15	17
From $3,000,001 and over	12	16	17

Estate Tax: Equal to federal credit for state death taxes. If an inheritance tax amounts to less than the maximum credit allowable under federal estate tax law, an additional tax is imposed by the state to make total death taxes collected by the state equal to the maximum allowable credit under federal estate tax law.

Gift Tax: Tax imposed

NORTH DAKOTA

Inheritance Tax: None

Estate Tax: Equal to federal credit for state death taxes

Gift Tax: None

OHIO

Inheritance Tax: None

Estate Tax:

AMOUNT OF TAXABLE ESTATE	RATE (%)
To $40,000	2
From $40,001 to $100,000	3
From $100,001 to $200,000	4
From $200,001 to $300,000	5
From $300,001 to $500,000	6
From $500,001 and over	7

(Exemptions: Spouse, all property; also, a credit of $500.)

If the estate tax amounts to less than the maximum credit allowable under federal estate tax law, the estate tax shall be increased to equal such maximum credit.

Gift Tax: None

OKLAHOMA

Inheritance Tax: None

Estate and Transfer Tax:
   Class 1 beneficiaries: Parent, child, child of spouse, descendant
   Class 2 beneficiaries: All others

AMOUNT OF NET ESTATE AFTER EXEMPTIONS RECEIVED BY EACH BENEFICIARY	CLASS 1 (%)	CLASS 2 (%)
To $10,000	0.5	1
From $10,001 to $20,000	1.0	2
From $20,001 to $40,000	1.5	3
From $40,001 to $60,000	2.0	4
From $60,001 to $100,000	2.5	5
From $100,001 to $250,000	3.0	6
From $250,001 to $500,000	6.5	13
From $500,001 to $750,000	7.0	14
From $750,001 to $1,000,000	7.5	14
From $1,000,001 to $3,000,000	8.0	15
From $3,000,001 to $5,000,000	8.5	15
From $5,000,001 to $10,000,000	9.0	15
From $10,000,001 and over	10.0	15

(Exemptions: Spouse, all property; Class 1 beneficiaries, $175,000.)

If the estate tax amounts to less than the maximum credit allowable under federal estate law, the estate tax shall be increased to equal such maximum credit.

Gift Tax: None

OREGON

Inheritance Tax: Equal to federal credit for state death taxes

Estate Tax: None

Gift Tax: None

PENNSYLVANIA

Inheritance Tax: All amounts received by grandparent, parent, spouse, descendant, spouse or surviving spouse of child, 6 percent; all amounts received by others, 15 percent. (Exemption: Property held jointly with spouse, unless coownership created within one year of death; $2,000 family exemption.)

Estate Tax: Equal to federal credit for state death taxes. If an inheritance tax amounts to less than the maximum credit allowable under federal estate tax law, an additional tax is imposed by the state to make total death taxes collected by the state equal to the maximum allowable credit under federal estate tax law.

Gift Tax: None

RHODE ISLAND

Inheritance Tax: None

Estate Tax: Equal to federal credit for state death taxes

Gift Tax: None

SOUTH CAROLINA

Inheritance Tax: None

Estate Tax: Equal to federal credit for state death taxes

Gift Tax: None

SOUTH DAKOTA

Inheritance Tax:

Class 1 beneficiary: Spouse

Class 2 beneficiaries: Issue, child to whom decedent stood in mutually acknowledged relationship of parent for 10 consecutive years, commencing before child was 15 years of age, or lineal issue of such child

Class 3 beneficiaries: Ancestor

Class 4 beneficiaries: Brother, sister, or issue of either, spouse of son or daughter

Class 5 beneficiaries: Aunt, uncle, or issue of either

Class 6 beneficiaries: Other than lineal issue or ancestors with respect to property used in business or farming enterprise in which such person was continuously engaged with decedent for at least 10 of 15 most recent years

Class 7 beneficiaries: All others

AMOUNT RECEIVED BY EACH	CLASS 2 (%)
To $30,000	-0-
From $30,001 to $50,000	3.75
From $50,001 to $100,000	6.00
From $100,001 and over	7.50

	CLASS 3 (%)	CLASS 4 (%)
To $500	-0-	-0-
From $501 to $3,000	-0-	4
From $3,001 to $10,000	3.0	4
From $10,001 to $15,000	3.0	4
From $15,001 to $50,000	7.5	10
From $50,001 to $100,000	12.0	16
From $100,001 and over	15.0	20

	CLASS 5 (%)	CLASS 6 (%)	CLASS 7 (%)
To $100	-0-	3.0	-0-
From $101 to $200	-0-	3.0	6
From $201 to $500	5.0	3.0	6
From $501 to $3,000	5.0	3.0	6
From $3,001 to $10,000	5.0	3.0	6
From $10,001 to $15,000	5.0	3.0	6
From $15,001 to $50,000	12.5	7.5	15
From $50,001 to $100,000	20.0	12.0	24
From $100,001 and over	25.0	15.0	30

(Exemptions: Spouse, all amounts. The rates shown are for amounts in excess of the exemptions.)

Estate Tax: Equal to federal credit for state death taxes. If an inheritance tax amounts to less than the maximum credit allowable under federal estate tax law, an additional tax is imposed by the state to make total death taxes collected by the state equal to the maximum allowable credit under federal estate tax law.

Gift Tax: None

TENNESSEE

Inheritance Tax:

AMOUNT PASSING IN EXCESS OF EXEMPTION OF $600,000	PERCENT
To $40,000	5.5
From $40,001 to $240,000	6.5
From $240,001 to $440,000	7.5
From $440,001 and over	9.5

(Exemptions: Spouse, all amounts.)

Estate Tax: Equal to federal credit for state death taxes. If an inheritance tax amounts to less than the maximum credit allowable under federal estate tax law, an additional tax is imposed by the state to make total death taxes collected by the state equal to the maximum allowable credit under federal estate tax law.

Gift Tax: Tax imposed

TEXAS

Inheritance Tax: None

Estate Tax: Equal to federal credit for state death taxes

Gift Tax: None

UTAH

Inheritance Tax: None

Estate Tax: Equal to federal credit for state death taxes

Gift Tax: None

VERMONT

Inheritance Tax: None

Estate Tax: Equal to federal credit for state death taxes

Gift Tax: None

VIRGINIA

Inheritance Tax: None

Estate Tax: Equal to federal credit for state death taxes

Gift Tax: None

WASHINGTON

Inheritance Tax: None

Estate Tax: Equal to federal credit for state death taxes

Gift Tax: None

WEST VIRGINIA

Inheritance Tax: None

Estate Tax: Equal to federal credit for state death taxes

Gift Tax: None

WISCONSIN

Inheritance Tax: None

Estate Tax: Equal to federal credit for state death taxes

Gift Tax: None

WYOMING

Inheritance Tax: None

Estate Tax: Equal to federal credit for state death taxes

Gift Tax: None

Appendix D

Laws of Descent and Distribution, by State

The listings that follow are intended to serve as a guide only and are not intended to be a complete statement of the laws on distribution of property when someone dies without a will. For example, the listings do not reflect state variations in defining *child*, *children*, or *next of kin*. Some states include an adopted child, a stepchild, children of an adopted child, and so on, in their definition. Some treat half-blood relatives (different set of parents) the same as whole-blood relatives (same set of parents).

Note: The word *or* is used to mean "but if all are not then living." For example, for Arizona under the heading No Spouse but Issue, this means: All to children equally but if all are not then living, to their issue *per stirpes*.

ALABAMA

Spouse and Issue: If all the children are those of the surviving spouse, $50,000 plus one-half to spouse. But if any of the children are not those of the surviving spouse, one-half only.

Balance to children or their issue per stirpes.

Spouse and No Issue: If no surviving parent, all to the surviving spouse. If surviving parent, $100,000 plus one-half to spouse, balance to parent(s).

No Spouse but Issue: All to children equally or to their issue per stirpes.

No Spouse or Issue but Parents: All to parents equally or to survivor.

No Spouse, Issue, or Parents: All to issue of parents per stirpes; if none, to grandparents or their issue per stirpes; and if none, to deceased spouse's next of kin.

ALASKA

Spouse and Issue: If all the children are those of surviving spouse, $50,000 plus one-half to spouse. But if any of the children are not those of the surviving spouse, one-half only. Balance to children or their issue per stirpes.

Spouse and No Issue: If no surviving parent, all to the surviving spouse. If surviving parent, $50,000 plus one-half to spouse, balance to parent(s).

No Spouse but Issue: All to children equally or to their issue per stirpes.

No Spouse or Issue but Parents: All to parents equally or to survivor.

No Spouse, Issue, or Parents: All to issue of parents per stirpes; if none, one-half to paternal grandparents or their issue per stirpes and one-half to maternal grandparents or their issue per stirpes.

ARIZONA

Spouse and Issue: If any issue are not those of surviving spouse, one-half of separate property and none of decedent's one-half interest in community property to spouse. Otherwise, all of separate property and one-half of community property to spouse. Balance to children or to their issue per stirpes.

Spouse and No Issue: All to spouse.

No Spouse but Issue: All to children equally or to their issue per stirpes.

No Spouse or Issue but Parents: All to parents equally or to the survivor.

No Spouse, Issue, or Parents: All to issue of parents per stirpes; if none, to next of kin.

ARKANSAS

Spouse and Issue: Real property—as to one-third, life estate to spouse. Balance to children equally or to their issue per stirpes. Personal property—one-third to spouse, balance to children equally or to their issue per stirpes (noncommunity property only).

Spouse and No Issue: All to spouse if married to decedent three years or more. One-half to spouse if married to decedent less than three years. Balance to parents equally or to survivor; if no parents, to brothers and sisters equally or to their issue per stirpes; if none, to ancestors (up to great-grandparents) and their issue; and, if none, all to spouse.

No Spouse but Issue: All to children equally or to their issue per stirpes.

No Spouse or Issue but Parents: All to parents equally or to the survivor.

No Spouse, Issue, or Parents: All to issue of parents per stirpes; if none, to grandparents and their issue.

CALIFORNIA

Spouse and Issue: All community property to spouse. As to other property, if only one child or issue of child, one-half to spouse and one-half to child or child's issue. If more than one child or issue of same, one-third to spouse and two-thirds to children or their issue per stirpes.

Spouse and No Issue: All community property to spouse. As to other property, one-half to spouse and one-half to parents or their survivor; if none, to brothers and sisters equally or to their issue per stirpes; and, if none, all to spouse.

No Spouse but Issue: All to children equally or to their issue per stirpes.

No Spouse or Issue but Parents: All to the parents equally or to the survivor.

No Spouse, Issue, or Parents: All to issue of parents per stirpes; if none, to next of kin.

COLORADO

Spouse and Issue: If all the children are those of the surviving spouse, $25,000 plus one-half to spouse. But if any of the children are not those of the surviving spouse, one-half only. Balance to children or to their issue per stirpes.

Spouse and No Issue: All to spouse.

No Spouse but Issue: All to children equally or to their issue per stirpes.

No Spouse or Issue but Parents: All to parents equally or to the survivor.

No Spouse, Issue, or Parents: All to issue of parents per stirpes; if none, to grandparents and their issue; and, if none, to nearest lineal ancestors and their issue.

CONNECTICUT

Spouse and Issue: If all children are those of the surviving spouse, $100,000 plus one-half to spouse. But if any of the children are not those of the surviving spouse, one-half only. Balance to children or to their issue per stirpes.

Spouse and No Issue: $100,000 plus three-fourths of balance to spouse. Balance to parents or surviving parent; if none, to spouse.

No Spouse but Issue: All to children equally or to their issue per stirpes.

No Spouse or Issue but Parents: All to parents equally or to the survivor.

No Spouse, Issue, or Parents: All to issue of parents per stirpes; if none, to next of kin.

DELAWARE

Spouse and Issue: Real property—a life estate (exclusive use and possession for life) only to spouse. Balance to children or to their issue per stirpes. Personal property—if all children are those of the surviving spouse, $50,000 plus one-half of personal property to spouse, but if any of the children are not those of surviving spouse, one-half only. Balance to children or to their issue per stirpes.

Spouse and No Issue: Real property—if no surviving parents, all to spouse. If surviving parents, life estate only. Balance to parents equally or to the survivor; if none, to issue of parents per stirpes. Personal property—if no surviving parents, all to spouse. If surviving parents, $50,000 plus one-half of balance. Balance to parents or to survivor of them.

No Spouse but Issue: All to children equally or to their issue per stirpes.

No Spouse or Issue but Parents: All to parents equally or to the survivor.

No Spouse, Issue, or Parents: All to brothers and sisters or to their issue per stirpes; if none, to next of kin.

DISTRICT OF COLUMBIA

Spouse and Issue: Real property—as to one-third, life estate to spouse. Balance to children equally or to their issue per stirpes. Personal property—one-third to spouse and balance to children equally or to their issue per stirpes.

Spouse and No Issue: Real property—as to one-third, life estate to spouse. Balance to parents or surviving parent; if none, to issue of parents per stirpes; and, if none, all to spouse. Personal property—one-half to spouse, balance same as for real property.

No Spouse but Issue: All to children equally or to their issue per stirpes.

No Spouse or Issue but Parents: All to parents equally or to the survivor.

No Spouse, Issue, or Parents: All to brothers and sisters or to their issue per stirpes; if none, to collaterals; and, if none, to grandparents.

FLORIDA

Spouse and Issue: If all children are those of the surviving spouse, $20,000 plus one-half to spouse. But if any children are not those of the surviving spouse, one-half only. Balance to children or to their issue per stirpes.

Spouse and No Issue: All to spouse.

No Spouse but Issue: All to children equally or to their issue per stirpes.

No Spouse or Issue but Parents: All to parents equally or to the survivor.

No Spouse, Issue, or Parents: All to brothers and sisters or to their issue per stirpes; if none, one-half each to maternal and paternal next of kin beginning with grandparents.

GEORGIA

Spouse and Issue: Children or their issue share equally with spouse, with spouse entitled to at least one-fourth.

Spouse and No Issue: All to spouse.

No Spouse but Issue: All to children equally or to their issue per stirpes.

No Spouse or Issue but Parents: All to parents, brothers and sisters equally or to their issue per stirpes.

No Spouse, Issue, or Parents: All to brothers and sisters or to their issue per stirpes; if none, to paternal and maternal next of kin.

HAWAII

Spouse and Issue: One-half to spouse and one-half to children equally or to their issue per stirpes.

Spouse and No Issue: One-half to spouse and one-half to parents equally or all to parent surviving; if none, all to spouse.

No Spouse but Issue: All to children equally or to their issue per stirpes.

No Spouse or Issue but Parents: All to parents equally or to the survivor.

No Spouse, Issue, or Parents: All to brothers and sisters or to their issue per stirpes; if none, to grandparents; and, if none, to uncles and aunts equally.

IDAHO

Spouse and Issue: Community property to spouse. One-half of quasi-community property to spouse; other one-half to spouse if not disposed of by will. If child or children are those of surviving spouse, $50,000 plus one-half of balance to spouse, but if not, one-half to spouse. Balance to surviving child or children or to their issue per stirpes.

Spouse and No Issue: Community property to spouse. Quasi-community property as where issue survive. If no surviving parent, all to spouse. Other-

wise, $50,000 plus one-half to spouse and balance to parents or to survivor of them.

No Spouse but Issue: All to children equally or to their issue per stirpes.

No Spouse or Issue but Parents: All to parents equally or to the survivor.

No Spouse, Issue, or Parents: To brothers and sisters or to their issue.

ILLINOIS

Spouse and Issue: One-half to spouse and one-half to children equally or to their issue per stirpes.

Spouse and No Issue: All to spouse.

No Spouse but Issue: All to children equally or to their issue per stirpes.

No Spouse or Issue but Parents: All to parents, brothers and sisters or issue of brothers and sisters per stirpes. One surviving parent takes a double share.

No Spouse, Issue, or Parents: One-half each to maternal and paternal grandparents equally or to survivor; if none, to their issue per stirpes, then to great-grandparents, as above, and then to next of kin without representation.

INDIANA

Spouse and Issue: If any issue, but none by spouse, life estate (exclusive use and possession for life) in one-third of real property to spouse and balance as below. If one or more children, or their issue, one-half to spouse and one-half to children or their issue per stirpes.

Spouse and No Issue: If no parents, all to spouse. If parents, one-fourth to parents or to survivor of them and three-fourths to spouse.

No Spouse but Issue: All to children equally or to their issue per stirpes.

No Spouse or Issue but Parents: One-half to parents if both survive or one-fourth to one surviving parent. Balance to brothers and sisters or to their issue per stirpes.

No Spouse, Issue, or Parents: All to brothers and sisters or to their issue per stirpes; if none, to grandparents; and, if none, to uncles and aunts per stirpes.

IOWA

Spouse and Issue: If issue are not those of spouse, one-half of all real property, all personal property exempt from execution, and one-half other personal property to spouse, but not less than $50,000. If issue are those of spouse, all to spouse.

Spouse and No Issue: All to spouse.

No Spouse but Issue: All to children equally or to their issue per stirpes.

No Spouse or Issue but Parents: All to parents equally or to the survivor.

No Spouse, Issue, or Parents: All to brothers and sisters or to their issue per stirpes; if none, to ancestors and

their issue; and, if none, to spouse or to heirs of spouse.

KANSAS

Spouse and Issue: One-half to spouse and one-half to children equally or to their issue per stirpes.

Spouse and No Issue: All to spouse.

No Spouse but Issue: All to children equally or to their issue per stirpes.

No Spouse or Issue but Parents: All to parents equally or to survivor.

No Spouse, Issue, or Parents: All to issue of parents per stirpes.

KENTUCKY

Spouse and Issue: Real property—life estate (exclusive use and possession for life) in one-third of real property of which decedent was seized of fee simple estate during marriage and one-half of surplus real estate; balance to children equally or to their issue per stirpes. Personal property—one-half to spouse and one-half to children equally or to their issue per stirpes.

Spouse and No Issue: One-half to spouse and one-half to parents equally or to survivor. But if neither parent survives, their one-half to their issue per stirpes; if none, to spouse.

No Spouse but Issue: All to children equally or to their issue per stirpes.

No Spouse or Issue but Parents: All to parents equally or to the survivor.

No Spouse, Issue, or Parents: To brothers and sisters or to their issue per stirpes, if none, one-half to maternal next of kin and one-half to paternal next of kin. Distribution to grandparents first; if none, to uncles and aunts or their issue per stirpes.

LOUISIANA

Spouse and Issue: All community property to descendants per stirpes, with the spouse having the right to the use or enjoyment of property unless spouse remarries. All separate property passes to children equally or to their issue per stirpes.

Spouse and No Issue: All community property to spouse. Separate property, to brothers and sisters or to their issue per stirpes; if none, all to the parents; and, if none, to spouse.

No Spouse but Issue: All to children equally or to their issue per stirpes.

No Spouse or Issue but Parents: All to brothers and sisters or to their issue per stirpes; if none, all to parents.

No Spouse, Issue, or Parents: All to brothers and sisters equally or to their issue per stirpes; if none, to more remote next of kin.

MAINE

Spouse and Issue: If all children are those of the surviving spouse, $50,000 plus one-half to spouse. But if any children are not those of surviving spouse, one-half only. Balance to children or their issue per stirpes.

Spouse and No Issue: $50,000 plus one-half to spouse. Balance to parents or to survivor of them or to their issue per capita; if none, all to spouse.

No Spouse but Issue: All to children equally or to their issue per stirpes.

No Spouse or Issue but Parents: All to parents or to the survivor.

No Spouse, Issue, or Parents: All to issue of parents per capita at each generation; if none, one-half to paternal grandparents or to their issue per capita and one-half to maternal grandparents or to their issue per capita.

MARYLAND

Spouse and Issue: If minor child survives, one-half to spouse and one-half to children equally or to their issue per stirpes. But if no minor child, additional $15,000 to spouse.

Spouse and No Issue: $15,000 plus one-half to spouse and one-half to parents or to the survivor. If neither parent survives, all to spouse.

No Spouse but Issue: All to children equally or to their issue per stirpes.

No Spouse or Issue but Parents: All to parents or to surviving parent.

No Spouse, Issue, or Parents: All to brothers and sisters equally or to their issue per stirpes; if none, to collateral next of kin.

MASSACHUSETTS

Spouse and Issue: One-half to spouse and one-half to children equally or to their issue per stirpes.

Spouse and No Issue: $200,000 plus one-half of the balance to spouse and other half to parents equally or to the survivor. But if neither parent survives, then one-half to brothers and sisters equally or to their issue per stirpes; if none, to next of kin, and if none, all to spouse.

No Spouse but Issue: All to children equally or to their issue per stirpes.

No Spouse or Issue but Parents: All to parents equally or to the survivor.

No Spouse, Issue, or Parents: All to brothers and sisters equally or to their issue per stirpes; if none, to next of kin.

MICHIGAN

Spouse and Issue: $60,000 plus one-half to surviving spouse and the balance to surviving issue per stirpes. But if any of the issue are not those of surviving spouse, surviving spouse does not get the $60,000.

Spouse and No Issue: $60,000 plus one-half the balance to surviving spouse. Remaining balance to parents equally or to the survivor. If there are no parents, all to spouse.

No Spouse but Issue: All to children equally or to their issue per stirpes.

No Spouse or Issue but Parents: All to parents equally or to survivor.

No Spouse, Issue, or Parents: All to brothers and sisters equally or to their children per stirpes; if none, one-half to maternal grandparents and one-half to paternal grandparents or to their issue per stirpes.

MINNESOTA

Spouse and Issue: If issue are also of spouse, $70,000 plus one-half of balance to spouse and balance to children or to their issue per stirpes; otherwise, one-half to spouse and balance to children or to their issue per stirpes.

Spouse and No Issue: All to spouse.

No Spouse but Issue: All to children equally or to their issue per stirpes.

No Spouse or Issue but Parents: All to parents equally or to survivor.

No Spouse, Issue, or Parents: All to brothers and sisters equally or to their issue per stirpes; if none, to next of kin.

MISSISSIPPI

Spouse and Issue: Property is divided into shares equal to the number of children (or issue of a child) and spouse living. Each takes one share.

Spouse and No Issue: All to spouse.

No Spouse but Issue: All to children equally or to their issue per stirpes.

No Spouse or Issue but Parents: All to parents, brothers and sisters equally or to their issue per stirpes. If no brothers or sisters or their issue, all to parents equally or to survivor.

No Spouse, Issue, or Parents: All to brothers and sisters equally or to their issue per stirpes; if none, to grandparents, uncles and aunts equally or to their issue per stirpes; and, if none, to next of kin.

MISSOURI

Spouse and Issue: If all the children are those of surviving spouse, $20,000 plus one-half to spouse. But if any children are not those of surviving spouse, one-half only. Balance to children or to their issue per stirpes.

Spouse and No Issue: $20,000 plus one-half of balance to spouse and the other half to parents or to the survivor of them; if none, all to spouse.

No Spouse but Issue: All to children equally or to their issue per stirpes.

No Spouse or Issue but Parents: All to parents, brothers and sisters equally or to their issue per stirpes; if none, all to parents or to survivor.

No Spouse, Issue, or Parents: All to brothers and sisters equally or to their issue per stirpes; if none, to grandparents, uncles and aunts and their issue per stirpes; and, if none, to nearest lineal ancestor and their issue.

MONTANA

Spouse and Issue: All to spouse if child or children are those of surviving spouse. If only one child is of spouse, one-half to spouse and one-half to child; if more than one child, one-third to spouse and the balance to children.

Spouse and No Issue: All to spouse.

No Spouse but Issue: All to children equally or to their issue per stirpes.

No Spouse or Issue but Parents: All to parents or to survivor.

No Spouse, Issue, or Parents: All to brothers and sisters equally or to their issue per stirpes; if none, one-half to paternal grandparents or to their issue per stirpes and one-half to maternal grandparents or to their issue per stirpes.

NEBRASKA

Spouse and Issue: $50,000 plus one-half to spouse. If any of the children are not of the surviving spouse, only one-half to spouse and the balance to children or to their issue per stirpes.

Spouse and No Issue: All to spouse, except when there is a surviving parent; then, $50,000 plus one-half to spouse and the balance to parents equally or to survivor.

No Spouse but Issue: All to children equally or to their issue per stirpes.

No Spouse or Issue but Parents: All to parents equally or to survivor.

No Spouse, Issue, or Parents: All to brothers and sisters equally or to their children per stirpes; if none, one-half to paternal next of kin and one-half to maternal next of kin.

NEVADA

Spouse and Issue: All community property to spouse. As to other property, if only one child or child's issue survive, one-half to spouse and one-half to child or such child's issue. If there is more than one child or issue, then one-third to spouse and the balance to such children or to their issue per stirpes.

Spouse and No Issue: All community property to spouse. As to other property, one-half to spouse and one-half to parents equally or to the survivor; if none, to brothers and sisters equally or to their children per stirpes; and, if none, all to spouse.

No Spouse but Issue: All to children equally or to their issue per stirpes.

No Spouse or Issue but Parents: All to parents equally or to survivor.

No Spouse, Issue, or Parents: All to brothers and sisters equally or to their issue per stirpes; if none, to next of kin.

NEW HAMPSHIRE

Spouse and Issue: $50,000 plus one-half to spouse. But if any of the children are not those of surviving spouse, only one-half. The balance to children or to their issue per stirpes.

Spouse and No Issue: $50,000 plus one-half to spouse. Balance to parents equally or to the survivor; if none, all to spouse.

No Spouse but Issue: All to children equally or to their issue per stirpes.

No Spouse or Issue but Parents: All to parents equally or to survivor.

No Spouse, Issue, or Parents: All to brothers and sisters equally or to their issue per stirpes; if none, one-half to paternal next of kin and one-half to maternal next of kin per stirpes.

NEW JERSEY

Spouse and Issue: $50,000 plus one-half to spouse. But if any of the children are not children of the surviving spouse, only one-half to spouse. The balance to children or to their issue per stirpes.

Spouse and No Issue: $50,000 plus one-half to spouse. Balance to parents equally or to the survivor; if none, all to spouse.

No Spouse but Issue: All to children equally or to their issue per stirpes.

No Spouse or Issue but Parents: All to parents equally or to survivor.

No Spouse, Issue, or Parents: All to brothers and sisters equally or to their issue per stirpes; if none, one-half to maternal grandparents or to their issue and one-half to paternal grand-parents or to their issue.

NEW MEXICO

Spouse and Issue: All community property to spouse. As to other property, one-fourth to spouse and three-fourths to children equally or to their issue per stirpes.

Spouse and No Issue: All to spouse.

No Spouse but Issue: All to children equally or to their issue per stirpes.

No Spouse or Issue but Parents: All to parents equally or to survivor.

No Spouse, Issue, or Parents: All to brothers and sisters equally or to their issue per stirpes; if none, one-half to maternal grandparents or to their issue and one half to paternal grand-parents or to their issue.

NEW YORK

Spouse and Issue: $50,000 plus one-half to spouse and the balance to children or to their issue per stirpes.

Spouse and No Issue: All to spouse.

No Spouse but Issue: All to children equally or to their issue per stirpes.

No Spouse or Issue but Parents: All to parents equally or to survivor.

No Spouse, Issue, or Parents: All to brothers and sisters or to their issue per stirpes; if none, to grandparents equally or to their issue per capita; and, if none, to next of kin.

NORTH CAROLINA

Spouse and Issue: If one child, $15,000 of personalty (if any) plus one-half to spouse and balance to child or such child's issue. If more than one child, $15,000 of personalty (if any) plus one-third to spouse and balance to children or to their issue per stirpes.

Spouse and No Issue: $25,000 of personalty (if any) plus one-half to spouse. Balance to parents equally or to the survivor; if none, all to spouse.

No Spouse but Issue: All to children equally or to their issue per stirpes.

No Spouse or Issue but Parents: All to parents equally or to survivor.

No Spouse, Issue, or Parents: All to brothers and sisters equally or to their issue per stirpes; if none, one-half to maternal grandparents or to their issue and one-half to paternal grand-parents or to their issue.

NORTH DAKOTA

Spouse and Issue: $50,000 plus one-half to spouse. If any of the children are not of the surviving spouse, only one-half to spouse and the balance to children or to their issue per stirpes.

Spouse and No Issue: $50,000 plus one-half to spouse and the balance to parents or to survivor.

No Spouse but Issue: All to children equally or to their issue per stirpes.

No Spouse or Issue but Parents: All to parents or to survivor.

No Spouse, Issue, or Parents: All to brothers and sisters equally or to their children per stirpes; if none, one-half to paternal next of kin and one-half to maternal next of kin.

OHIO

Spouse and Issue: $60,000 if spouse is natural or adoptive parent of any child; if not, $20,000. In addition, one-half to spouse if there is only one child or issue of a child; otherwise, one-third to spouse. The balance to child or children or to their issue per stirpes.

Spouse and No Issue: All to spouse.

No Spouse but Issue: All to children equally or to their issue per stirpes.

No Spouse or Issue but Parents: All to parents equally or to the survivor.

No Spouse, Issue, or Parents: All to brothers and sisters or to their issue per stirpes; if none, one-half to maternal grandparents or to the survivor or to their issue per stirpes, and one-half to paternal grandparents or to the survivor or to their issue per stirpes; and, if none, to next of kin.

OKLAHOMA

Spouse and Issue: One-half to spouse and balance to children per stirpes. But if any issue are not of surviving spouse, one-half of property acquired during marriage by joint industry and equal part with children per stirpes as to balance.

Spouse and No Issue: All property acquired during marriage by joint industry and one-third of balance to spouse. Balance to parents equally or to survivor per stirpes; if none, one-half to maternal grandparents or to the survivor or to their issue per stirpes and one-half to paternal grandparents or to the survivor or to their issue per stirpes; and, if none, to next of kin.

No Spouse but Issue: All to children equally or to their issue per stirpes.

No Spouse or Issue but Parents: All to parents equally or to survivor.

No Spouse, Issue, or Parents: All to brothers and sisters equally or to survivor per stirpes; if none, one-half to maternal grandparents or to survivor or their issue per stirpes and one-half to paternal grandparents or to survivor or their issue per stirpes; and, if none, to next of kin.

OREGON

Spouse and Issue: All to spouse, except when there are any children not of surviving spouse. Then, only one-half to spouse and one-half to children or to their issue per stirpes.

Spouse and No Issue: All to spouse.

No Spouse but Issue: All to children equally or to their issue per stirpes.

No Spouse or Issue but Parents: All to parents equally or to survivor.

No Spouse, Issue, or Parents: All to brothers and sisters equally or to their issue per stirpes; if none, to next of kin.

PENNSYLVANIA

Spouse and Issue: $30,000 plus one-half to surviving spouse. The balance to the surviving issue per stirpes. But if any issue are not of surviving spouse, surviving spouse does not get the $30,000.

Spouse and No Issue: $30,000 plus one-half of the balance to surviving spouse. The balance to parents equally or to survivor; if none, all to spouse.

No Spouse but Issue: All to children equally or to their issue per stirpes.

No Spouse or Issue but Parents: All to parents equally or to survivor.

No Spouse, Issue, or Parents: All to brothers and sisters equally or to their issue per stirpes; if none, one-half to maternal grandparents and one-half to paternal grandparents or to survivor; and, if none, to aunts and uncles or to their issue.

RHODE ISLAND

Spouse and Issue: Real property: life estate to spouse; balance to children equally or to their issue per stirpes. Personal property: one-half to spouse and one-half to children equally or to their issue per stirpes.

Spouse and No Issue: Real property: life estate (exclusive use and possession for life) to spouse plus, with the

court's discretion, $75,000; balance to parents equally or to survivor; if none, to brothers and sisters equally or to survivor; if none, one-half to maternal grandparents and one-half to paternal grandparents or to survivor; if none, to aunts and uncles equally or to their issue per stirpes; if none, to next of kin; and, if none, to spouse. Personal property: $50,000 and one-half to spouse; balance to parents equally or to survivor; if none, to brothers and sisters equally or to their issue per stirpes; if none, one-half to maternal grandparents and one-half to paternal grandparents; if none, to next of kin; and, if none, to spouse.

No Spouse but Issue: All to children equally or to their issue per stirpes.

No Spouse or Issue but Parents: All to parents equally or to survivor.

No Spouse, Issue, or Parents: All to brothers and sisters equally or to their issue per stirpes; if none, one-half to maternal grandparents and one-half to paternal grandparents; and, if none, to next of kin.

SOUTH CAROLINA

Spouse and Issue: One-half to spouse and one-half to children or to their issue per stirpes.

Spouse and No Issue: All to spouse.

No Spouse but Issue: All to children equally or to their issue per stirpes.

No Spouse or Issue but Parents: All to parents equally or to survivor.

No Spouse, Issue, or Parents: All to brothers and sisters equally or to their issue per stirpes; if none, one-half to maternal grandparents and one-half to paternal grandparents or to survivor; if none, to their issue per stirpes; and, if none, to great-grandparents and their issue.

SOUTH DAKOTA

Spouse and Issue: The greater of $100,000 or one-third of augmented estate to spouse and, if one child, one-half to spouse and one-half to child or such child's issue. If more than one child, one-third to spouse and two-thirds to children equally or to their issue per stirpes.

Spouse and No Issue: $100,000 plus one-half to spouse. Balance to parents equally or to survivor; if none, to brothers and sisters equally or to their issue per stirpes; and, if none, to spouse.

No Spouse but Issue: All to children equally or to their issue per stirpes.

No Spouse or Issue but Parents: All to parents equally or to survivor.

No Spouse, Issue, or Parents: All to brothers and sisters equally or to their issue per stirpes; if none, to next of kin.

TENNESSEE

Spouse and Issue: Homestead and year's support allowance plus child's share to spouse, but not less than one-third if issue survive. Balance to children equally or to their issue per stirpes.

Spouse and No Issue: All to spouse.

No Spouse but Issue: All to children equally or to their issue per stirpes.

No Spouse or Issue but Parents: All to parents equally or to survivor.

No Spouse, Issue, or Parents: All to brothers and sisters equally or to their issue per stirpes; if none, one-half to maternal grandparents and one-half to paternal grandparents or to survivor; and, if none, to their issue per stirpes.

TEXAS

Spouse and Issue: One-half of community property to spouse and one-half to children equally or to their issue per stirpes. As to separate real property, life estate in one-third to spouse. As to separate personal property, one-third to spouse. Balance of real property and personal property to children equally or to their issue per stirpes.

Spouse and No Issue: All community property and personal property to spouse. As to other property, one-half of realty and all of personality to spouse and balance to parents equally; if only one parent, one-half (of such balance) to such parent and one-half to brothers and sisters equally or to their issue per stirpes; if neither brothers and sisters nor any of their issue survive, the entire one-half to surviving parent; if no parent, to brothers and sisters or to their issue per stirpes; if none, to grandparents and their descendants; and, if none, to spouse.

No Spouse but Issue: All to children equally or to their issue per stirpes.

No Spouse or Issue but Parents: All to parents equally or one-half to survivor and one-half to brothers and sisters equally or to their issue per stirpes; if none, to surviving parent.

No Spouse, Issue, or Parents: All to brothers and sisters equally or to their issue per stirpes; if none, one-half to maternal grandparents and their issue and one-half to paternal grandparents and their issue.

UTAH

Spouse and Issue: $50,000 plus one-half to surviving spouse and the balance to surviving issue per stirpes. But if any issue are not of surviving spouse, surviving spouse does not get the $50,000.

Spouse and No Issue: $100,000 plus one-half of the balance to surviving spouse. The balance to parents equally or to survivor; if none, all to spouse.

No Spouse but Issue: All to children equally or to their issue per stirpes.

No Spouse or Issue but Parents: All to parents equally or to survivor.

No Spouse, Issue, or Parents: All to brothers and sisters equally or to their

issue per stirpes; if none, one-half to maternal grandparents or their descendants and one-half to paternal grandparents or their descendants per stirpes, or all to survivor; and, if none, to next of kin.

VERMONT

Spouse and Issue: If spouse with one child, who is issue of spouse, or spouse with issue of child, with respect to real property, one-half to spouse and one-half to child or such child's issue; with respect to personal property, one-third to spouse and two-thirds to child or such child's issue. Otherwise, one-third to spouse and two-thirds to children equally or to their issue per stirpes.

Spouse and No Issue: $25,000 plus one-half to spouse. The balance to parents equally or to survivor; if none, to brothers and sisters equally or to their issue per stirpes; if none, to next of kin; and, if none, to spouse.

No Spouse but Issue: All to children equally or to their issue per stirpes.

No Spouse or Issue but Parents: All to parents equally or to survivor.

No Spouse, Issue, or Parents: All to brothers and sisters equally or to their issue per stirpes; if none, to next of kin.

VIRGINIA

Spouse and Issue: All to spouse if child or children are of surviving spouse;

otherwise, one-third to spouse and balance to children or to their issue per stirpes.

Spouse and No Issue: All to spouse.

No Spouse but Issue: All to children equally or to their issue per stirpes.

No Spouse or Issue but Parents: All to parents equally or to survivor.

No Spouse, Issue, or Parents: All to brothers and sisters equally or to their issue per stirpes; if none, one-half (or all if there is no maternal next of kin) to paternal next of kin and one-half (or all if there is no paternal next of kin) to maternal next of kin, but first to grandparents or to survivor or to their issue.

WASHINGTON

Spouse and Issue: All community and quasi-community property to spouse. As to other property, one-half to spouse and one-half to children equally or to their issue per stirpes.

Spouse and No Issue: All community and quasi-community property to spouse. As to other property, three-fourths to spouse and one-fourth to parents equally or to survivor or their issue; if none, all to spouse.

No Spouse but Issue: All to children equally or to their issue per stirpes.

No Spouse or Issue but Parents: All to parents equally or to survivor.

No Spouse, Issue, or Parents: All to brothers and sisters equally or to their

children per stirpes; if none, to grandparents or to their issue.

WEST VIRGINIA

Spouse and Issue: If all issue are of decedent and surviving spouse, all to spouse. If any issue are of surviving spouse and decedent left other issue, (that is, issue sired with someone other than with surviving spouse), three-fifths to surviving spouse, otherwise one-half to surviving spouse; balance to issue per stirpes.

Spouse and No Issue: Three-fourths to spouse. The balance to parents equally or to the survivor; if none, all to spouse.

No Spouse but Issue: All to children equally or to their issue per stirpes.

No Spouse or Issue but Parents: All to parents equally or to survivor.

No Spouse, Issue, or Parents: All to brothers and sisters equally or to their issue per stirpes; if none, one-half (or all if there is no maternal next of kin) to paternal next of kin and one-half (or all if there is no paternal next of kin) to maternal next of kin, but first to grandparents or to survivor, then uncles and aunts or their issue.

WISCONSIN

Spouse and Issue: If all children are those of decedent and surviving spouse, all to spouse. If any child is not of surviving spouse, one-half of the estate to surviving spouse and the balance to the surviving children or their issue per stirpes.

Spouse and No Issue: All to spouse.

No Spouse but Issue: All to children equally or to their issue per stirpes.

No Spouse or Issue but Parents: All to parents equally or to survivor.

No Spouse, Issue, or Parents: All to brothers and sisters equally or to their issue per stirpes; if none, all to grandparents or survivor; and, if none, all to next of kin.

WYOMING

Spouse and Issue: One-half to spouse and one-half to children equally or to their issue per stirpes.

Spouse and No Issue: All to spouse.

No Spouse but Issue: All to children equally or to their issue per stirpes.

No Spouse or Issue but Parents: All to parents, brothers and sisters equally or to their issue per stirpes.

No Spouse, Issue, or Parents: All to brothers and sisters equally or to their issue per stirpes; if none, to grandparents, uncles and aunts or to their issue per stirpes.

APPENDIX E

Age and Witness Requirements for Valid Wills, by State

In most states, the minimum age necessary to make a will is 18, and the number of witnesses required is two. The exceptions are:

STATE	MINIMUM AGE	NUMBER OF WITNESSES
Georgia	14	2
Idaho	18 or emancipated child (any age)	2
Louisiana	16	2 plus notary
New Hampshire	18 or married (any age)	2
Oregon	18 or married (any age)	2
South Carolina	18	3
Texas	18 or married (now or before) or member of U.S. armed forces or merchant marine (any age)	2
Vermont	18	3

APPENDIX F

Compensation Allowed to Fiduciaries, by State

Note: The listings that follow are intended to serve as a guide only and are not intended to be a complete statement of the applicable laws.

In many states, local court rules fix the amount of compensation; in others, custom prevails as to the amount of compensation. Reasonable compensation for trusts may include annual minimum fees, account maintenance, acceptance or distribution fees, fees for preparing tax returns, and fees for nonprobate assets that are included in the estate for tax purposes. For estates, real estate that is not sold usually is not considered part of the compensable estate. Customs and laws also vary as to whether attorneys' fees are permissible extra charges, in addition to reasonable compensation for fiduciaries. Also, in virtually every state the compensation may vary according to special circumstances such as extensive litigation.

The reader is urged to consult with local counsel to determine the appropriate compensation and fees.

STATE	EXECUTOR, ADMINISTRATOR, OR PERSONAL REPRESENTATIVE	TRUSTEE UNDER WILL
Alabama	Just and fair but not in excess of 2½% of receipts and disbursements	No statutory provision
Alaska	Reasonable compensation	No statutory provision
Arizona	Reasonable compensation	No statutory provision

STATE	EXECUTOR, ADMINISTRATOR, OR PERSONAL REPRESENTATIVE	TRUSTEE UNDER WILL
Arkansas	Reasonable compensation not to exceed 10% of first $1,000, 5% of next $4,000, and 3% of excess over $5,000	No statutory provision
California	Commissions, as well as fees, of attorneys are 4% of $15,000; 3% on next $85,000; 2% on next $900,000; and 1% on next $9,000,000; ½ of 1% on next $15,000,000; reasonable compensation on excess	Reasonable compensation
Colorado	Reasonable compensation	Reasonable compensation
Connecticut	No statutory rates provided; customarily based on percentage of gross estate administered	Reasonable compensation
Delaware	Provided by court rules and based on value of gross estate; in summary as follows: $10,000, $905; $60,000, $3,205;$150,000, $6,150; $300,000, $9,900; $500,000 and over, 2.8%	On income, 6% of first $20,000, 3.5% on next $10,000, 3% on next $270,000, 2% on excess. On principal annually 5/10 of 1% of $100,000, 3/10 of 1% of next $100,000, 2/10 of 1% of next $500,000, 1/10 of 1% on excess

STATE	EXECUTOR, ADMINISTRATOR, OR PERSONAL REPRESENTATIVE	TRUSTEE UNDER WILL
District of Columbia	Reasonable compensation	No statutory provision
Florida	Reasonable compensation	No statutory provision
Georgia	2½% on money received and 2½% on money paid out; on property distributed in kind, reasonable fee not to exceed 3%	Same as for executors, etc.
Hawaii	On income, 7% on first $5,000 and 5% on excess; on principal, 4% on first $15,000, 3% on next $85,000, 2% on next $900,000, 1½% on next $2,000,000, 1% on excess over $3,000,000	On income, same as executors, etc.; on principal, 1% at inception, 1/10 of 1% of principal annually and 1% of principal on final distribution, 2½% received after inception, 2½% on payments before termination
Idaho	Reasonable compensation	Reasonable compensation
Illinois	Reasonable compensation	Reasonable compensation
Indiana	Reasonable compensation	Reasonable compensation
Iowa	Reasonable compensation not to exceed 6% on first $1,000, 4% on next $5,000, 2% on excess; attorney's fees based on above	Reasonable compensation

STATE	EXECUTOR, ADMINISTRATOR, OR PERSONAL REPRESENTATIVE	TRUSTEE UNDER WILL
Kansas	Reasonable compensation	Reasonable compensation
Kentucky	Not to exceed 5% of personal estate plus 5% of income collected	6% of income plus $\frac{3}{10}$ of 1% of principal annually or, at option of fiduciary, 6% of principal when distributed
Louisiana	2½% of gross estate, but in absence of agreement, reasonable compensation	Reasonable compensation
Maine	Reasonable compensation	Reasonable compensation
Maryland	Reasonable compensation not exceeding 9% of first $20,000 of gross estate plus 3.6% of excess; real estate excluded, but if sold, commission not to exceed 9%	6% on income of real estate; other income, 6½% on first $10,000, 5% on next $20,000, 4% on next $10,000, 3% on excess; annual principal commissions, $\frac{4}{10}$ of 1% on $250,000, ¼ of 1% on next $250,000, $\frac{1}{10}$ of 1% on excess ½ of 1% on final distribution
Massachusetts	Reasonable compensation; following considered reasonable: 6–7% on gross income; for principal, 5% of first $100,000, 4%	Reasonable compensation

STATE	EXECUTOR, ADMINISTRATOR, OR PERSONAL REPRESENTATIVE	TRUSTEE UNDER WILL
	on next $200,000, 3% on next $700,000, 2% on next $2,000,000, and 1% on balance	
Michigan	Reasonable compensation	Reasonable compensation
Minnesota	Reasonable compensation	Reasonable compensation
Mississippi	Not to exceed 7% of gross estate	Reasonable compensation
Missouri	5% on first $5,000; 4% on next $20,000; 3% on next $75,000; 2¾% on next $300,000; 2½% on next $600,000; 2% on excess	Reasonable compensation
Montana	Reasonable compensation not to exceed 3% of first $40,000, 2% on excess; attorneys' fees not to exceed 1½ times above amounts	Reasonable compensation
Nebraska	Reasonable compensation	Reasonable compensation
Nevada	4% on first $15,000; 3% on next $85,000; 2% on excess	Reasonable compensation
New Hampshire	Reasonable compensation	Reasonable compensation

STATE	EXECUTOR, ADMINISTRATOR, OR PERSONAL REPRESENTATIVE	TRUSTEE UNDER WILL
New Jersey	On income, 6%; on principal, 5% up to $200,000, 3½% on excess to $1,000,000, and 2% on excess	On income, 6%; on principal, annually, ⁵⁄₁₀ of 1% on first $400,000, ³⁄₁₀ of 1% on excess
New Mexico	10% on first $3,000; 5% on excess (less for life insurance, CDs, U.S. government bonds, bank accounts)	Reasonable compensation
New York	For receiving and paying out first $100,000, 5%; next $200,000, 4%; next $700,000, 3%; next $4,000,000, 2½%; over $5,000,000, 2%; also, 5% of gross rents on real property. If gross estate is $300,000 or more, each fiduciary (up to 3) allowed full commission; if $100,000 to $300,000, each fiduciary (up to 2) allowed full commission	Annual commissions of $10.50 per $1,000 on first $400,000 of principal, $4.50 per $1,000 on next $600,000, $3 per $1,000 on balance; for paying out principal, 1%; on accumulated income, 2% on first $2,500, 1% on balance; also, 6% of gross rents on real property; same provisions as for executors, etc., for allocation where more than one trustee
North Carolina	At discretion of clerk of court, not to exceed 5% of receipts and expenditures fairly made	Same as for executors, etc.

STATE	EXECUTOR, ADMINISTRATOR, OR PERSONAL REPRESENTATIVE	TRUSTEE UNDER WILL
North Dakota	Reasonable compensation	Reasonable compensation
Ohio	On personal property, real property sold, and income, 4% on first $100,000; 3% on next $300,000; 2% on balance; 1% on unsold real estate subject to Ohio estate tax when not jointly owned	Reasonable compensation
Oklahoma	5% on first $1,000; 4% on next $4,000; 2½% on excess	Reasonable compensation
Oregon	On estate, including income, 7% on first $1,000; 4% on next $9,000; 3% on next $40,000; 2% on excess; 1% on other property subject to estate taxation	Reasonable compensation
Pennsylvania	Reasonable compensation, but custom is to allow 5% on small estates (not defined) and 3% on large estates	Reasonable compensation
Rhode Island	Reasonable compensation	Reasonable compensation
South Carolina	5% on personal property and 5% on income	Reasonable compensation

STATE	EXECUTOR, ADMINISTRATOR, OR PERSONAL REPRESENTATIVE	TRUSTEE UNDER WILL
South Dakota	5% on first $1,000, 4% on next $4,000, 2½% on excess; real property included in above when sold; otherwise, just compensation	Reasonable compensation
Tennessee	Reasonable compensation	Reasonable compensation
Texas	5% each on sums paid and received in cash, other than cash on hand (but not to exceed 5% of value of estate)	Reasonable compensation
Utah	Reasonable compensation	Reasonable compensation
Vermont	Reasonable compensation (minimum of $4 per day)	Reasonable compensation
Virginia	Reasonable compensation	Reasonable compensation
Washington	Reasonable compensation	Reasonable compensation
West Virginia	Reasonable compensation, usually 5% of receipts	Reasonable compensation
Wisconsin	2% of estate	Reasonable compensation
Wyoming	10% on first $1,000, 5% on next $4,000, 3% on next $15,000, 2% on excess	Reasonable compensation

APPENDIX G

Asset Update

By responding to the following questions and keeping a record of your responses, you can help your loved ones receive the maximum value from your assets with minimum delay and cost to them.

Even after answering every question, you still may not have a complete listing or have enough information about your assets. Going through this process, however, may remind you about other information you should record.

RESIDENCE

Where do you keep the deed?
When did you purchase the property?
What was the purchase price?
Where do you keep a copy of the settlement sheet?
If you had a lawyer represent you, what is the name and address of the lawyer?
What do you believe is the fair value of the residence?
If you wanted to sell the house today, how would you go about selling it?

Which real estate agent would you choose? Do you know a private buyer?
If you are survived by a spouse, would you advise your spouse to sell the house or live in it for a specific period of time?
If there is a mortgage, would you advise your spouse to pay it off? If so, when?
When you purchased or acquired the house, did you buy title insurance? If so, where is the policy?

HOUSEHOLD FURNISHINGS

Do they belong to you or your spouse?
What do you think they are worth?
Do you recommend selling any valuable paintings, silver, furniture, rugs, or jewelry?
If you were to sell them, how would you go about it?

VALUABLE COLLECTIONS (GUNS, JEWELRY, COINS, STAMPS, CLOCKS, WATCHES, STONES, ETC.)

What do you think the items are worth?

Do you recommend selling them now or later?

If your spouse or family needed the cash, how would you advise they go about making the sale?

Do you know a possible buyer?

Who is the owner of the collection?

Who acquired it? When? From whom? At what cost?

What proof do you have of ownership?

Where do you keep the proof?

Should the valuables be sold in one lot or piecemeal?

OTHER REAL ESTATE

Do you have deeds? If so, where do you keep them?

If you do not have deeds, identify the location of each parcel and specify the *liber* (book or volume where deeds are recorded) and page where the deed is recorded, the date acquired, the purchase price, and the lawyer who represented you.

What do you believe each parcel is worth?

Do you know someone who would be a likely buyer? If so, give a name, address, and phone number.

If you wished to sell a parcel, which agent would you use?

Would you recommend that your family hold the property or sell?

If a sale is made, and there is a large parcel, should the sale be in one lot or piecemeal?

PARTNERSHIP INTERESTS

What are the names and addresses of your partners?

Where do you keep a copy of the partnership agreement and financial statements or reports?

What does the partnership own?

Are there any other agreements affecting your interest that specify what happens to your interest when you die? If oral, consider getting them in writing.

How does your estate benefit from your partnership interest? Is your interest to be redeemed? If so, by whom?

What do you believe your interest to be worth?

Are there any written agreements providing your spouse with a continuation of your guaranteed payments (if any)? If so, where are these agreements?

Who is the lawyer and who is the accountant for the partnership?

Do you have written evidence of your percentage interest?

Does the partnership owe you any money, or vice versa? Where do you keep such records?

CLOSELY HELD BUSINESS INTERESTS

Identify such interests.

What do you believe they are worth?

What documentation do you have establishing your interests?

If you own a percentage interest in a corporation, where is the stock certificate kept (if stock was ever issued)?

What guidance can you give your family to help them convert the stock certificate into cash or its equivalent?

Can you require the corporation or the other stockholders to purchase your stock? If so, at what price? When does your estate get paid?

Is there a stockholders' agreement?

Do you have an executed copy of the agreement?

Where do you keep it?

Do you have an employment agreement?

If so, where do you keep it?

Is the agreement up-to-date?

Does the corporation (or other business entity) have insurance on your life?

If so, is your estate or beneficiary entitled to the proceeds?

What assurance do you have that the corporation will not use the life insurance proceeds for general corporate purposes?

Do you have a copy of the policy or, at least, the name of the insurance company and policy number?

Where do you keep them?

What do you consider your interests to be worth?

If the corporation is a foreign one, who should your estate contact to secure information about your holdings?

If the corporation owes you money, do you have a record of it? Where do you keep such evidence?

PUBLICLY TRADED STOCKS OR BONDS

Where are the stock certificates or bonds held?

If a broker has them, where is the most recent brokerage statement?

If you have joint-ownership securities, do you have a record of where they were acquired or purchased from, and when?

If purchased, who supplied the funds?

If you loaned the securities to an individual or used them as collateral for a loan (personal or business), where do you keep the receipt?

MONEY OWED TO YOU

Do you have a promissory note?

Where do you keep it?

What is the principal balance due?

Where do you keep a record of the balance due?

Do you have a written statement from the debtor as to what is now owed for principal? For interest?

If the note is from a family member, do you want your estate to collect or forgive the balance due?

Obligations that are many years old may not be enforceable unless some payments have been made on account or a written promise to pay has been made. Do you have such documentation?

If a corporation, partnership, or other entity is indebted to you, what evidence do you have?

Where do you keep this evidence?

BANK ACCOUNTS
(Checking, Savings, and CDs)

Who is the registered owner?

If the accounts are joint, do you want the joint owner to become the sole owner on your death?

Do you have a written statement, signed and dated, showing your intent?

MUTUAL FUNDS AND BROKERAGE ACCOUNTS

Where do you keep the records?

Do you understand that the ownership of the funds or accounts is based on the original application form and not on whose name is listed first (for a joint account), whose Social Security number is listed, or what name is on the monthly or other periodic statements?

Do you have a copy of the application you made when the account was opened?

Where do you keep this copy?

LIFE INSURANCE

Where do you keep the policies and certificates?

Do you have a written record from the insurance company that shows the beneficiary for each policy?

If you died today, considering any outstanding loans or reinvested dividends, how much money would your loved ones be entitled to?

Is there a written record of what they are entitled to?

Do you recommend that your loved ones withdraw the funds in a lump sum, leave them at interest with the insurance company (if available), or exercise other available options, such as receiving the funds in equal amounts over a period of years or over the lifetime of the surviving spouse or other beneficiary?

TRUSTS

Where do you keep documents relating to any trusts in which you have an interest?

Where do you keep the most recent statement of assets the trust owns?

Where do you keep a record of the income generated by the trust?

Do you have a written record as to what control you may exercise over the trust? For example, can you remove the trustee? Do you have a right to withdraw all or part of the principal? Do you have a right to designate who shall have an interest in the trust, either by will or during your lifetime?

INTEREST IN RETIREMENT PLANS

(IRA, HR-10, 401(k), contractual, pension, profit-sharing, ESOP, deferred, defined benefit, etc.)

Do you have a written record of your interest?

Where do you keep it?

Who is the obligor (the one who is obligated to pay you)? What is the obligor's address?

Who is the administrator of the plan?

Who is the trustee of the plan?

Where do you keep a written record of what your successor in interest is entitled to?

OTHER FINANCIAL INTERESTS

Do you have records of any royalty interests due you?

Will your estate know what its rights are and against whom they may be enforced for any oil, timber, gas, copyright, or patent interests you have?

Will your estate know what rental property you may own, with names and addresses of the tenants?

Do you keep a record of any remainder or reversionary interests you may have?

OTHER IMPORTANT MATTERS

If you signed a power of attorney, did you give possession of the power to your attorney-in-fact? If not, where do you keep it?

Does your family know your wishes with respect to your burial? Do you wish to donate your body or organs for medical science? Is there a written record of this?

If you signed a living will or a medical power of attorney, does your family know where you keep these documents?

Set forth the name, address, and telephone number of your attorney, accountant, insurance broker, and stockbroker. Provide a list of what records or documents each may have.

INDEX